# THE WOOD HANDBOOK FOR CRAFTSMEN

**David Johnston**

A James Latham/ B T Batsford book

*This book is dedicated to all those who have worked to
recover the Mary Rose, a unique legacy of Tudor craftsmanship*

*Illustrations:* John Williams
*Coloured photographs:* Tony Anderson

First published 1983
© David Johnston 1983

ISBN 0 7134 3425 0

Printed in Great Britain by The Anchor Press Ltd
Tiptree, Essex
for the publishers, B T Batsford Ltd
4 Fitzhardinge Street, London, W1H 0AH

# THE WOOD HANDBOOK FOR CRAFTSMEN

*By the same author:*

The Craft of Furniture Making (*Batsford, 1979*)

# Contents

# Introduction

The word 'craftsmen' in the title of this book embraces all those who work with wood, and especially those who work with hand tools at traditional crafts. No one can use a variable, biological material like wood to its best advantage without a broad understanding of its characteristics and properties, and the object of this book is to help provide such an understanding for the craftsman. There are chapters on timber properties and defects, seasoning and storage, glues and finishes, preservatives, panel products, the sources and purchase of wood and on wood-based crafts. Well over one hundred species of hardwood and softwood timber are described in detail and all the hardwood species are illustrated with photographs. It is not, therefore, a textbook on wood science but a practical manual for practical woodworkers.

I have an interest in wood both as a professional forester and as an amateur furniture maker, but I relied upon the help of many people, including friends and colleagues, in the compilation of this book. For the sake of brevity and clarity and to focus attention on the essentials I have simplified some of the complexities and omitted inessential detail. I am therefore responsible for the statements and opinions in the book.

It is not practicable to mention every source of information but I am particularly indebted to The American Plywood Association for permission to reproduce Figure 83, B. T. Batsford Ltd for permission to reproduce some passages from *The Craft of Furniture Making* by David Johnston, John Brazier and Tom Harding of The Building Research Establishment, The British Standards Institution for permission to reproduce parts of B.S.565, 1972, The Building Research Establishment for permission to reproduce Figures 3a, 3b, 6, 7a, 7b, 8a, 8b, 13, 14, 15a, 15b, 18, 19, 20(b) and 21 and the photomicrographs in Chapter 8, all of which are Crown copyright, M. Byford of Sadolin (UK) Limited, J. Crisp of J. Crisp and Sons Limited, English Abrasives Ltd., J. K. Evling and Miss P. C. Naismith of The London College of Furniture for information and permission to reproduce Figures 87 and 88, C. Faulkner, The Fibre Building Board Development Organisation Ltd for permission to reproduce Figure 82, The Finnish Plywood Development Association for permission to reproduce Figures 84 and 85, the Forestry Commission for permission to reproduce Figure 20 (a), which is Crown copyright, Gavin Hall of the Timber Research and Development Association, S. D. Holmes of Bordon (UK) Ltd, F. L. Jackson for permission to reproduce Figure 2, D. Kinsey of Fiddes & Son, James Latham of James Latham Limited, John Levy of Imperial College, R. Lewis of R. Graefe Ltd, R. A. (Sandy) Mackilligan, John Makepeace, A. M. Parsons of E. Parsons & Sons, R. Rustin of Rustins Ltd, J. M. Shipman of The Furniture Industry Research Association, C. Wainwright of The Victoria and Albert Museum, the Editor of Unasylva for permission to reproduce Figures 27 and 28, and to a number of my colleagues in the Forestry Commission including John Williams who drew most of the diagrams, Tony Anderson who took the colour photographs, Jack Aaron, Dermot Bevan, David Burdekin, Julian Evans, Arnold Grayson, Colin King, Mike Locke and Alan Mitchell. Finally, I am most grateful to my wife for doing all the typing and secretarial work.

# CHAPTER 1
# Structure and properties

Wood is not only one of the most beautiful and versatile of natural materials, it is also one of the most variable. It varies from species to species and, within a species, from region to region, from site to site and even from one part of a tree to another. Wood is also affected by changes in temperature and humidity and by the rays of the sun. It provides food and growing space for many living organisms, especially for insects and fungi. Some knowledge of the nature and properties of timber is, therefore, essential to those who work with wood if they are to use it to the best advantage.

There is a relationship between growth and structure and between structure and properties, and those relationships are briefly described, from a practical point of view, in this chapter.

## Growth

The stem of a tree is a gentle paraboloid with, generally, a swelling at the base which becomes more pronounced with age and which, in some tropical species, may take the form of massive buttresses extending several metres up the tree. This shape is shown in an exaggerated form in Figure 1.

Just below the bark and forming a complete sheath around all the branches and the stem is a thin layer of tissue known as the cambium, which produces wood cells towards the centre of the tree and bark cells towards the outside. The wood cells of the stem perform three functions. They provide mechanical support for the crown, they conduct water and nutrients from the roots to the leaves and they store food made by the leaves.

Water conduction and food storage occur in the sapwood. This is an outermost zone of wood which, depending upon the species, age and condition of growth of the tree, is usually between about 12mm ($\frac{1}{2}$in) to 75mm (3in) wide. Inside the sapwood is the heartwood. This is generally more durable than the sapwood, contains less moisture

and is usually darker in colour, although in some species the sapwood and heartwood are visually indistinguishable.

In the temperate regions growth is almost entirely restricted to the spring and summer. In most coniferous and some broadleaved species

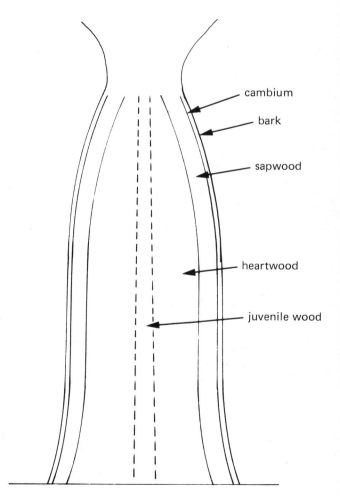

**1** The stem of a tree

7

**2** Spiral growth

(page 9), such as oak and ash, the wood cells produced in the spring differ in size and sometimes in shape from those produced in the summer, and there is a very conspicuous growth ring. In other species, such as beech and sycamore, there is far less contrast in the cell structure, and growth rings, although present, are less obvious. Wood grown in the spring is referred to as early wood and wood grown in the summer as late wood.

In the tropics, if growth is more or less continuous throughout the year, the annual rings cannot easily be identified, but if there is a pronounced dry season some cyclical pattern of growth may be detected.

As the stem of a tree grows it encloses the branches, which form knots in the wood. While the branch is still living the enclosed knot is, structurally, part of the stem and is known as a live knot. But after a branch has died the dead wood enclosed by the stem has no structural connection with the surrounding tissue and is known as a dead knot. In conifers dead knots often fall out after the tree has been felled and sawn, while in broadleaves they are less common and tend to rot rather than fall out.

For any given species the pattern of growth can, to a considerable extent, be influenced by the forester who can select, for example, for vigour, straightness and branching habit in his tree-breeding programme, and who can influence growth rate by his choice of planting site and by the use of fertilizers. Diameter growth and branchiness, but not height growth, can be influenced by spacing, so that trees planted wider apart, or given more space by the removal of their neighbours, become larger in girth and more tapered; they have thicker branches, and hence larger knots, than trees grown more closely together. Much of the wood used in furniture making, however, comes from natural or semi-natural forests in which the growth of individual trees has been little, it at all, influenced by management practices.

Generally, the new cells produced by the cambium are more or less parallel with the long axis of the stem or branch. Sometimes however, they grow at an angle, thus forming a spiral round the tree. This is illustrated in Figure 2, which is a photograph of a sweet chestnut planted by John Evelyn in 1660 to commemorate the restoration of Charles II.

Spiral growth is more common in some species

than others and frequently occurs, for example, in sweet chestnut. In some tropical species, such as sapele, the direction of the spiral changes every few years. This results in an interlocked grain which produces a striped or banded effect on a planed radial surface.

Wood from near the centre of the tree, known as juvenile wood, tends to be less dense, less strong and more knotty than the more mature wood, and in conifers tends to have a more spiral grain. The boundary between the two is gradual but the juvenile characteristics are only pronounced in the ten to twenty growth rings in the centre of the stem.

All wood is composed of small cells, the principal structural material of which is cellulose, which forms the cell walls. This is reinforced with hemicellulose and lignin, which add stiffness to the walls. Various other chemicals occur in different species and these affect the colour, smell and durability of the wood. There are significant differences in structure between conifers, such as pine and spruce, and broadleaves, such as oak and birch.

The wood of conifers is usually referred to as softwood and that of broadleaves as hardwood. These descriptions are generally valid, but some hardwoods such as poplar or obeche are softer than some softwoods such as yew or pitch pine. With the exception of yew the principal high quality furniture timbers are all hardwoods.

## The structure of conifers

There are two types of cell in conifers. Most of them are tracheids, which serve both to conduct water and nutrients and to provide mechanical strength. The others are food storage cells (or parenchyma) which occur in very small quantities. The tracheids formed at the beginning of the growing season are relatively larger in diameter and have thinner walls than those formed later in the year. They range in length from 3mm (almost $\frac{1}{8}$in) to 7mm (just over $\frac{1}{4}$in) with an average length of 3.5mm (just over $\frac{1}{8}$in). Their length is about one hundred times their diameter.

The boundary between the early and late wood may be abrupt as in larch, Douglas fir and most pines, or gradual, as in the firs and spruces.

For any given species, density – which is closely correlated with strength – depends upon cell diameter, cell-wall thickness and upon the proportions of early and late wood. Fast-growing trees have wider annual rings and tend to have larger and thinner-walled tracheids than slower-growing trees. They also have a greater proportion of lighter-weight early wood than of denser late wood. Fast growth does not necessarily, however, result in wood of low density. On some favourable sites and under good growing conditions trees continue to grow until late into the season and produce a relatively large proportion of thick-walled, late-wood tracheids. This is particularly true of species showing a clear differential between spring and summer wood, such as Douglas fir.

The storage cells, which are inconspicuous in conifers, occur among the tracheids or in the form of rays extending radially through the wood. The rays are several cells deep, but typically only one cell wide unless they contain a resin duct. They are barely visible to the naked eye. Of the conifers, pines, spruces, larches and Douglas fir contain resin ducts, which give the characteristic resin smell to the wood and which, on occasions, make the wood sticky to work. These ducts are lined with resin-producing parenchyma cells.

## The structure of broadleaves

The wood cells in broadleaves are generally shorter than those in conifers, and there is a greater difference between the cells which conduct water and nutrients and those which provide strength and rigidity. The storage cells are similar in structure and function to those in conifers but they are more abundant and more variable.

The principal conducting cells, which are called vessels, range in diameter from 0.02mm (less than $\frac{1}{1000}$in) to 0.5mm (about $\frac{1}{50}$in) so that in some species they are large enough to be seen easily by the naked eye. They always occur in vertical series which form tube-like structures extending vertically for some distance in the tree.

In most species there is little contrast in the size or pattern of the vessels across the growth ring and these are known as diffuse-porous species. In some species, however, the transition from large early-wood vessels to smaller late-wood vessels is abrupt and the early-wood vessels form a series of distinct rings which are clearly visible on the end grain of the wood. These are the ring-porous species which include oak, elm and sweet chestnut. In oak, for example, the diameter of the early-wood vessels can be as much as ten times that of those in the late

9

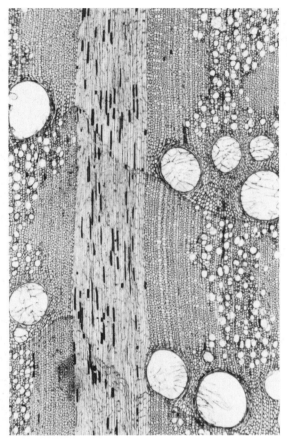

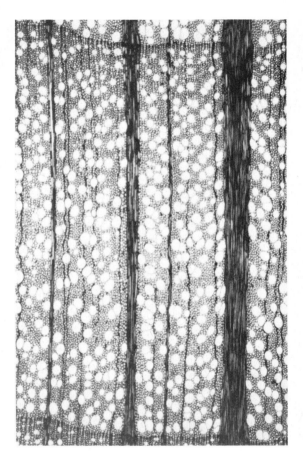

3(a) Ring-porous wood (oak)

3(b) Diffuse-porous wood (beech)

wood. Unlike diffuse-porous species, faster growth in the ring-porous group is normally associated with denser and stronger wood because of the larger proportion of the denser late wood. Ring-porous wood and diffuse-porous wood are shown in Figures 3(a) and 3(b).

The cells which provide most of the strength in hardwoods are called fibres. They are similar to the late-wood tracheids in conifers although they are shorter, averaging 1mm (about $\frac{1}{25}$in) to 1.5mm ($\frac{1}{16}$in) in length. They vary greatly in cell-wall thickness, but are typically thick walled. The thickness of the fibre wall and its physical and chemical properties are major factors in determining the strength and working properties of wood.

The storage tissue, or parenchyma, occurs both vertically, and radially in the form of rays. The vertical parenchyma forms various patterns on the end grain of the wood and can be used as an aid to identification (page 20). The rays are generally larger and more conspicuous than those in conifers and their size, shape and distribution are characteristics which are also used in the identification of timber.

Resin ducts are not usually present in broad-leaves but they occur in a few families, notably the *Dipterocarpaceae* which includes various species of meranti.

The storage tissue of many species contains crystals, usually of calcium oxalate and, less frequently, of silica. The presence of silica in such species as keruing and teak is an undesirable feature because it rapidly blunts the cutting edges of tools.

10

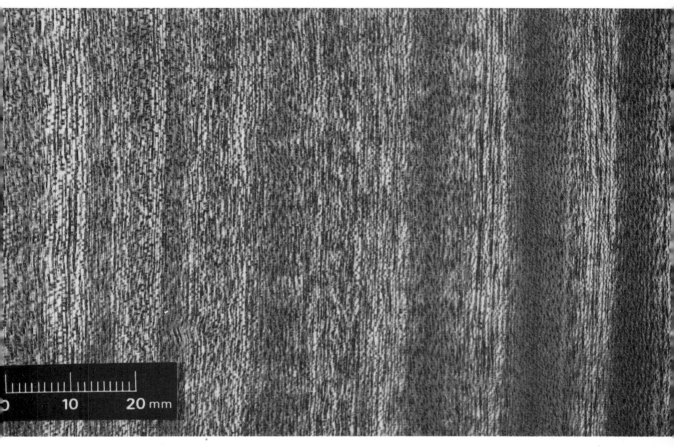

## Grain, texture and figure

### Grain

Grain is the direction of the fibres relative to the long axis of the tree or of a particular piece of wood. Straight grain is self-explanatory, but there are various forms of irregular grain, some of which have a decorative value. In a number of species the grain is irregular, but follows no particular pattern, as in English elm. A not uncommon form of irregularity is spiral grain, which has no decorative value.

In some hardwood species the direction of a spiral grain changes every few years, as in Figure 4. This is known as interlocked grain, which may be steep and regular as in sapele, or shallow and irregular as in utile. Another form of irregularity is wavy grain which occurs almost always in the radial plane (Figure 5). It is found, for example, in sycamore. The two patterns are sometimes combined in the same tree, as in makoré (Figure 7(b)).

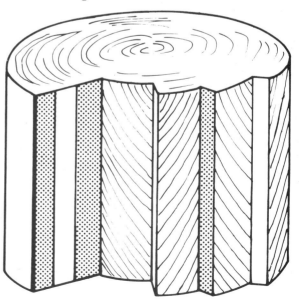

4 Interlocked grain

11

5 Wavy grain

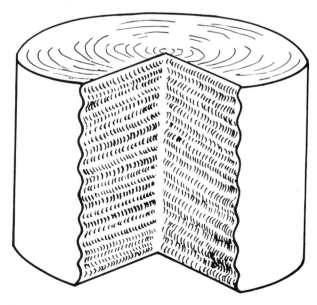

In other species patches or areas of the cambium grow more quickly or more slowly than the surrounding areas and produce slight depressions or undulations in the grain. These irregularities may be caused by the natural growth of the tree, by damage inflicted by insects or fungi or, possibly, by physical stresses imposed on the tree.

If a stem divides into two separate stems the joint where the two stems separate is known as a crotch and the grain in this area is distorted. The grain is also highly contorted within the burrs which sometimes grow on species such as walnut.

Sloping grain occurs when timber is not sawn parallel with the long axis of the tree, and is particularly common when the tree has a pronounced butt-swell or when the stem is bowed. Knots are also a cause of irregular grain.

## Texture

Texture in hardwoods depends primarily upon the size and distribution of the wood cells and, to a much lesser extent, upon the rays. Wood with large vessels, such as oak, is said to be coarse textured, while wood with small vessels is said to be fine textured. As well as being coarse or fine the texture may be even or uneven. If the cells are consistent in size throughout the annual growth ring the texture is even, but if there are pronounced differences between the early and late wood the texture is uneven.

In softwoods the texture depends mainly upon the contrast between early and late wood and upon the rate of growth. Conifers do not contain cells of large diameter, such as the vessels of hardwoods, but many of them, such as pines, larches and Douglas fir, show a marked contrast in tracheid size and sometimes in cell-wall thickness from early to late wood, and have a fine or medium but uneven texture. The faster the rate of growth the more uneven the texture becomes because the early wood tends to be relatively wider and the early wood cells relatively larger in fast-grown than slow-grown softwoods.

## Figure

Figure is the pattern produced on the longitudinal surfaces of wood by variations in the colour, by the arrangement of various forms of tissue such as tracheids, vessels and parenchyma and by growth rings, rays, grain and knots.

### Colour variation

A perfectly uniform colour does not contribute to the figure of wood. There has to be variation and contrast which is very marked in some species of the pea family such as the rosewoods, laburnum, muninga and padauk. Although the colour of a particular species is often variable, it is nevertheless a characteristic which is a major factor in the subjective identification of timber and probably contributes more than anything else to its beauty and value. In most hardwoods and some conifers descriptions of colour refer to the heartwood and not the sapwood which, even in the highly decorative species, is usually pale and without interest. Occasionally, however, as in ebony, zones of sapwood become included in the heartwood, probably due to cambial damage, and produce a highly contrasting pattern of very light and very dark wood.

### Tissue arrangement

Tissue of contrasting texture, colour or light reflectance, such as vessels or parenchyma, is sometimes arranged in a characteristic and visible pattern. In elm, for example, the late-wood vessels appear as faint zig-zag lines on tangential surfaces, and in iroko and African padauk the parenchyma shows a similar pattern.

When the rays are arranged in a regular pattern, like tiles on a wall, they are sometimes visible to the naked eye or with a hand lens as a fine pattern on tangential surfaces. This storied arrangement is described as ripple marking and is particularly characteristic of American mahogany and the rosewoods (pages 100 and 115).

### Growth rings

In many species the growth rings are very distinct. In conifers this is usually because there is a zone of late wood in each annual ring composed of smaller and thicker-walled tracheids, which are often harder and darker in colour than the early-wood cells. In ring-porous hardwoods, especially if they are fast grown, the large early-wood vessels are clearly differentiated from the very much smaller late-wood vessels. In some diffuse-porous species there is a discernible difference between early wood and late wood in the number, size or pattern of the vessels. But even if there is no change in the vessels throughout the growth ring, it is possible to detect the periodic growth patterns in many species owing to the presence of terminal or initial bands of parenchyma which mark the boundaries of the rings.

If a plank is sawn radially and parallel with the grain the growth rings do not produce a decorative figure on the surface of the wood but appear simply as a series of parallel lines. But because trees are parabaloidal or conical in shape a tangentially sawn plank is likely to show some growth ring figure if growth rings are present.

A plank sawn parallel with the outside of the tree will tend to show a sharp conical growth ring figure, while if it is sawn parallel with the long axis of the tree it is more likely to show a blunter conical pattern. An example of growth-ring figure is shown in colour plate 29.

An irregular, wavy figure on tangential or rotary-peeled surfaces is characteristic of some species such as Douglas fir (Figure 6). This is because neither the stem nor the growth rings are perfectly regular or circular.

**6** Tangentially cut Douglas fir

*Rays*

Rays sometimes produce a highly decorative figure on radial surfaces, the most notable examples being the white oaks and the Australian silky oaks which have deep, silvery rays. Many other species, such as beech and London plane, also have a characteristic figure on radial surfaces caused by conspicuous rays which contrast in colour, texture and direction of grain with the vessels and fibres. If the ray figure is a decorative feature, as in oak, the most valuable boards are those sawn radially. For very high class work the wood is sometimes cleaved radially in the plane of the rays and then planed true in order to show as much of the ray tissue as possible. Some species, such as hornbeam, have quite deep rays, but they do not give a figure to the wood because they are the same colour as the surrounding tissue and are not, therefore, easily visible.

*Grain*

Almost any irregular grain produces some figure on longitudinal surfaces, but the more attractive type of figure is usually the result of an identifiable pattern in the grain. Interlocked grain (page 11) produces a banded or striped effect on radial surfaces. If the interlocking is steep and the direction of growth changes regularly and frequently, the result is a sharply defined, narrow-banded figure (colour plate 21). A more shallow interlocking and a less regular or frequent change in direction give a less sharply defined pattern (colour plate 1).

Wavy grain (page 12) produces a fiddle-back figure (Figure 7(a)) so called because fiddle-back maple is used for making the backs of violins. If interlocked and wavy grain occur together in the same tree the result is a roe or mottled figure on radial surfaces (Figure 7(b)). There are endless variations of this figure according to the angle, frequency and regularity of the interlocking and to the pattern of waviness.

Irregular grain caused by differential growth in the cambium (page 12) produces a variety of different types of figure on tangential or rotary cut surfaces. If they are small, deep indentations they appear as a bird's-eye figure as in bird's-eye maple (Figure 8(a)) while larger and less steep undulations may produce a blister or a quilted figure (Figure 8(b)).

The extremely contorted grain in the burrs and stumps of such species as elm and walnut and in the crotches of species such as mahogany is rarely used in the solid, but provides highly decorative and valuable veneers for furniture making and panelling.

7(a) Fiddle-back figure

7(b) Roe figure

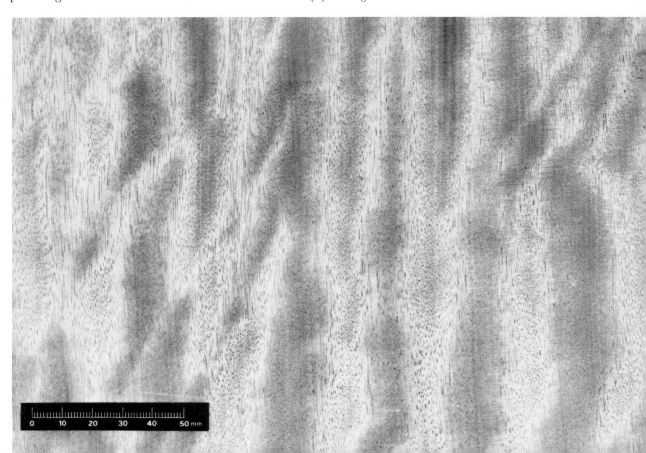

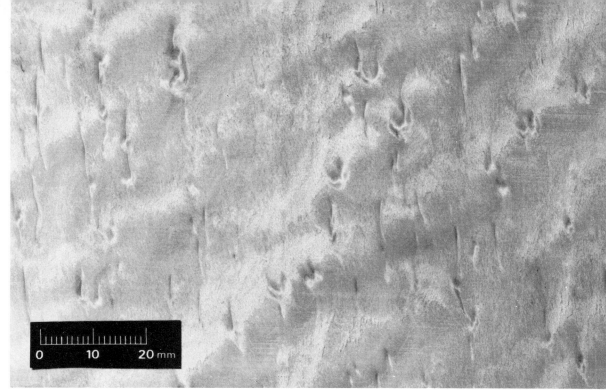

**8(a)** Bird's-eye maple          **8(b)** Blister figure

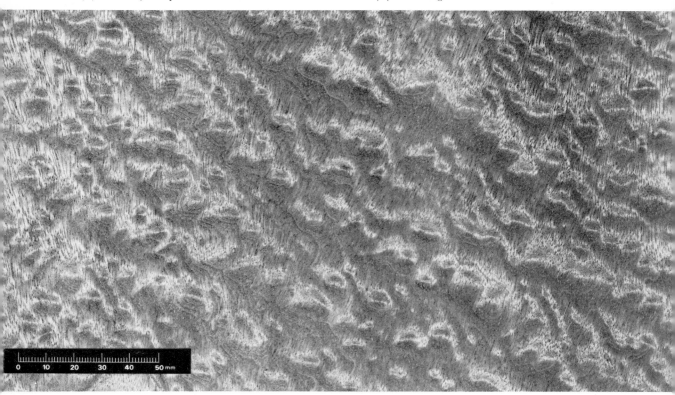

*Knots*

Knots give a figure to wood partly because the grain is deflected around them, but mainly because of the shapes of hard, dark tissue. For most purposes knots are regarded as technically undesirable and aesthetically unsightly, but they are occasionally exploited as a desirable feature in situations where strength and stability are not of major importance. Knotty pine, for example, is used for panelling, and the knots are even reproduced in some melamine simulations of wood. The small pin knots which occur in yew are regarded as desirable features in yew veneers.

## Equilibrium moisture content

The moisture content of wood varies with the temperature and relative humidity of the atmosphere and adjusts itself to a change in either of these variables. For a given combination of temperature and relative humidity there is a corresponding equilibrium moisture content as indicated in Figure 9 where the equilibrium moisture content for a temperature of 27°C and a relative humidity of 60 per cent is seen to be 11 per cent.

It will also be seen from the temperature curves that for a given humidity the moisture content declines as the temperature rises. If there is a change in either temperature or humidity the new equilibrium moisture content is attained more quickly by thin than by thick pieces of wood, and more quickly at the surface than in the interior. Therefore, during the process of gaining or losing water there is a moisture gradient from the outside to the centre of a piece of wood.

The moisture content for a given combination of temperature and humidity varies from one species to another. For example, at a temperature of 40°C and a relative humidity of 70 per cent the equilibrium moisture content of oak is about 14 per cent and of teak about 11 per cent.

If wood is dried and then allowed to reabsorb moisture the reabsorbtion curve does not follow the drying curve. This is shown by the dotted line in Figure 9 for the 27°C temperature curve. For a given combination of temperature and humidity, wood which has been dried and re-wetted contains less moisture than when it was originally drying. In other words, it becomes less hygroscopic and this characteristic, which makes wood more stable, can also be induced by steaming or boiling.

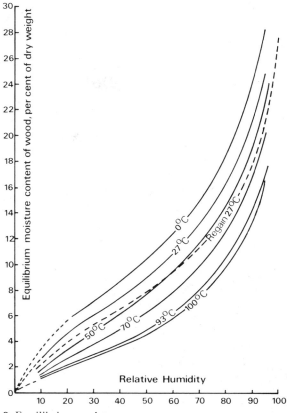

**9** Equilibrium moisture content

### Response to changes in moisture content

When freshly felled, the moisture content of wood may be more than 100 per cent of its dry weight, but when completely air dry, under cover in a temperate climate, the equilibrium moisture content falls to about 20 per cent in winter and about 15 per cent in summer. In very arid regions it can fall to as low as 6 per cent. In centrally heated homes the equilibrium moisture content varies between about 12 per cent in the summer and 10 per cent in the winter. In houses without central heating the figures are about 14 per cent in the winter and about 12 per cent in the summer.

Wood does not begin to shrink until it reaches fibre saturation point. At this stage the cell walls are completely saturated but the interior cavities of the cells are empty. For most species the moisture content at fibre saturation point is about 30 per cent. Below this level shrinkage is approximately proportional to moisture content so that the shrinkage from 30 per cent to 20 per cent moisture content is the same as that between

17

20 per cent and 10 per cent. Shrinkage in the tangential plane is 1.5 to 2.0 times that in the radial plane, while in the longitudinal plane it is almost negligible, except in reaction wood, in which it may be considerable. As an example, normal English oak in drying from 14 per cent to 10 per cent moisture content shrinks almost 2 per cent tangentially and 1 per cent radially. Stability is related to the change in equilibrium moisture content for a given change in humidity; the more stable the timber the smaller the change.

A particular problem arises in fitting high class joinery into a new building. As the mortar and plaster dry a large volume of water is released and the humidity of the building may be so high for a time that the equilibrium moisture content of the wood can be as high as 16 per cent to 20 per cent. Later, when the building has dried, the moisture content falls to between about 10 per cent and 14 per cent. If dry timber is used it may at first swell and distort and acquire a compression set (page 18). The ideal solution is to allow the building to dry before fitting high class joinery. A compromise solution is to use timber with a somewhat higher than average moisture content, say, 14 per cent to 15 per cent instead of 12 per cent.

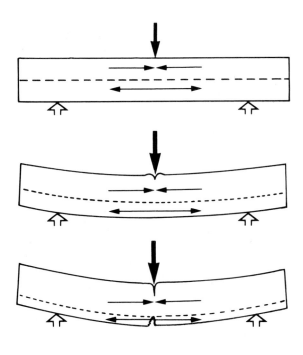

**10** The stresses in a beam

### Set

If wood is dried or wetted under restraint it acquires a set. That is to say, it develops a new equilibrium between moisture content and volume. Wood with a compression set has a smaller volume for a given moisture content than it had originally, while wood with a tension set has a greater volume. Wood can acquire a cumulative compression set if the process of wetting under compression and then drying is repeated a number of times. This happens, for example, each time a dry axe handle is tapped tightly into the blade and then wetted and re-dried. The same thing occurs if dry flooring blocks are fitted tightly together and then wetted. When they dry they shrink below their original size and leave cracks. If the cracks are filled with fillets of wood and the process repeated the blocks will become still smaller.

A tension set cannot develop cumulatively to the same degree as a compression set because sooner or later the wood will rupture under the stress.

### Strength

Timber possesses various strength qualities. It may withstand a sustained load, a sudden impact or a shear stress, or resist compression parallel with or across the grain. It may be hard and it may resist bending and cleaving. There is a high correlation between density and strength so that fast-grown conifers and diffuse-porous hardwoods are likely to produce weaker timber than slower-growing trees (page 9). Faster grown ring-porous hardwoods, on the other hand, tend to produce stronger timber than slower-growing trees.

With the exception of impact strength, seasoned wood is stronger than wet wood, especially in compression parallel with the grain. At about the equilibrium moisture content in houses the stiffness of wood is increased by about 2 per cent for each 1 per cent decrease in moisture content. There is a correlation, but not a consistent or simple one, beteeen stiffness and bending strength, which is the ability to resist breaking under a load. For practical purposes, therefore, the index of stiffness (the modulus of elasticity) is used as an indirect index of breaking strength (the modulus of rupture) because it can be measured without destroying the wood.

The strength of a beam is a combination of three aspects of strength – tensile, compression and shear. If a load is applied to a beam the upper half of the beam is compressed and the lower half is stretched, and there is a neutral plane of shear stress in between. Wood is from two to nearly four times stronger in tension than in compression and a beam always fails intially on the upper surface. As the load is increased on a beam the neutral plane moves downwards towards the lower surface (Figure 10).

The stiffness of a beam is proportional to its width and to the cube of its depth, while the breaking strength is proportional to its width but to the square of its depth. Stiffness is inversely proportional to the cube of the span, while breaking strength is inversely proportional to the span. These relationships are illustrated in Figure 11.

Wood varies greatly in its resistance to cleaving. Generally, the species which most resist cleaving have an irregular grain, such as English elm. Straight-grained wood tends to be easy to cleave in either plane but wood with interlocked grain is more easily split tangentially than radially. Timbers with a very low density have little resistance to cleaving but tend not to split when nailed.

For a given density there is a tendency for tropical timbers to be relatively stronger in compression and for temperate timbers to be relatively stronger in breaking strength.

The desirable strength qualities depend upon the use to which the wood is to be put. Furniture timber should be reasonably stiff and hard. Rafters and joists in buildings need to be stiff to avoid distortion in ceilings and roofs and strong enough to provide a good safety margin. The

timbers used for boat frames and planks need to be stiff and strong and to resist impact. Wood used for tool handles and sports goods has to resist impact and, for some purposes, has also to be hard. The ability to resist splitting is important for wheel hubs and nailed boxes. In general, stiffness is more important than strength because if a member is stiff enough not to bend unacceptably it is usually strong enough for most purposes.

## Elasticity

No timber is perfectly elastic, so that if it is subjected to a load it never completely recovers its original shape. The longer the load is applied and the higher the temperature the greater will be the permanent distortion. This quality may be exploited to re-shape wood which has become distorted for any reason. If, for example, a piece of wood has become twisted it may be straightened by cramping it for a period of time to a firm base over a diagonal rod, such as a broom handle, so that it is twisted in the opposite direction. This straightening is a matter of trial and error, but as the wood is not weakened by the process the movement can be reversed if necessary. The process can be hastened by putting wet towels on the concave surface, but if this is done the wood must be held rigid after it has been straightened while it regains its equilibrium moisture content.

## Variability

There is considerable variation in appearance and properties within many timber species. This variation depends upon a number of factors such as genetic variability, geographical location, rate of growth, soil type and age of tree. For many genera, especially in the conifers, the variation within a species is as great or greater than the variation between species, assuming the different species to have grown under comparable conditions. For this reason it is often difficult to identify the timber of individual species of such genera, as spruce, fir, larch, birch, or ash; for other genera such as oak, maple or pine it is often only possible to identify broad species groups within each genus.

## Identification

Timber can be identified at various levels of precision and objectivity. At the one extreme

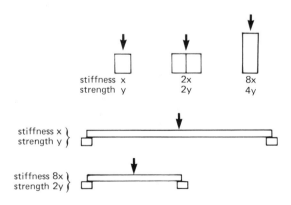

11 The strength of wood

people who work with wood come to recognise a species in much the same way that they recognise another human being. They rely upon an almost subconscious assessment of a number of easily observed features such as colour, grain, texture, figure and perhaps weight and feel. At the other extreme an electron microscope can be used to study the detailed structure of the cell walls. It is obvious that neither of these methods is satisfactory for the craftsman who wants to be able to identify perhaps thirty to forty species, species groups or genera with reasonable certainty but without elaborate equipment and training.

If a clean cut is made on the end grain of a piece of wood a number of diagnostic features can be identified with the aid of a hand lens. It is possible by using a punch-card system or a dichotomous key to track down any species, but the use of these methods is neither very easy nor very certain without considerable practice. Frequently, however, the craftsman has some idea of the name of a species and he wants only to check his identification. For this reason a dichotomous key is not included in this book, but descriptions of a number of timbers are given in Chapters 8 and 9, and for each hardwood timber there is a microscopic photograph of a transverse section. Some of the more important species are illustrated by coloured plates of radial or tangential surfaces. The diagnostic features of the end grain, which are visible with an ordinary hand lens, are listed for each species. It is very much easier and more certain to use this method of identification with hardwoods than with conifers because hardwood tissue is more variable.

The features which can be used for the identification of hardwoods with the aid of a hand lens are:

a) growth ring pattern
b) vessels
c) rays
d) parenchyma
e) resin canals (for some species).

For conifers the only features are:

a) annual ring pattern
b) resin canals.

## Growth rings

Growth rings are almost always visible in temperate hardwoods and in almost all conifers. They are absent in some tropical species where growth is continuous throughout the year. The contrast between early and late wood is a diagnostic feature in conifers and also distinguishes between ring-porous and diffuse-porous hardwood species.

## Vessels

Wood is described as ring porous or diffuse porous according to the differentiation in size of vessel from early to late wood (p. 9). This distinction is not always completely unequivocal because in some species the vessels change in size gradually from the early spring wood to the late summer wood. For practical purposes, however, any species in which the early wood vessels are markedly larger than the late wood vessels is described as ring porous. In both groups the vessels are arranged in various patterns. These are:

a) Solitary     see opepe (p. 111)
b) Clustered    see plane (p. 113)
c) In chains
   (i) radial     see afrormosia (p. 72)
   (ii) tangential   see English elm (p. 86)

## Rays

Rays are so small in conifers that they are of no value in diagnosis with a hand lens. In hardwoods, however, they are usually visible and they vary from species to species in width and depth, in spacing and in variation in size within a piece of wood. Sometimes a number of narrow rays are aligned close together, as an aggregate ray, so that they give the impression of being one large ray.

In some species rays are arranged in a storied pattern on the tangential surface, giving a rippled appearance to the naked eye or when viewed through a hand lens. (See also parenchyma in the next section.)

Reference is made in Chapter 8 to the number of vessels per ray or the number of rays per vessel for each species. This is because when seen in cross section some species have several rays between each radial row of vessels (Indian laurel, page 98) some have one ray (obeche, page 109) and some have several rows of vessels between adjoining rays (oak, page 108).

## Parenchyma

Parenchyma appears as a light-coloured tissue on the end grain and occurs in various patterns for which there is a standardised terminology. Unless there is a well-defined, regular pattern it is not always visible with a hand lens. A somewhat simplified classification is given below:

**a)** Apotracheal — not touching the vessels
  (i) terminal or initial — occuring in a thin band at the beginning or end of the growth ring. Figure 12(a).
  (ii) diffuse — individual cells or fine strands distributed irregularly, often not visible with a hand lens. Figure 12(b).

**b)** Paratracheal — touching the vessels
  (i) vasicentric — forming borders round the vessels. Figure 12(c).
  (ii) partially vasicentric — forming discontinuous borders to the vessels. Figure 12(d).
  (iii) aliform — forming a well defined border round the vessels which is extended tangentially into wings. Figure 12(e).
  (iv) confluent — aliform with the wings joining to form complete or partial bands. Figure 12(f).

**c)** Banded — used in this book to describe conspicuous bands which do not fit into the category of confluent. Figure 12(g).

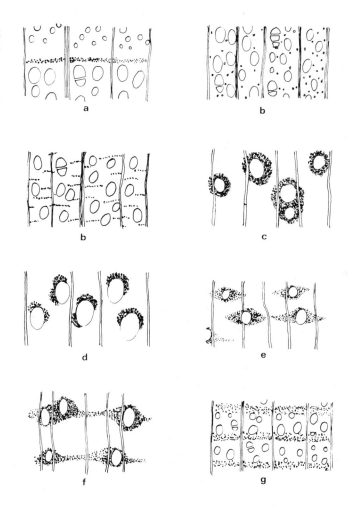

12(**a**) Parenchyma: terminal or initial
(**b**) diffuse
(**c**) vasicentric
(**d**) partially vasicentric
(**e**) aliform
(**f**) confluent
(**g**) banded

In some species such as obeche the parenchyma is arranged in a storied pattern which is visible with the naked eye or with a lens as a minute rippled pattern on the tangential face (Figure 13). When this occurs there is a tendency for the rays to be arranged in a similar pattern (page 13).

## Resin canals

Resin canals are not common in hardwoods but in some species they are visible as a tangential line of cells as in meranti (Figure 14).

## Classification

In the past it was very difficult for botanists to exchange information about plants because plant names varied not only from country to country but from region to region within a country. Moreover, similar names were given to genetically quite unrelated plants having only a superficial resemblance to each other. Over the past three hundred years or so a system has been developed which enables botanists to classify plants according to their genetical relationships. This system is based upon Latin (or pseudo-Latin) names, because this was the international

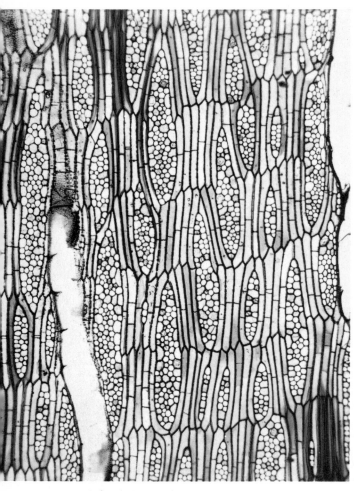

**13** Storied parenchyma

**14** Resin canals

language when the system was evolving.

There are seven principal levels in the classification. These are the division, the subdivision, the class, the order, the family, the genus and the species.

All timber trees belong to one of two subdivisions: the angiosperms or broadleaves and the gymnosperms or conifers. At a more detailed level the plants within an order are grouped into families. All the plants within a family are genetically related and have, in particular, similar flowering and fruiting characteristics, although they may differ greatly in their forms of growth and general appearance. The pea family or *Leguminosae*, for example, includes beans and peas, lupins, wisteria, gorse and broom as well as timber trees such as the various rosewoods, laburnum and robinia. All these plants, however, have the typical pea flower and they all produce their seed in pods.

The genus is a subdivision within a family and comprises groups of plants which are obviously related to each other. Within the beech family or *Fagaceae*, the oaks *Quercus*, the beeches *Fagus* and the sweet chestnuts *Castanea* each comprise a separate genus. As an example from the conifers, the pine family or *Pinaceae* comprises 29 genera including the pines *Pinus*, the spruces *Picea*, the larches *Larix*, the firs *Abies* and the hemlocks *Tsuga*.

Finally, a particular plant, such as English oak, is an individual species and has a specific name. The botanical name of a species is always identified by two names: the genus and the specific name. The genus is written first with a capital letter and the specific name second with a lower case letter, both in italics. The botanical name of English oak is *Quercus robur* and the name distinguishes it from any other oak in the world. Colloquial names are often misleading or imprecise. White oak is a name given in the USA to about ten quite similar species, but the names *Quercus alba, Quercus prinus* or *Quercus lyrata* refer to particular identifiable species within the group.

The usual convention with common names is to write the specific name first with a lower case initial letter followed by the generic name, also with a lower case letter. This applies both to a true species such as sweet chestnut and to a group of similar species bearing only one common name, such as white oak. If the specific name is a proper name, as in Douglas fir, a capital letter is used.

The botanical system of nomenclature is based upon characteristics of the living plant, although wood properties are increasingly being used to establish genetical relationships. A botanical name, therefore, applies strictly speaking to the tree rather than to its timber. In practice, however, names are applied equally to the timber as to the tree from which it comes.

23

# CHAPTER 2

# Defects

The types of defect found in wood may be subdivided into the six categories listed below:

**a**) natural
**b**) seasoning
**c**) conversion
**d**) weathering
**e**) insect
**f**) fungal.

This classification is somewhat arbitrary because the defects which may develop during the period of seasoning and, to some extent, during conversion, are due to patterns of growth within the tree and may be the result, therefore, of natural defects.

From the point of view of the craftsman the first three types of defect are more important than the last two, but it is useful to be able to recognise the more common examples of insect and fungal damage in wood, to understand their significance and to know how to prevent the development of such damage in service.

## Natural defects

### Knots

Knots, as has been mentioned already, are sections of branches which have been enclosed in the stem. They cause irregular grain and reduce the strength of the wood. The irregular grain is not only weaker than straight-grained wood but is difficult to work and tends to tear when planed. Knots are particularly troublesome if they occur where joints have to be cut. It is quite impracticable to cut mortices and undesirable to cut tenons or dovetail joints through large knots. But perhaps the most serious disadvantage of knots, because of the associated irregularity of grain, is their tendency to cause distortion of the wood with changes in moisture content.

Very knotty timber is sometimes used for decorative panels where strength is a minor consideration, and knots are relatively unimpor-tant in large-dimensioned structural timber. Moderately knotty timber can be used for softwood joinery and for utility furniture which is to be painted, provided no knots or knot clusters form a large proportion of the cross-sectional area of any structural member. For many purposes, however, knots have to be considered a serious defect.

### Irregular grain

Irregular grain has been discussed on page 11. Some irregular grain such as interlocked or bird's-eye grain is, for some purposes, considered to be a desirable decorative feature despite the fact that it is difficult to work and requires careful finishing to achieve a smooth surface. Other forms of irregular grain such as spiral, knotty or sloping grain have no merit, but considerable disadvantages. They are all liable to cause serious distortion with changes in moisture content, and wood with pronounced spiral or sloping grain should not be used in furniture making or for any work where stability is important. Irregular grain is likely to be particularly troublesome in large, thin sheets.

### Reaction wood

Stems which are not growing vertically, and branches, produce reaction wood. In conifers the reaction wood occurs on the underside of the leaning stem and is known as compression wood, while in broadleaves it occurs on the upper side and is known as tension wood. Reaction wood has different strength properties from normal wood. Seasoned compression wood is stronger in compression but weaker in tension than normal wood, while tension wood is stronger in tension but weaker in compression. These characteristics cannot, however, be exploited because the wood is so variable and unpredictable. Unlike normal wood, reaction wood has a very high longitudinal shrinkage, which causes planks to bow or spring with changes in moisture content. Compression wood is usually easy to recognise because it is

15(**a**)  Compression wood in a conifer

darker in colour than the surrounding wood and tends to occur in longitudinal streaks. There is usually, also, a lack of contrast in colour between the early and late wood. Tension wood, on the other hand, can be paler or darker than normal wood and tends to be rather woolly and brittle to work. Another indication of the likely presence of reaction wood is very eccentric growth as seen on the cross section of the log in Figure 15.

### Brittleheart
Brittleheart is a defect which is likely to occur in the centre of fast-growing, low- to medium-density tropical broadleaved species such as

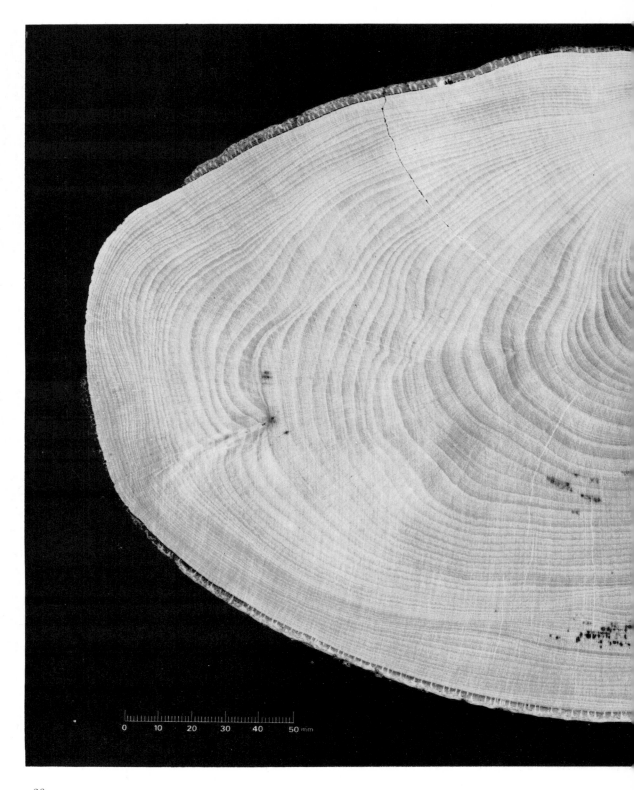

15(b) Tension wood in a broadleaved species

African mahogany. In a large tree the outer part of the stem is in a state of tension which the central portion may be unable to withstand. This leads to numerous minute failures in the cell walls of the wood. Wood with brittleheart has a somewhat carroty texture which is easy to detect. It should not be used in furniture.

### Compression failures

Compression failures, or hairline cracks across the grain in the centre of the tree, are associated with brittleheart. Compression failures are also caused by the tree bending in the wind or when it is felled. They occur in such species as African mahogany and meranti and often only become apparent when the wood is converted and used.

### Bark pockets

Bark pockets occur when a patch of cambium is killed and the bark becomes incorporated into the wood as new cambium grows over the dead patch.

### Pitch pockets

Pitch pockets are found mainly in conifers but also in the dipterocarp family. Damage to the cambium leaves small leaf-shaped pockets in the wood which become filled with resin. They normally follow the line of an annual ring.

## Seasoning defects

### Warping

Even without any natural defects sawn wood becomes distorted during seasoning because the tangential shrinkage is about twice the radial shrinkage (page 18). Tangentially sawn planks cup towards the external face because the wood is more nearly tangential on the outer than on the inner face. Square sections become diamond shaped and round sections become oval shaped for the same reason (Figure 16).

The various natural defects described on page 24 cause additional distortion when the moisture content falls below fibre saturation point, about 30 per cent. Spiral grain leads to twisting, while reaction wood and sloping grain cause bow and spring in the longitudinal plane (Figure 17).

### Case-hardening

As wood is seasoned the outer layer dries first and comes under a tension stress, but is restrained

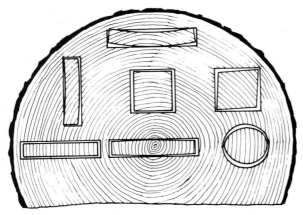

**16** Warping due to drying

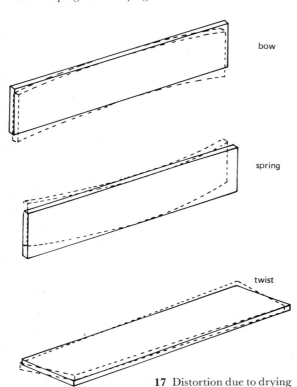

bow

spring

twist

**17** Distortion due to drying

from shrinking by the wetter, interior portion, thus acquiring a set (page 18). This is known as case-hardening, which is aggravated by rapid drying and is more likely to occur with thick pieces of wood. Some degree of case-hardening is, however, very common in any wood which is air dried, and furniture components which are cut to approximate dimensions and then left for some time in a heated house are likely to become case-

hardened. When they are subsequently planed an outer zone of tension-set wood is removed and the components tend to bow towards the planed faces. A case-hardened piece of wood may bow slightly when one face is planed but return to its original shape when the opposite face has been planed.

Reverse case-hardening is possible if case-hardened wood is over-steamed to relieve the condition. If this happens the core becomes drier than the surface and comes under a tension stress. This puts a compression set on the outer skin and if the case-hardening is removed from one face of a board the other face will bow outwards.

### Collapse

Collapse may occur when fully saturated wood with relatively thin walled cells is dried rapidly. A very high tension is created in the water inside the cells and this sucks the cell walls together, causing distortion and abnormal shrinking, which often takes the form of a surface corrugation known as washboarding (Figure 18).

With severe collapse some physical damage is almost inevitable but collapsed wood can, to a remarkable degree, be restored by steaming at a temperature close to the boiling point of water. Collapse will not occur at the second drying because the cell walls are no longer full of water and the wood is more permeable.

### Honeycombing

Honeycoming is the development of ruptures in the wood as a result of tension stresses created by collapse or case-hardening (Figure 19).

### Checks and splits

Checks and splits are longitudinal cracks caused by shrinkage in the course of seasoning and are particularly likely to occur with rapid air-drying. A check is a crack which does not extend right through the wood, whereas a split extends from one face to the other. Splits develop particularly at the ends of dense hardwood logs and planks if they are left unprotected in drying conditions. This is because the diffusion of water is very much more rapid longitudinally than radially or tangentially, so that the ends of a log or plank tend to dry more rapidly than the middle and are therefore subjected to transverse tension, which causes them to split. For this reason the ends of the wood should be waterproofed during the process of air-drying.

**18** Washboarding

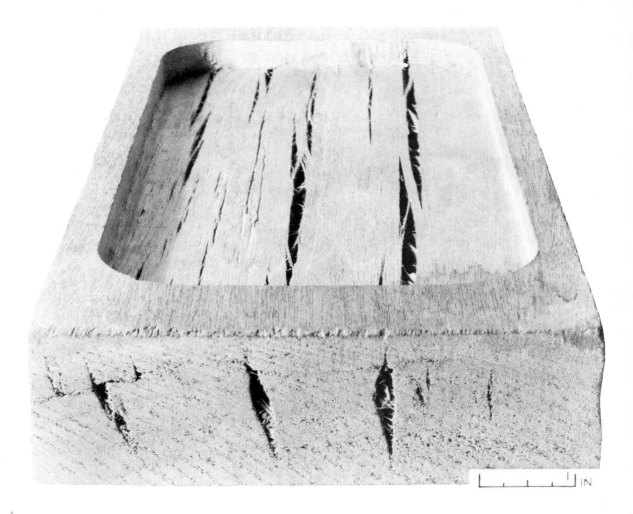

### Shakes

A shake is an internal split which develops in the growing tree or is caused at the time of felling. Splits radiating from the pith are known as star shakes, and splits occurring along the junctions of annual rings are called ring shakes. These sometimes occur when over-mature sweet chestnut or oak trees fall very heavily when they are felled.

## Conversion defects

### *Sloping grain*

If straight-grained wood is cut in such a way that the grain is not parallel with the long axis of the plank this can be regarded as a conversion defect, because the plank will tend to spring or bow as it dries.

**19** Honeycombing

### *Raised grain*

If wood is planed before it is fully seasoned there is a differential shrinkage between the early and late wood and the surface becomes corrugated. This defect can often be seen in painted joinery in new houses after the wood has been in a warm, dry atmosphere for some time.

### *Response to sawing*

It has been shown that wood, for a number of reasons, may be subjected to various forms of internal stress. If a piece of timber having an internal stress is sawn or planed true on all faces and then sawn into two parts, each part immediately becomes bowed, sprung or twisted, or even acquires a combination of all these defects.

### Torn grain

If wood is planed against the grain the fibres of the wood are likely to be torn away from the surface. This is most likely to occur with interlocked, sloping or undulating grain, or in the immediate vicinity of knots. It may sometimes be avoided by reversing the direction of planing or by planing at right angles to the grain.

## Weathering defects

Wood which is exposed to the weather is subjected to alternate swelling and shrinking as the humidity and temperature change, and also to the action of sunlight. These factors cause a physical degradation of the surface layers of the wood, which can be prevented by well maintained paintwork.

## Insect damage

Of the numerous species of insect which can damage healthy, sickly or diseased trees or converted timber there are only four groups, all of them beetles, which are likely to be of importance to the craftsman. These are furniture beetles, ambrosia beetles, powder-post beetles and long-horn beetles.

### Furniture beetles; family *Anobiidae*

*Anobium punctatum*; the common furniture beetle. The common furniture beetle, which has been introduced into many countries from Europe, bores into wood and makes extensive tunnels with clean-cut exit holes about 1.6mm ($\frac{1}{16}$in) in diameter. Damage is confined mainly to the sapwood of conifers and hardwoods and is usually most severe in the outer sapwood, nearest to the bark, where there is a higher protein content. Infestation is more likely to occur in damp climates or in the damper parts of houses. The older type of birch plywood made with blood or casein glue is particularly susceptible because of the high protein content of the glue. Tropical hardwoods, except mahogany, and chipboard, hardboard and insulating board seem to be immune. Eggs are laid on end grain or in cracks or fissures so that wood with a smooth, finished surface is less likely to be attacked. The eggs hatch in about five weeks and the larvae then immediately bore into the wood and emerge as adults about three years later between the months of May and August.

Active infestation may be recognised by the presence of fine, granular bore dust outside the exit holes.

*Ptilinus pectinicornis.* This is a European species which has no popular name and which is specialised in its choice of timbers. It is mainly restricted to beech, elm, hornbeam, maple and sycamore. The damage is similar to that caused by the common furniture beetle except that the very fine bore-dust is tightly packed in the tunnels.

*Xestobium rufovillosum*; the death-watch beetle. The death-watch beetle occurs in Europe, but not in Scotland, and is unimportant in North America. It attacks the sapwood and heartwood of partly decayed beech, sweet chestnut, elm, walnut and especially oak in old buildings, where it can cause serious damage in wood joints and in the bearing ends of beams and joists which are in contact with damp walls. Very slight fungal infection such as blue stain is sufficient to render the timber susceptible to attack, which may then continue at a moisture content too low for normal fungal development, that is about 12 per cent. It is, therefore, unwise to re-use infected timber from an old building. The exit holes are larger than those of the other furniture beetles being about 3mm ($\frac{1}{8}$in) in diameter and the tunnels are filled with a coarse bore-dust.

The name 'death-watch' is due to the tapping noises made by the adults during the mating period. This was believed to herald an approaching death.

*Control of furniture beetle damage.* Damage by various species of furniture beetle may involve structural repair, but the infestation is relatively easily controlled with proprietory brands of preservative (page 51) or by fumigation.

### Ambrosia beetles; families *Platypodidae*, *Scolytidae* **and** *Lymexylidae*

There are hundreds of species of ambrosia beetles belonging to the families *Platypodidae*, *Scolytidae* and *Lymexylidae*. They occur throughout the world but are most common in the tropics. They have in common the characteristic that the adults bore tunnels into the wood in which they lay their eggs and deposit fungi which form a dark-coloured growth on the walls of the tunnels. The fungus provides food for the larvae after they have hatched and sometimes discolours the surrounding wood. The tunnels of the various species vary between 0.5mm and 3.0mm ($\frac{1}{50}$in and $\frac{1}{8}$in) in diameter and run mainly across the grain at right angles to the outer surface of the tree.

Both the sapwood and heartwood of hardwoods and softwoods are susceptible. Some species attack standing trees but ambrosia beetles are primarily pests of felled trees and even sawn timber so long as the moisture content is more than 30 per cent. When the wood has dried below this level, even if it is subsequently re-wetted, the fungus, and therefore the beetle, is no longer able to survive and the wood is then safe from attack.

Species particularly susceptible to infestation by ambrosia beetles are antiaris, afara, obeche, abura and agba in West Africa; the merantis, the lauans and keruing in the Far East; Douglas fir and western hemlock in North America; Parana pine in South America and oak and softwoods in Europe.

### Powder-post beetles; families Lyctidae and Bostrychidae

The term powder-post beetle is restricted in Britain to species of the families *Lyctidae* and *Bostrychidae* which are world-wide, but in the USA it is sometimes applied to wood-boring insects in general.

Powder-post beetles attack the sapwood of any hardwoods which contain sufficient starch and have sufficiently large vessels to receive the female beetle's ovipositor. Species commonly attacked are ash, elm, hickory, oak and walnut from temperate regions, agba, antiaris, afara, iroko, mahogany and obeche from Africa and ramin and seraya from the Far East.

One species of conifer, *Pinus canariensis*, is also known to be susceptible. Species with very small vessels, such as lime and cherry, or with low levels of starch, such as beech and birch, are immune.

The tunnels of the *Lyctidae* are about 1.6mm ($\frac{1}{16}$in) in diameter but those of the *Bostrychidae*, in some tropical timbers, may be as large as 6mm ($\frac{1}{4}$in).

Unlike furniture beetles, some *Lyctus* beetles can breed in very dry wood. It is important, therefore, not to use infected wood in furniture or structures. *Lyctus* tunnels can be distinguished from furniture-beetle tunnels because *Lyctus* bore dust is a very fine powder while furniture beetle dust is granular. One furniture beetle, *Ptilinus pestinicornis*, produces fine bore dust but unlike the *Lyctus* dust it is tightly packed in the tunnels.

### Longhorn beetles; family Cerambycidae

There are thousands of species of longhorn beetles occurring throughout the world but many of them are purely forest insects.

With one notable exception, *Hylotrupes bajulus*, almost all longhorn beetles can only enter green or partially seasoned wood with the bark on. The larvae bore tunnels into the sapwood and heartwood and few if any tree species are immune. Most of the important species of longhorn beetles bore relatively large, oval shaped tunnels, having an average diameter of about 5.0mm to 10mm ($\frac{3}{16}$in to $\frac{3}{8}$in). Some species produce bore dust, some produce wood fibres, while with some species the tunnels are empty.

Larvae already present may continue to work within the wood for many years, especially in cooler climates, and cause some structural damage.

The house longhorn beetle, *Hylotrupes bajulus*, occurs naturally in Europe and has been introduced into South Africa, Australia and South and North America, where it is known as the old house borer. It typically attacks structural timbers and joinery in new houses and has given some trouble in South East England. The tunnels are 6mm to 10mm ($\frac{1}{4}$in to $\frac{3}{8}$in) in diameter and are loosely filled with chips, wood fibres and sausage shaped pellets of bore-dust, unlike the powder-post tunnels which are filled with a fine powder.

### The significance of beetle damage

Furniture beetle is not likely to be present in new wood but may occur during service, particularly under damp conditions and in roughly finished wood. It is easily dealt with by using an appropriate preservative.

Death-watch beetle can be damaging to structural timbers, such as oak and sweet chestnut, in damp conditions.

Ambrosia beetle damage will not increase after the wood has been seasoned and if the damage is acceptable at the time of conversion the timber may safely be used.

Powder-post beetles are primarily a pest of timber yards, where they may be dealt with by methods of kiln sterilisation. The larvae of both powder-post and longhorn beetles can continue to work in the wood for a number of years after the wood has been sawn. The craftsman, therefore, should check that these larvae are not present in his timber.

Furniture, powder-post, house longhorn and death-watch beetles can all attack structural timbers in service which should therefore be treated with a permanent preservative before being used. The residual effects of other longhorn larvae already in the wood at the time of conversion are unlikely to be of much importance in structural timbers.

## Fungal decay

### Types of decay

Fungal decay varies according to the species of fungus and timber but all decay leads to:

**a**) changes in colour
**b**) a change of texture
**c**) a reduction in density
**d**) softening.

There is an accompanying loss in strength which is proportionally greater than the reduction in density, and there is often an appreciable loss in strength before the decay is readily apparent.

All decay can, rather loosely, be described as brown rot or white rot. Brown rot destroys the cellulose and leaves a brown-coloured, crumbly, cubical structure, having cracks both parallel with and across the grain (Figure 20(a)). White rot destroys both the lignin and the cellulose and is less consistent than brown rot in its effects upon the wood. Typically, it produces a pale-coloured, fibrous or stringy structure which often becomes white in the later stages, (Figure 20(b)).

Both brown and white rots can occur in flecks or bands, or throughout the wood, and dark-coloured zone lines are sometimes produced along the periphery of the rot, (Figure 21).

Decay should not be confused with various forms of staining which are also usually caused by fungi but which have little or no effect upon the mechanical properties of the wood.

### Occurrence of decay

Decay fungi can attack wood at the following stages:

**a**) in the growing tree
**b**) in the felled log
**c**) during conversion and storage
**d**) in use.

Given the right conditions the heartwood, but not the sapwood, of almost any species of growing tree can be attacked by decay fungi which enter through dead roots or branches. The fungi which attack living trees very rarely infect, or continue to develop in, the felled tree.

**20(a)** Brown rot

After a tree is felled infection depends upon the species of timber, the moisture content of the wood and, to a lesser extent, the temperature. Wood with a moisture content of 20 per cent or less is not at risk. After felling, no sapwood has much resistance to infection but the heartwood of many species, particularly if it is dense and dark coloured such as teak, afrormosia, iroko, pitch pine and yew, is very resistant and is almost immune to attack even in situation favourable to infection.

Other species, such as beech, birch and many conifers, which have an ill-defined heartwood, have virtually no resistance and are liable to

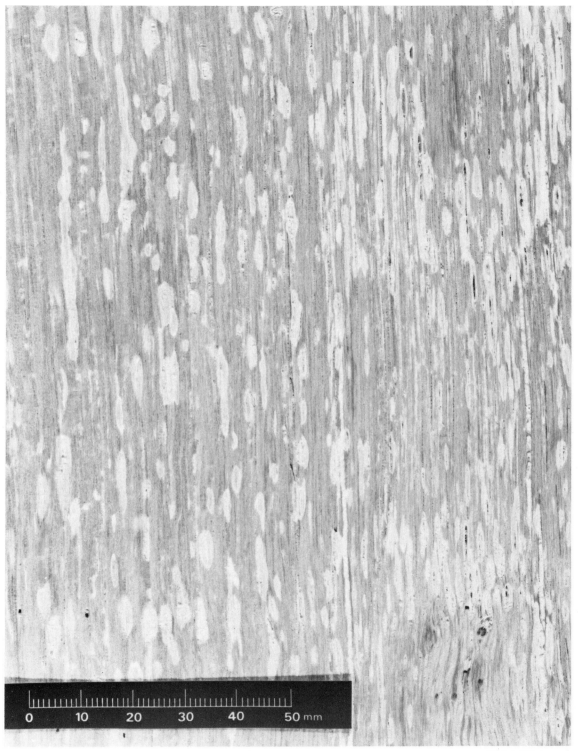

**20(b)** White rot

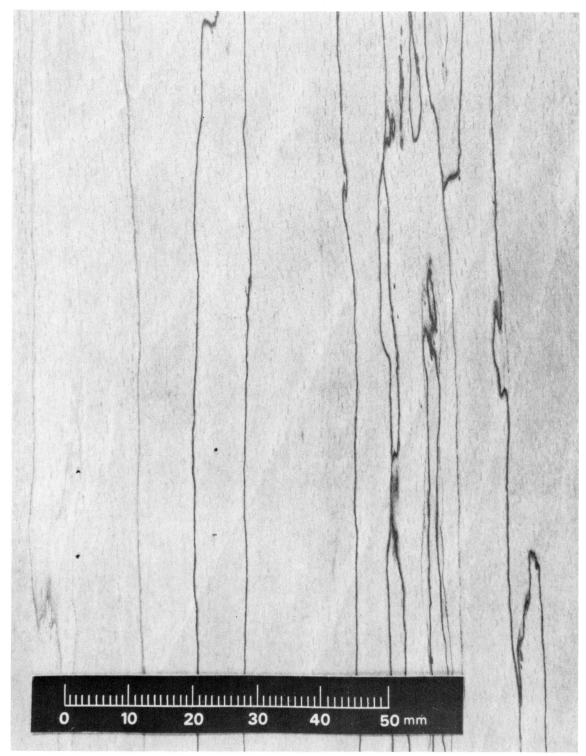

**21** Dark zone lines caused by rot

infection if the moisture content of the wood is above about 20 per cent and the temperature well above freezing. Well seasoned timber in dry, well ventilated conditions is safe from infection by decay fungi.

The rots which enter the standing tree or, subsequently, the timber during the processes of logging, conversion and storage are more the responsibility of the forester and the timber merchant than the craftsman, who is mainly concerned to avoid buying and using timber already damaged by decay fungi. The wood worker may, however, be involved in wood storage and it is therefore important to realise that decay fungi can infect carelessly stored wood which is allowed to remain damp for any length of time, especially in warm weather (page 40).

It is not practicable to describe the large number of fungi which can attack various timber species under a range of different conditions. But examples of a few of the more important and representative fungal species are described below.

### Rot in exposed situations

*Lentinus lepideus* is a brown rot widely distributed in Europe and North America. It attacks coniferous timbers such as railway sleepers, transmission poles and fences. It can enter the heartwood and is tolerant of low concentrations of creosote.

*Daedalea quercina* is a brown rot which occurs throughout temperate regions of the world. It is found in a number of hardwood species but is particularly common in the sapwood of oak, the heartwood being relatively resistant.

### Rot in buildings and structures

There is no clear-cut distinction between the rots found in buildings and those occurring in the open. Some of the so-called wet rots which infect saturated timber in buildings also occur out of doors. But the most common and serious of the structural rots, the dry-rot fungus, is not found in the open.

*Merulius lacrymans*, the dry-rot fungus. The dry rot fungus causes serious damage in Europe but is unimportant in North America, where its place is taken by a similar rot, *Poria incrassata*. The dry-rot fungus cannot develop in wood having a moisture content of less than 20 per cent and it flourishes best with a mosture content between about 30 per cent and 40 per cent. It causes a brown, cubical rot and attacks mainly softwoods, but also hardwoods, such as mahogany.

The fungus extends some distance along the grain, perhaps 450mm (18in) beyond the visible rot. It also penetrates brickwork, from which it is difficult to eradicate. It may, therefore, on occasions be preferable not to replace an affected structure with wood but with an alternative material. Generally, however, if the source of moisture and the infected wood are removed and both the remaining wood and the replacement member treated with a preservative the damaged wood can be replaced.

*Poria vaillantii*, the wet-rot fungus. The name of the dry-rot fungus is misleading because it only occurs in damp conditions but, in contrast, *Poria vaillantii* is a fungus of really wet wood and only occurs in buildings if there has been a persistent water leak. The fungus causes a light brown cubical rot on softwoods similar to that caused by dry-rot fungus. It is widely distributed in Europe but is relatively uncommon in America. *Poria vaillantii* is easier to eradicate than the dry-rot fungus because it will not persist when the leakage of water has been stopped, and it does not penetrate deeply into brickwork.

*Phellinus megaloporous* can be regarded as the hardwood equivalent of *Poria vaillantii* because it attacks hardwoods under very wet conditions. It is a white, stringy rot which is common in Europe and which is particularly associated with the decay of oak structures in buildings and with subsequent attack by death-watch beetles. *Phellinus megaloporus* only thrives in very damp and warm conditions and does not enter brickwork. It is, therefore, relatively easy to eradicate.

### Fungal staining

*Sap or blue stain*. A number of different fungi can cause sap or blue stain in softwoods and some hardwoods. The staining is almost always restricted to the sapwood but occasionally occurs in the heartwood of softwoods. Among the softwoods pine is particularly susceptible; more so, for example, than spruce, fir or Douglas fir. Temperate hardwoods are generally not susceptible although ash and aspen are occasionally infected. Blue stain does occur, however, in a number of pale-coloured tropical hardwoods such as obeche, limba and ramin.

The stain has little effect upon the compression or bending strength of the timber but it reduces, to some extent, its hardness and impact strength. It has no effect upon the permeability of wood to preservatives.

Blue stain is less likely to occur in temperate regions if trees are felled in the winter and, in any climate, if the logs are quickly converted and dried. If logs have to be left unsawn infection can be prevented by keeping them perpetually saturated in a pond or under a permanent spray,or by treating exposed surfaces of wood with an appropriate antiseptic solution of which there are several on the market.

Damp sawn timber should not be stacked without sticks and particular care should be taken not to close-stack timber which is superficially dry but wet inside. Blue stain in sawn timber can be prevented by dipping in a fungicidal solution immediately after conversion.

*Brown oak.* The heartwood of oak is sometimes stained a uniform medium-brown colour by the beef-steak fungus, *Fistulina hepatica*, which enters the tree via wounds in the stem. The staining is sometimes streaky but may colour the whole stem. The strength of the wood is only slightly affected and after seasoning there is no further spread of the fungus. Brown oak is highly prized for furniture making and panelling but should not be used in situations where strength is a critical factor.

*Green wood.* Several species, including oak, ash and hazel, are occasionally stained a vivid green by the fungus *Chlorosplenium aeruginosum.* Like other staining fungi it has little effect on the strength properties of the wood although the fungus can occur in combination with a wood rot.

Sound wood stained with *chlorosplenium aeruginosum* is sometimes used for marquetry and inlay work.

*Iron stain.* Timbers with a high tannin content such as oak and sweet chestnut react with iron to form a bluish dye. This dye is an iron salt of gallic acid, which is the basis of ordinary writing ink.

### The significance of fungal decay

With the exception of a relatively small number of species with a high degree of natural durability, decay in timber is closely associated with moisture content. Decay does not occur in any timber at a moisture content of less than 20 per cent so that furniture and other portable wooden articles kept indoors are not liable to decay. Well ventilated wood in the open, provided it is not in contact with the ground, is also safe from infection.

If wood which does not have a high natural durability is used in damp situations it should be impregnated with an appropriate preservative (page 51) and all structures involving the use of timber should be designed in such a way that water cannot be trapped in contact with the wood.

Seasoned wood which contains decayed or partially decayed tissue should not be used because its strength and working properties will have been impaired. Wood staining, however, is almost entirely a matter of appearance and stained wood can be used in situations where the appearance is of little or no importance.

# CHAPTER 3
# Seasoning and storage

## Reasons for seasoning

Seasoning is the process of reducing the moisture content of green timber and may be done by air drying or kilning. There are a number of reasons for seasoning:

**a**) To achieve a moisture content approximately equal to that which will be maintained in service so that there will be relatively little subsequent movement (page 17).

**b**) To reduce the warping and distortion which normally occurs when timber dries (page 27). This is achieved by holding the timber under a physical constraint as the moisture content is reduced.

**c**) To reduce the liability of infection by decay fungi (page 33).

**d**) To prevent the development of blue stain (page 36).

**e**) To reduce the liability to attack by such insects as ambrosia beetles (page 31).

**f**) To increase the strength of the wood (page 18).

**g**) To make the wood suitable for gluing and finishing (page 42).

**h**) To reduce transport costs by reducing weight.

## Factors affecting seasoning

Whether seasoning is done by air drying or kilning there are four factors which control the rate of drying:

**a**) humidity
**b**) temperature
**c**) the rate of air flow
**d**) the permeability of the species.

Since warm air can absorb much more water vapour than colder air it is possible to achieve a considerable degree of drying, even in a humid atmosphere, provided the temperature is suffi-ciently high. For this reason timber can dry more rapidly and to a lower equilibrium moisture content in a moderately humid, tropical climate than under drier, temperate conditions. In temperate regions seasoning is unlikely to be rapid enough to cause serious case hardening, collapse, honeycoming or splitting except, possibly, in exposed conditions during a hot summer and especially at the ends of planks exposed to the sun.

If there is no draught the air becomes saturated close to the drying wood and in the absence of a moisture gradient from the wood to the air the drying process slows down or ceases. It is indeed self-evident that the drying process is accelerated if the rate of airflow is increased.

Some species of timber, such as oak, are naturally slower to season than other species, such as obeche, because they are less permeable to water vapour. In general, hard, dense, timbers are likely to be less permeable than softer and lighter timbers and to be more difficult to season, although they tend to be more stable in service.

Seasoning does not start properly until logs are sawn into planks and battens but some changes do take place in the wood if logs are left unsawn for a long time. Longitudinal splits and tension set may develop as a result of a steep moisture gradient from the outside to the centre of the log. This is particularly liable to happen at the ends of logs because wood dries very much faster from the end grain than across the grain. Under some circumstances the longitudinal water movement through freshly cut end grain may be up to one thousand times faster than radial movement. There is also a likelihood of degradation by insects and fungi. But not all the changes are undesirable. The food storing parenchyma cells remain alive for a considerable time in the log and while they are alive respiration reduces the quantity of nutrients in the cells, thus making the wood less susceptible to subsequent infection by blue stain fungi.

Some species, such as teak, are girdled, and therefore killed, several years before they are felled. This causes some seasoning to take place before the trees leave the forest. The degree of drying is small but the density of the wood is reduced sufficiently to allow the logs to be floated down the rivers. Without this preliminary drying they would sink.

If logs are immersed for a time in water, before conversion, the sawn timber is less likely to be attacked subsequently by powder-post beetles.

## Air seasoning

In many situations there is no alternative to air seasoning, which has some disadvantages and advantages compared with kiln drying. The rate of natural drying cannot be controlled but depends broadly upon the climate and, more specifically, upon the weather so that very high temperatures or, to a lesser extent, very dry or windy conditions, may cause some species to dry too quickly and to suffer some of the defects described on page 27. It is equally a disadvantage that the final moisture content cannot always reliably be predetermined and unless wood is finally dried in a heated building the moisture content can rarely be reduced to a level suitable for internal use. In very hot, dry climates wood seasoned in the open or under cover may reach an equilibrium moisture content as low as 6 or 7 per cent but in temperate regions the moisture content of air-dried wood is unlikely to fall below about 17 per cent in summer and 25–30 per cent in winter. This has to be compared with the equilibrium moisture content in heated buildings of 10 to 14 per cent.

Many craftsmen believe, however, that wood which is seasoned naturally is more stable in service than kiln-dried timber, and there may well be a logical explanation for this belief, especially for wood with an irregular grain in a temperate climate, provided the wood is dried carefully and brought by degrees to a suitable moisture content. The reason for this is that almost every piece of wood has some internal stresses, and commercial kiln drying, which is designed to dry wood to a predetermined but approximate moisture content as quickly as possible, does not necessarily result in a uniform moisture content throughout every piece of wood, even after conditioning (page 41). As the kiln-dried wood subsequently becomes uniformly dry in service some of the small residual stresses are released and the wood moves slightly. Natural seasoning is a very much longer process and in the final stages the moisture content of the wood fluctuates slightly with changes in the ambient humidity. In this process the moisture content and the internal stresses are gradually brought to an equilibrium.

The same result could probably be achieved by a very gentle and slow kiln-drying schedule and is achievable with a dehumidifer.

If timber is to be dried in the open it should be protected against damp from below and rain from above. The ends of the wood should not be exposed to direct sunlight and the end grain should, desirably, be coated with a relatively impermeable end sealer such as wax or bitumen. The planks or battens have to be separated by wooden sticks about 12–25mm ($\frac{1}{2}$–1in) thick to allow a circulation of air and these should be

**22** Stacking sawn timber for drying

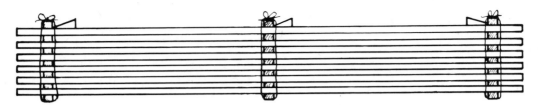

23 Restraining sawn timber while drying

placed in vertical series, as in Figure 22, to avoid distorting the wood. The thickness of the sticks to some extent controls the rate of drying; the thicker the sticks the more rapid the loss of water.

The weight of the overlying wood in a large stack prevents or reduces warping during seasoning but there is inadequate weight for the upper layer of wood in a large stack or for any of the wood in a small stack. It is therefore desirable to put heavy weights on the top planks in line with the sticks.

The stacking area should be kept clean and tidy because old logs and pieces of wood left lying on the ground are sources of insect and fungal infection.

The time taken to air dry wood depends not only upon the atmospheric conditions and the species of timber but also upon the thickness of the wood. Thick battens take very much longer to season than thin boards and massive pieces of wood may not reach an equilibrium moisture content for many years. A common rule of thumb is to allow one year for each 25mm (1in) of thickness.

In commercial practice wood is often partially air seasoned before being kiln dried. It is rare for small-scale craftsmen or amateurs to have access to kilning facilities but they may have occasion to season wood to a moisture content suitable for internal use. This can be done if the freshly sawn wood is stacked in a shed or under cover in the open, as described above. After one or two seasons, depending upon the thickness of the wood, it needs to be stored indoors for 6 to 12 months under the conditions of temperature and humidity approximating to those it will ultimately experience in service. This is particularly true for wood to be used for high quality work.

The author has found it convenient when stacking small quantities of sawn timber to put sticks across the top plank and to lash the top and bottom sticks together with binder twine. This can be tightened by tapping wooden wedges under the top sticks, thereby preventing the boards from moving during the drying process (Figure 23).

There is a particular problem in seasoning a large block of timber to be used for wood carving, which is to be kept indoors, especially if it is a dense hardwood. A steep moisture gradient will be established in the wood and the centre may not reach an equilibrium moisture content for many years, during which time the outer layers are subjected to constant stress. One partial solution is to hollow out the block. This will accelerate drying and reduce the moisture gradient. But a more certain method is to cut the block into slices and dry each slice to the required equilibrium moisture content. When they have reached this condition they are trued and glued together.

## Kiln drying

The reasons for kiln drying are to season timber quickly to a pre-determined moisture content under controlled conditions. As with air seasoning the rate of drying is determined by the temperature, the relative humidity and the airflow, all of which are directly under the control of the operator; a high temperature, a low relative humidity and a fast airflow all increase the rate of drying and thereby set up a steep moisture gradient from the surface to the middle of the timber.

The acceptable rate of drying depends upon several factors. These are:

a) timber species
b) timber quality
c) timber thickness
d) timber use
e) direction of sawing.

Some species can tolerate a faster rate of drying than others without damage, and any species of wood which has a straight and even pattern of growth and is free from knots can safely be dried faster than poorer quality material. A steep moisture gradient can occur in thick pieces of wood and this leads to tension set (page 18) and splitting. Therefore thick planks have to be dried more slowly than thinner planks. The use to which timber is to be put also has a bearing on the rate of drying. If it is to be cut into wide, flat planks which need to be stable in use the rate of drying has to be carefully controlled. Finally, the direction of sawing has some effect upon drying because moisture vapour diffuses more rapidly in a radial than in a tangential direction. Temperatures above about 60°C (140°F) may slightly reduce the strength of wood, especially the impact strength, although this is unlikely to be important, and some species such as sycamore become darkened at temperatures above 50°C (120°F).

Standardised schedules have been worked out for a range of different species and these may be modified in the light of local experience. If a particular type of material is inclined to split, the relative humidity is increased to reduce the moisture gradient in the wood, and timber which shows a pronounced tendency to distort is dried at a relatively low temperature.

## Conditioning

It is usual to dry wood to an equilibrium moisture content of 12 per cent in temperate climates because this is about the average of the range of moisture contents likely to be attained in service. It is not possible to dry a load in a kiln uniformly, so it is the normal practice to dry each load so that the drier wood reaches a lower moisture content. The temperature and humidity are then adjusted to a combination appropriate to a 12 per cent moisture content. Figure 9 shows, for example, that this could be 50°C (120°F) and 73 per cent relative humidity. The load is then left in this condition for a time during which period the moisture content of the drier and wetter portions of the load tend to converge on 12 per cent.

## Dehumidifying

Kiln drying gives a perfectly satisfactory result for most purposes and if kiln-dried timber is stored for a time, before being worked, in the conditions it will experience in service there will be little or no difference between kiln drying and careful air drying.

It is often not possible, however, for the craftsman to have his timber kiln dried, especially if he buys standing trees or logs and has them sawn by a local sawmill. A commercial kiln cannot be operated economically for small parcels of wood, even if there is one in the vincinity, and a small consignment of a particular species cannot be included in a larger load of another species requiring a different drying schedule. This can be a problem if it is not convenient to wait for a year or more for the timber to dry. There is, however, a compromise method known as dehumidifying. A dehumidifier can be regarded as a form of refrigerator which cools the air, thereby causing the moisture to condense. The cold, dry air is then warmed by the heat released in the cooling process and blown by a fan through the chamber containing the timber to be dried. The cost of a dehumidifier, which is not unlike a refrigerator in appearance, is of the order of £500 to £1000 at 1980 costs and the chamber containing the timber can be a relatively cheap and simple structure.

The process of dehumidifying is more akin to accelerated air drying than to kilning and because it is slow and gentle it is possible to accommodate several species of timber simultaneously. Because of its modest cost it is also suitable for small-scale working.

## Care of seasoned timber

When timber has been seasoned to a predetermined equilibrium moisture content it should, desirably, be stored immediately in conditions of temperature and humidity which will maintain the equilibrium.

This counsel of perfection is often impracticable but it is necessary to protect seasoned timber from extremes of temperature or humidity. If wood is to be stored in the open it should be protected against rain and sun. Provided it is stored soon after kilning and is not to be left for very long periods it is best piled without sticks. In this way the wood inside the stack is partially protected against atmospheric changes.

# CHAPTER 4
# Glues

## Properties required

Glue used by craftsmen has to satisfy different criteria for different jobs. For any purpose it must retain its strength more or less indefinitely under the conditions for which it is intended. It has, therefore, to be resistant to decaying organisms and, in temperate climates, to moderate changes in humidity and temperature. In some tropical regions a glue has to retain its strength over quite wide ranges of humidity and temperature and to accommodate considerable stress on the glue line resulting from movement in the timber.

It is generally an advantage for the glue used by craftsmen to be colourless, but it need not normally be resistant to prolonged weathering, to extremes of temperature or to the action of chemicals. For some applications, such as veneering, a glue has to provide some degree of immediate adhesion before it has set. Glue used by the amateur needs to be strong enough for the job even in an imperfect joint. It therefore has to be a filler as well as an adhesive. Within reason expense is only of moderate importance because the glue used in a piece of furniture, for example, is likely to account for only a very small proportion of the total cost.

## The strength of glued joints

The principal strength of a glued joint is its resistance to shear, not to tension. The lap joint illustrated in Figure 24 is very much stronger in the direction A than in the direction B.

Nevertheless, glue joints have a considerable strength in the direction B as is demonstrated in the construction of a violin, where the pressure of the strings, acting through the soundpost, is exerting a considerable stress at right angles to the glued interface between the back of the instrument and the liners on the ribs.

In general, less dense woods glue more easily than denser species and oily woods, such as teak and iroko, are particularly difficult, especially if

water-based glues are used. These difficult species are best glued immediately after the joints have been cut and the oil in the wood has been removed with a solvent such as methanol, although the oil can be removed later by the same method before applying the glue. It is, however, a wise precaution with any species lightly to sand the surfaces to be glued if they have been exposed to the air for a considerable time or if, due to dull cutting tools, the gluing surfaces have become burnished.

All glues, no matter how moisture resistant they may be in service, are more effective on wood that has been well seasoned. The optimum moisture content for the types of glue likely to be used for indoor work is about 12 per cent.

The thickness of the glue line is important. The thinner the glue line the stronger the bond, and unless the glue contains a filler the glue line should not be thicker than 0.125mm (0.005in). Although a gap-filling glue can be used with a glue line not exceeding 1.25mm (0.05in) it is still preferable to keep the glue gline as thin as possible.

All conventional wood joints are inherently well designed because they provide an adequate area of bonding, and they constrain the wood in such a way that it is virtually only a shear stress that can be applied to the joint.

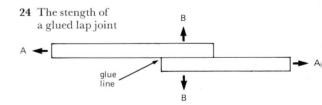

**24** The stength of a glued lap joint

## Natural glues

### *Animal glues*

Various types of animal glue derived from bone, skin and hide have been used from prehistoric times and no other types were available until about 1930.

Animal glue, such as Scotch glue, makes a strong bond but is not resistant to decaying organisms or to heat and moisture and is rather more troublesome to use than synthetic resin glues. These are not usually major disadvantages and animal glue is still widely used for musical instrument making and for veneering. It is used for making musical instruments because they occasionally have to be dismantled for maintenance and repair and a skilled worker can, for example, separate the back and belly of a violin from its ribs with a thin blade without damaging the instrument (page 146). This would be impossible with a synthetic resin glue. Animal glue is used for veneering because it provides an immediate and adequate bond between the veneer and the groundwork as soon as the veneer is pressed into position, without the need for sustained pressure while the glue is setting.

Animal glue is sold in cake or pearl form and has then to be mixed with water and heated in a glue pot. It is applied hot and sets by cooling.

Animal blood glues are moisture resistant if hot pressed and they are still used in some cheap plywood. Casein glue, which is made from milk, is strong and easy to use and is moderately resistant to heat and moisture, but being alkaline in character is liable to stain timbers having a high tannin content. Since it has no particular qualities not possessed by the better synthetic resin glues it is rarely used by craftsmen.

### Vegetable glues

The only glue derived from a vegetable source which is widely used to-day is the contact-type glue made of rubber, dissolved in a solvent. This may, however, be made of synthetic rubber, in which case it is strictly incorrect to refer to it as a vegetable glue. The rubber-based glues are used for bonding sheet materials together but are not suitable for bonding wood to wood.

For bonding baize to wood the best choice is a white latex-based product of the type used for gluing backing strips and edges to carpets.

Leather is bonded to wood with a water-soluble cellulose paste similar to that used for heavy wallpaper. This type of adhesive does not harden the leather but holds it firmly in position with no tendency to curl or lift at the edges.

Attempts are being made, notably in China, to develop from plant materials alternatives to oil-based resin glues. This is because some countries, like China, have poorly developed chemical industries and have to import the bulk of their synthetic resin glues from abroad. Resins have been synthesised from resin extracts from trees, and lignin, a constituent of wood, has been used as a source of phenolic compounds as a partial or complete replacement for phenol derived from petroleum. Adhesives derived from these materials are cheaper than phenol formaldehyde glues (see below) but, generally speaking, are less moisture resistant.

## Synthetic resin glues

A number of synthetic resin glues have been developed since about 1930 and most of them are stronger and more resistant to heat and moisture than the natural glues. With the exception of polyvinyl acetate glues they all require a hardener to accelerate setting although they will set very slowly without a hardener and therefore have a limited shelf life.

With some types of glue the hardener is applied to one face of the joint and the glue to the other so that setting does not start until the two faces of the joint are brought together. They are known as separate-application glues. With combined-application glues the glue and hardener are mixed in the correct proportions before use, while some glues have the hardener incorporated with the glue in the form of a powder. These are known as one-shot glues in which the hardener is not activated until the powder is mixed with water.

All the synthetic resin glues, apart from the polyvinyl acetates, are thermosetting, which means that once they are set they will not soften again under the influence of heat. All synthetic resin glues set more quickly the higher the temperature, but polyvinyl acetate, which is themoplastic, requires a cooling period to harden before the cramps are removed.

The synthetic resin glues are all completely resistant to decaying organisms.

### Phenol formaldehyde (PF)

Phenol formaldehyde glues are extremely strong and virtually indestructible. They will withstand more exposure, moisture and heat than the wood itself, and they form an extremely strong bond. The temperature has to be carefully controlled during the gluing process and for most types of PF glues a high temperature is required. They form a dark glue line and are used almost always only for plywood and chipboard manufacture.

### Resorcinol formaldehyde (RF)

Resorcinol formalydehyde has similar properties to phenol formaldehyde but is easier to use and its only real disadvantages are its high price, which is several times that of urea formaldehyde, and the fact that it forms a dark glue line. It is the only type of assembly, or jointing, glue which is both completely water, weather and heat resistant and suitable for home use.

### Urea formaldehyde (UF)

Urea formaldehyde is considerably less weather and heat resistant than phenol or resorcinal formaldehyde. It is, however, more than adequate for articles to be used indoors and is indefinitely resistant to the range of heat and moisture changes normally encountered in a building. It is colourless, relatively cheap and can be used at normal room temperatures, but should not be used below 10°C (50°F). A number of different types of urea formaldehyde glue are commercially available and they include separate-application, combined-application and one-shot varieties, some with a filler and some without.

### Polyvinyl acetate (PVA)

Polyvinyl acetate glues are white, water-soluble emulsions. They can form bonds of high dry strength but are less strong than urea formaldehyde and they are thermoplastic, which means that they soften in high temperatures. Although they re-set when the temperature is reduced, movement in the joint can rupture the glue line. They are less resistant than urea formaldehyde to water but they are very clean and easy to use and have a long shelf and pot life. They form transparent glue lines. One of their disadvantages is a tendency to creep when subjected to sustained loading, but this is of little importance in most situations.

### Epoxy resins

Epoxy resins used as adhesives are combined-application glues. The glue and hardener are stiff creams which are mixed together before use. They are strong and durable, and are used for bonding a wide variety of materials such as metal, wood, china and glass. They can be used for furniture making but are very expensive and have a short pot life once the two components are mixed together.

## Choice of glue

The choice of glue depends upon the job. Bearing in mind the qualities mentioned at the beginning of this chapter the most suitable types of glue for wood joints are urea formaldehyde and polyvinyl acetates. Neither of them is particularly expensive, they both have adequate bonding strength and permanence under normal conditions and they both form colourless glue lines. They are also easy to use. Of the two types urea formaldehyde has the advantage of being themosetting so that it is completely unaffected by heat. Of the numerous forms of urea formaldehyde on the market the author has found a one-shot, gap-filling type such as Cascamite One Shot consistently successful.

For amateur work on large boats or for external structures there is no really satisfactory alternative to a resorcinol formaldehyde glue, although a one-shot urea formaldehyde glue has been used successfully for a number of years on dinghies which are not continually immersed in the water and which are protected by paint or varnish.

For stringed instruments, for the working parts of keyboard instruments and for wood veneering there is no satisfactory alternative to animal, or Scotch, glue and for laminating melamine or other thin films *in situ* a rubber based glue is used.

The wood craftsman occasionally has to bond other materials such as metal, leather and baize to wood. An epoxy resin is the best choice for bonding metal to wood. A white latex-based emulsion is used for bonding cloth and a cellulose paste for laying leather.

# CHAPTER 5

# Sanding and finishing

## Sanding

Sanding is a traditional word used to describe the operation of smoothing wood with abrasive paper, none of which is any longer made with sand. The abrasive paper is also often referred to colloquially as sandpaper.

### Types of abrasive material

Of the various types of abrasive material used in different trades and industries the wood worker is concerned primarily with glass, garnet and aluminium oxide. Silicon carbide and wire wool are also used on occasions, especially on hard lacquer finishes.

Glasspaper, with the exception of the 00 or flour grade, is a very inferior material for sanding hardwoods. It is relatively soft and the coarser grades, in particular, quickly lose their cutting surfaces. But flour grade glasspaper is a valuable material because it gives a smoother and finer finish then any other paper. Although the equivalent in grain size of 5/0 garnet paper, it gives the impression of being as fine, if not finer, than 9/0 garnet paper because it is much softer and does not bite so sharply into the wood.

Garnet paper, which is a reddish orange colour, is much harder than glass, cuts more quickly, and retains its cutting surface longer than glass.

Aluminium oxide, which is the same mineral as ruby, is tougher and harder than garnet. Woodworking aluminium oxide is usually a light sandy colour.

Silicon carbide is harder than aluminium oxide and is nearly as hard as diamond. It is familiar to many people as the black wet-and-dry paper used for rubbing down hard surfaces such as car bodies.

The 000 grade of wire wool is the finest of all the commonly used abrasive materials.

In addition to the abrasive material itself there are three other variables to be taken into account.

**Table 1**  *Common types of abrasive paper for woodworking*

| Aluminium oxide | | Garnet | | | Glass | | |
|---|---|---|---|---|---|---|---|
| grit size | backing paper | grade | backing paper | | grade | backing paper | |
| | | 9/0 | A | | | | |
| | | 8/0 | A | | | | |
| | | 7/0 | A | | | | |
| | | 6/0 | A | | | | |
| 180 | C | 5/0 | A | C | 00 (flour) | A | |
| 150 | C | 4/0 | A | C | 0 | A | C |
| 120 | C | 3/0 | A | C | 1 | | C |
| 100 | C | 2/0 | A | C | $1\frac{1}{2}$ | | C |
| 80 | C | 0 | A | C | F2 | | C |
| 60 | C | $\frac{1}{2}$ | | C | M2 | | C |
| 50 | C | 1 | | C | S2 | | C |
| 40 | C | $1\frac{1}{2}$ | | C | $2\frac{1}{2}$ | | C |
| 36 | C | | | | 3 | | C |

The grit size of silicon carbide paper is classified in the same way as that of aluminium oxide

These are grade or grit size, the density of the grit on the paper, and the thickness of the paper.

### Grade or grit size

The most important of these three variables is grade or grit size which is a measure of the coarseness of the cutting surface. Different units of grading are used for each of the three types of paper and the equivalent grades are set out in Table 1. The higher the number the finer the grade (except for glass paper).

### Density of grains

There are two patterns of grit on abrasive papers: open and closed. The grains on open-coat paper occupy about 50 per cent of the surface and on close-coat paper virtually all the surface. In theory, the close-coat paper should cut more rapidly because it has more cutting edges, but in practice open-coat paper is more suitable for woodwork because it is less liable to clog.

### Backing paper

Backing papers are of several thicknesses of which 'A' grade is the thinnest and, therefore, the most flexible. An 'A' grade paper should always be chosen for fine-grade finishing papers while the coarser papers for the preparatory work should have a 'C' grade backing. A 'D' grade is sometimes used for machine sanding-discs.

### Sizes of abrasive papers

Most papers are available in a standard size of 280mm by 230mm (11in by 9in), but aluminium oxide and garnet papers are also available in a number of specialized sizes and shapes for powered sanding machines. A convenient size, which is sold in packets for small orbital sanders, is 235mm by 94mm ($9\frac{1}{4}$in by $3\frac{11}{16}$in).

### Use of abrasive papers

When the work has been cleaned and trimmed up after gluing, the surfaces are prepared for finishing by a series of sanding operations. It is both ineffective and a waste of effort to use a fine paper too soon and to jump from a coarse to a fine grade. The coarse paper makes relatively deep scratches which the fine paper will not remove without a great deal of effort. The secret is to sand the work several times using a successively finer grade each time.

For almost all work the preliminary cleaning and smoothing is best done with open-coat aluminium oxide paper having a C grade backing. The first sanding is done with a 60 or 80 grade paper followed successively with 100 and 120 grade paper. The later stages of sanding are better done with garnet paper varying from about 4/0 to 6/0 or 7/0 grade, and the final finish given with 00 grade glass paper.

Wood is cut down most quickly by sanding across the grain, but this makes deep scratches, especially with the coarser grades, and the sanding with each grade should be finished with the grain.

The paper is most conveniently wrapped round a wooden block for sanding. Some workers prefer to fix a wad of hard rubber or some other resilient material to the working surface of the block. This is said to make the paper last longer, but it is not really necessary, although very fine papers accumulate small, hard patches of wood dust which can mark the surface of the wood unless they are scraped off. These are less likely to occur if a more resilient sanding block is used.

Sanding always tends to wear away the sharp edges of wood, and the more resilient the sanding block the more likely is this to happen, as shown in Figure 25(a). It can be prevented by cramping pieces of waste wood along the edge of the work as in Figure 25(b).

When sanding any two pieces of wood which are joined at right angles, sanding across the grain is unavoidable. Provided a series of successively finer papers is used, the final stages of sanding with 6/0 or 7/0 garnet paper produces only superficial scratching, and this is removed by final sanding with the grain using 00 glass paper or wire wool (Figure 26).

Even open-coated paper is continually clogged with sawdust, but this can easily be removed by tapping the sanding block firmly against a hard surface.

### Machine sanding

There are three types of sanding machine which can be operated with a small hand drill. These are disc sanders with a fixed spindle, disc sanders with a universal joint, and orbital sanders. Disc sanders with a fixed spindle are very liable to make deep grooves in the wood and are not suitable for fine work. Discs with a universal joint are less likely to cause damage, but even these have to be used with great care. Orbital sanders are safe but slow. After using all three types the author has come to the conclusion that the most satisfactory sequence is a

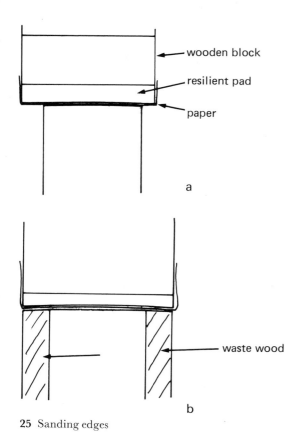

a

b

25 Sanding edges

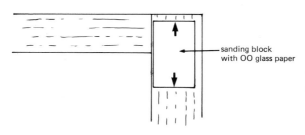

sanding block
with OO glass paper

26 Sanding to remove cross-grain scratches

finely set smoothing plane followed by a cabinet-maker's scraper, followed in turn by coarse and fine sanding by hand.

## Finishing

Almost all wooden articles made by craftsmen are treated with some form of finish to enhance the natural colour and figure of the wood and usually, also, to seal and protect the surface.

Various waxes, oils and natural varnishes were used until shellac-based french polish became popular in Britain in the early nineteenth century, having been developed in France towards the end of the previous century. Today, most factory-made furniture and other wooden articles are finished with various forms of nitrocellulose and catalysed lacquers. Many of these synthetic finishes are unsuitable for the amateur or small-scale craftsmen either because they are unobtainable in small quantities or because they have to be used under carefully controlled conditions both to achieve satisfactory results and to ensure safe and healthy working conditions. Some synthetic lacquers such as certain formulations of polyurethane are, however, suitable for use in the house or small workshop.

The number of different lacquers is enormous and it is quite outside the scope of this book either to classify them or to describe them comprehensively. For this reason two references are given in the bibliography for the benefit of those who wish to study the subject in more detail. There is no particular finish which can be regarded as ideal. The choice depends upon circumstances but it is possible to achieve perfectly satisfactory results for any situation by choosing from the five main types of finish which are available to, and suitable for the domestic craftsmen. These are wax, shellac resin, oil, nitrocellulose lacquer and some forms of catalysed lacquer.

As a generalisation, the natural products like wax, oil and shellac resin, and to some extent also, nitrocellulose finishes, are easily damaged by heat and moisture, but being soluble they are also easily repaired. The various catalysed lacquers which set into hard, insoluble films are resistant to damage but they are also difficult to repair. Before applying the finish it is sometimes desirable to fill or stain the wood.

## Filling

A wood filler is used to fill the grain and sometimes, also, to stain the wood. It is only necessary when a very smooth finish is wanted on coarse-grained wood, and since it is usually desirable to retain the natural colour of the wood a filler is chosen which matches as closely as possible the colour of the wood. It is applied after sanding and before waxing or varnishing. The filler itself, however, has to be sanded smooth before the final finish is put on.

47

### Staining

Staining is not normally a recommended treatment for hand-made furniture but it may occasionally be worthwhile staining light coloured pieces of wood if there is a pronounced variation in colour within a piece of furniture. Staining has to be done very carefully and it should first be tested on some small offcuts before being applied to a furniture component. The stain is applied after sanding.

### Wax

Many people consider that the soft lustre of wax is the most beautiful of all wood finishes, but wax gives no protection at all against heat and moisture and a wet glass will leave a permanent stain which can only be removed by re-sanding the surface. Silicone waxes are said to be less vulnerable, but this is only a matter of degree, and no wax gives any real protection to wood.

The recommended type of wax for new wood is beeswax dissolved in turpentine to give a consistency of soft butter. The author has used this and also various proprietary brands of furniture polish, and has been able to detect little or no difference between them. Whatever type of wax is used it is important to apply several coats and to buff surface energetically with a soft duster.

Wax can also be applied over heat and water-resistant finishes with the advantage that stains will not penetrate to the wood. If the wax is marked it is easily cleaned off to the varnish layer with turpentine or white spirit and then replaced.

Some craftsmen consider that a thin coat of french polish or nitrocellulose lacquer should be used as a form of filler and sealer before applying wax. This has the effect of giving a somewhat richer looking finish and preventing the slightly dry look which can occur until the wood has been waxed many times. An application of oil has a similar effect.

### Shellac resin

Shellac, which is the main spirit-soluble resin, is made by dissolving the excretion of an insect in methylated spirit. It is available in a range of grades and colours and is marketed, for example, as button, garnet, pale or transparent polish. French polish is a form of shellac resin.

French polishing is a time-consuming and skilful process, and it is doubtful whether it is worth attempting without instruction and some experience. It involves building up a smooth, lustrous surface with a series of thin coats, each of which is applied with a cotton pad. A very small quantity of oil is also used in the process. It is interesting to note that when french polishing was introduced at the beginning of the nineteenth century it was regarded as a cheap substitute for the earlier practice of using oils, waxes and varnishes as wood finishes.

A single coat of shellac makes a good base for subsequent waxing or, by itself, acts as a natural looking sealer. It can be used, for example, on softwood or hardwood panelling to give a more natural finish than is obtained with varnish. Some commercial shellac sealers differ slightly in composition from shellac polishes. No form of french polish is very resistant to heat or moisture but a french polish base under wax protects the wood to some extent against moisture.

### Oil

Linseed oil, when rubbed into wood, slowly oxidises to give a glossy and moderately protective coat. About a dozen applications spread over several months are required to give a substantial finish. Some more recent products, such as teak oil, incorporate an oxidising agent, and these can be built up into an adequate coat with only two or three applications. An oil finish is relatively resistant to heat and moisture but both linseed oil and teak oil tend to give a yellowish colour to the wood. A lighter oil, such as walnut oil, which is used on gun stocks, gives a more natural colour.

### Lacquers

The words 'lacquer' or 'varnish' are used in a general sense to describe any finish which dries as a transparent film. Lacquer is becoming the preferred term but it has no particular chemical meaning and it is not easy to make a simple classification of the innumerable products which are used as wood finishes. Paint, for example, is merely a pigmented lacquer.

The principal subdivision is between finishes which consist primarily of nitrocellulose and which harden mainly by the evaporation of their solvents, and finishes which harden mainly by chemical action and which are known as catalysed lacquers, or sometimes as synthetic resins.

There are several major differences between the nitrocellulose and the catalysed lacquers. As mentioned previously, the former are soluble in appropriate solvents and are, partly for this reason, more susceptible to damage but easier to

symbol that follows the species name indicates
ther the illustrated wood surface is tangential ◯
al ⊖ or in between ⊝

*ht* afrormosia ◯

*ow* ash, European ◯

*ow right* beech, European ⊝

4  cherry, European

5  chestnut, sweet

6  elm, English

7  iroko

8  mahogany, African

9  mahogany, American

10  makoré

11  mansonia

12 muninga

13 oak, English

14 obeche

15 padauk, Andaman

16 plane

17 ramin

18 robinia

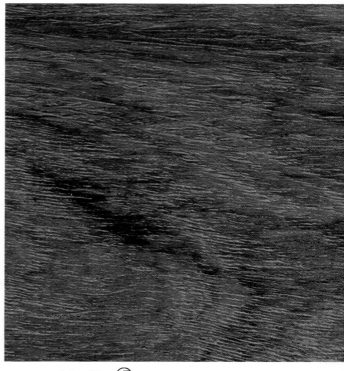

19 rosewood, Brazilian

**20** rosewood, Indian

**21** sapele

**22** satinwood, Ceylon

**23** sycamore

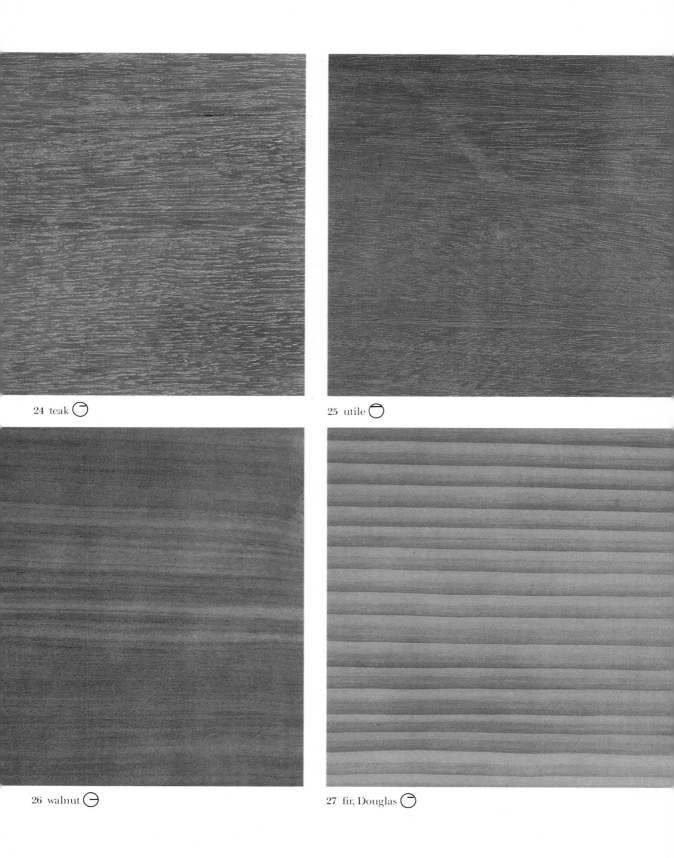

24 teak

25 utile

26 walnut

27 fir, Douglas

28 pine, Parana ⊖

29 pine, Scots ⊖

30 *left* spruce, Norway ⊖

31 *above* yew; desk of solid yew made by the author

repair. The catalysed lacquers cannot be re-dissolved after they have hardened and are generally tougher in service but more difficult to repair.

Catalysed lacquers may be either two-pack or one-pack finishes., In the two-pack type a catalyst (or hardener), usually an acid, has to be mixed with the lacquer immediately before use, whereas with a one-pack or precatalysed finish the hardening agent is premixed and only begins to take effect when the lacquer is applied to the wood. The one-pack or precatalysed finishes are easier to use but they have the disadvantage of a more limited shelf life and, generally, a slower drying time. A particular example of a precatalysed finish is a one-pack polyurethane/alkyd formulation of the type freely available from wholesale shops. An example of an acid-catalysed, two-pack, formulation is a butylated urea-formaldehyde which is most easily identified by its commercial name of Rustin's clear plastic coating.

Most lacquers can be bought as clear or matt finishes or they can be given a matt finish after they have set. This is done by rubbing with a fine abrasive such as 000 wire wool.

Fo the reasons stated earlier, only four types are described below as being easily obtainable and suitable for the small-scale craftsman. These are nitrocellulose finish, a one-pack polyurethane alkyd, an alkyd and a two-pack acid-catalysed butylated urea-formaldehyde.

### Nitrocellulose

Nitrocellulose is widely used by the furniture industry but can also be used domestically. It is a finish which hardens by the evaporation of its solvents and is therefore easily removed and repaired. It gives a clear finish which is only relatively resistant to heat and moisture.

A very thin solution of nitrocellulose is sometimes used as a colourless sealer.

### Polyurethane

There are three main types of polyurethane finish. These are an air-drying one-pack precatalysed polyurethane alkyd, more properly called a urethane alkyd, a two-pack acid-catalysed polyurethane and a one-pack moisture-curing polurethane. Of these the only one generally available in the retail shops is the one-pack (poly)urethane alkyd. The polyurethanes are never completely colourless and some tend to

yellow more than others. They are extremely resistant to heat and moisture and are available in glossy, eggshell or matt finishes.

The matt finish is obtained by mixing fine particles, such as silica, in the lacquer to scatter the light rays., This has a slight dulling effect and it is probably better to use a glossy formulation and to achieve a natural, matt surface by rubbing with a very fine abrasive such as 000 wire wool. The surface can then be waxed to give a lustrous finish. If the wax is marked it can be removed with white spirit down to the polyurethane surface and then replaced.

### Alkyd

Alkyd-based lacquers have a number of desirable properties. They have little tendency to yellow or darken, are easy to apply and, if rubbed down with 000 wire wool, give a pleasant, natural looking matt finish. They have less resistance to heat than polyurethanes or urethane alkyds but considerably more than a nitrocellulose lacquer. They have good resistance to water and alcohol, being comparable with urethane alkyds, and far superior to nitrocellulose. An example of an alkyd-based lacquer which is easily obtainable in Britain is Sadolin's Holdex.

### Two-pack acid-catalysed finish

Examples of this type of finish are Rustin's Clear Plastic Coating and Sadolin's PV-67. These lacquers are forms of urea/melamine formaldehyde and the two-pack product comprises a lacquer and hardener plus, usually, thinners and a burnishing cream. The lacquer is applied with either a brush or a spray and it gives a very hard clear finish which is highly resistant to heat and moisture and which does not darken with age. A fine matt surface can be obtained by rubbing with 000 wire wool. This type of finish has the disadvantage that any imperfection is not easily made good. If a patch of one coat is oversanded down to the underlying coat there is likely to be an optical imperfection even if the lacquer is replaced. It is therefore necessary to apply the finish with care.

### Choice of finish

The most suitable finish depends upon circumstances. Many craftsmen prefer a wax finish which may be applied either directly to the wood, over oil or a thin coat of shellac if the article is not to be subjected to heat and moisture, or over a urethane alkyd or other catalysed lacquer if a more resistant finish is required. If a surface, like a table top, is likely to be subjected frequently to heat and moisture, one of the more resistant finishes without wax is the most practicable.

Of the resistant finishes a matt urethane alkyd gives a tough, natural looking surface but it is liable to yellow somewhat with age. The two-pack acid-catalysed lacquer described above is probably a better finish but is rather more expensive and troublesome to apply. Clear nitrocellulose is colourless and easy to apply but it is not very heat resistant and is unsuitable for surfaces likely to experience hard treatment. A good compromise for most situations is an alkyd-based lacquer.

A thin coat of shellac or nitrocellulose makes an effective and natural looking sealer. An oiled surface has a rich, natural appearance, is easy to maintain and has a moderate resistance to heat and moisture. It is particularly suitable for outdoor use on, for example, nameplates and garden furniture. In such situations an oiled surface is easier to maintain than any lacquer which is liable to deteriorate due to the effects of sunlight and the physical movement of the wood with changes in moisture content.

Although shellac is useful as a sealer and as a base for waxing it is doubtful if french polishing, especially if done by an amateur, has any advantages compared with other types of finish. If it is attempted by an inexperienced craftsman it is advisable to work only on small objects because considerable skill is required to achieve good results on large surfaces.

## Application

Detailed instructions for applying various types of finish are best obtained from the manufacturers but some general advice can be given.

Good surface preparation and cleanliness are perhaps the two most important factors. The surface has to be carefully cleaned with a brush or rag after sanding, and the finish should not be applied in a dusty atmosphere. The cleanliness of the brush is particularly important and if it has to be cleaned in white spirit or a paint remover it should be thoroughly washed in a detergent and water before use.

It is always better to apply several thin coats rather than one thick one, and any imperfections, or nibs, should be removed with fine sandpaper or flour paper before applying the next coat. The lacquer should be applied with light brush strokes in the direction of the grain.

Some lacquers set more quickly in a warm than in a cold atmosphere and it is inadvisable to apply a finish in very cold conditions. Some lacquers will not set in a very cold temperature and in any case the longer it takes to dry the longer it has to collect dust and insects.

All finishes will dry more quickly if there is good ventilation. Solvent vapours are heavier than air and tend to accumulate on the surface in still air, thus slowing down the drying process.

# CHAPTER 6

# Preservatives

## Durability

Under certain conditions timber in service is liable to be attacked by fungi and insects (see Chapter 2). Sapwood has no natural durability, but the durability of heartwood varies greatly from species to species and depends upon the presence of naturally occurring chemical substances in the wood. There are five classes in the conventional classification of natural durability which are based upon the average life of a $50 \times 50$mm ($2 \times 2$in) stake driven into the ground. These classes are:

| Class | | Life in ground | Examples |
|---|---|---|---|
| Very durable | (1) | more than 25 years | teak, greenheart |
| Durable | (2) | 15–25 years | white oak, utile |
| Moderately durable | (3) | 10–15 years | sapele, Douglas fir |
| Non durable | (4) | 5–10 years | elm, Scots pine |
| Perishable | (5) | less than 5 years | beech, birch |

Wood preservatives are chemicals which are deposited on or in wood to give it an artificial durability. The sapwood of any species is more permeable than the heartwood and with most species is easily penetrated by preservatives provided an appropriate method is used. There are, however, differences in permeability between species both of the sapwood and, to a greater extent, of the heartwood. In general, if the wood is dense and the heartwood dark in colour it is likely neither to be permeable nor to require preservation. Information about the durability of particular species is given in Chapters 8 and 9 and in references 9 and 10 in the bibliography.

## Properties of a preservative

A number of desirable properties of a preservative are listed below. No preservative possesses all these properties and it would be very unusual for all of them to be required in a given situation. There are some, however, which are almost always necessary or desirable and these are shown towards the top of the list.

1) Toxic to fungi and insects
2) Harmless to human beings and animals
3) Capable of effective penetration
4) Reasonably cheap and easily obtainable
5) Persistent
6) Easy to apply
7) Non-inflammable
8) Colourless
9) Odourless
10) Able to take paint and other finishes and glue
11) Non-contaminating to food
12) Harmless to other materials such as metal and plastic

## Types of preservative

There are three main types of wood preservative:

1) Tar oils
2) Water-borne preservatives
3) Organic solvent preservatives

With the exception of some specialised formulations, these are all effective against insects and fungi.

### Tar oils

Tar oils are by-products of the carbonisation of coal to produce gas and coke. The oils vary in their viscosity and chemical composition and are referred to generically as creosote. The most viscous type of creosote, which conforms to British Standard BS 144, is used for vacuum pressure impregnation and has to be heated. The more mobile mixture, which can be applied with a brush, conforms to British Standard BS 3051.

Creosote is an effective fungicide and insecticide and is resistant to leaching. It does not corrode metals and the mobile formulation is easy to apply. These properties make it a suitable preservative for many outdoor situations but it is not suitable for internal use because it has a strong odour and colour and cannot easily be painted. It temporarily increases the inflammability of wood but this effect gradually wears off as the volatile oils evaporate. Creosote is, to some extent, a water repellent. It therefore has the effect of evening out the changes in moisture content of timber with changes in humidity and temperature. For this reason it slows down the physical deterioration of wood in the open.

### Water-borne preservatives

There are two main types of water-borne preservative: those which do not remain fixed in the wood and can therefore be leached out by water, and those which are fixed by chemical changes on penetrating the wood and are not washed out by water. Boron compounds are an example of the former type, while formulations containing copper, chromium and arsenic salts are the most widely used examples of the latter.

Boron compounds are used to preserve freshly felled timber. The boron salts are applied to the timber by immersing it in a concentrated solution and stacking under sealed conditions so that the salts gradually diffuse into the water in the wood and are then deposited as the wood dries. The salts remain soluble in the dried wood so that the method is suitable only for a timber which is to be used inside, or for painted joinery out of doors. The method cannot be used for a timber in contact with a permanent source of moisture. The advantages of the method are that the salts are colourless and can be painted.

Copper chrome arsenic (CCA) preservatives are applied to partially seasoned timber by a vacuum pressure impregnation. The salts are deposited on the walls of the wood cells in such a way that they become insoluble in water and the treated timber is therefore suitable for external situations and can be successfully used in contact with water, as in water cooling towers.

Some species such as Sitka spruce are relatively impermeable to the salt solutions because the small valves, or pits, which allow the transfer of materials from tracheid to tracheid (see Chapter 1) in the living tree become permanently closed as the wood dries. Attempts to overcome this difficulty include the use of bacteria to break down the pit membranes and the use of more mobile or permeable salts.

The copper chrome arsenic salts are not toxic to plants or animals when once deposited in the wood. Because the salts are carried in solution in water the process causes wood to swell and gives it a greyish-green colour.

### Organic solvent preservatives

There are numerous chemicals dissolved in an organic solvent which are applied to seasoned wood, and although they differ in their individual properties they have a number of characteristics in common. These are:

a) With a suitable solvent they are easily absorbed by wood and can therefore be effectively applied with a brush as well as by more elaborate methods.
b) They can be painted and glued after the solvent has evaporated.
c) They do not cause wood to swell.
d) They are usually non-staining.
e) They do not corrode metals.
f) They may taint food even when the solvent has evaporated.
g) They render the wood temporarily more inflammable than untreated wood.

## Choice of preservative

For amateurs or operators without industrial equipment creosote is the only practicable preservative to use for exterior timber and one or other of the proprietory organic solvent formulations for interior work.

Adequate penetration of an organic solvent into dry wood can be achieved for most interior furniture and fittings by applying liberally with a brush. The effective preservation of structural timber likely to be attacked by insects or to be in frequent contact with a source of moisture is more difficult. Ideally the wood should first be cut to size and then treated industrially with creosote or CCA for outside use. CCA can also be applied industrially to pre-cut timber for inside use, but if boron formulations are used for inside work they cannot be applied to seasoned timber; the wood must have been treated before purchase. A small degree of penetration can be obtained by soaking seasoned wood for a day or so in creosote. The least effective method is brushing, which will not achieve much penetration although, if liberally applied, it is better than nothing in difficult situations and is perfectly satisfactory with periodic retreatment for protecting well ventilated wood such as weatherboarding.

# CHAPTER 7
# Sources of wood

## The world's forests
### Area

The world's total forest area is about 3800 million hectares or approximately one third of the land surface of the globe. Of the 3800 million hectares (9390 million acres) about 2800 million hectares (6919 million acres) are classified by the Food and Agriculture Organisation of the United Nations (FAO) (1966) as closed forest and about 1000 million as open or savanna type woodland of low stocking.

For various reasons not all of the closed forest is productive. Some is inaccessible or uneconomic to harvest under present day conditions while some is set aside for protection, conservation and recreation. On the other hand not all of the open forest is unproductive since in some parts of the world it supplies large quantities of wood for fuel. It is perhaps reasonable to think that about 2500 million hectares (6178 million acres) of closed forest are exploitable or potentially exploitable for the production of wood.

The total area of man-made forest is believed to be about 100 million hectares (247 million acres), which is about 2.6 per cent of the total forest or 3.6 per cent of the closed forest area.

With an estimated world population of approximately 4500 million people there are about 0.8 hectares (2 acres) of forest or about 0.6 hectares (1.5 acres) of closed forest per head. Applying this same calculation to Britain, the amount of forest per person works out to be in the region of 0.06 hectares (0.14 acres).

The distribution of forest throughout the world is very uneven. The greatest areas of closed forest occur in North America, South America and the USSR, each of which has almost a quarter of the world's total. Asia has about 15 per cent, Africa about 7 per cent and Europe about 5 per cent. There is a greater disparity between the developed and developing regions in the proportion of coniferous and non-coniferous forest. About 90 per cent of the coniferous, or softwood, forest is in the developed, predominantly temperate, regions and about 70 per cent of the non-coniferous, or hardwood, forest is in the developing, predominantly tropical regions. There are large areas in northern Africa, Asia and China which have very little forest but which support about one third of the world's population.

There is little reliable information for the world as a whole on the rate of change in forest area. The forest area in Europe and North America is increasing but it seems reasonably certain that the net forest area of the world as a whole is decreasing. This is due to the destruction or degradation of forest, especially in South America, Africa and parts of Asia, by permanent clearance for agriculture, over-grazing and over-cutting, often for fuelwood. Subjective estimates by FAO staff suggest that the area of the world's forest is decreasing at the rate of about 5 million hectares (12.3 million acres) per annum, most of it from the tropical hardwood forests.

Of the 2800 million hectares (6919 million acres) of closed forest about 1100 million hectares (2718 million acres) consisted, in 1980, of tropical hardwood forest. It is estimated, therefore, that this area will have been reduced to about 1000 million hectares (2471 million acres) by the end of the century, as shown in Table 2.

The total area of new tropical hardwood plantations likely to be established during this 20-year period is estimated to be about 6 million hectares (15 million acres) or about 6 per cent of the loss, but the new conifer plantations in the tropical regions may amount to a further 4 million hectares (10 million acres). Since the commercial productivity of the new plantations is likely to be about seven times as high as that of the natural forest the net loss in potential production will not be very great.

**Table 2** *Areas of closed tropical forest*

|          |                          | million hectares | acres |
|----------|--------------------------|------------------|-------|
| A.D. 1980 | Central and South America | 620              | 1532  |
|          | Africa                   | 200              | 494   |
|          | Asia                     | 280              | 692   |
|          |                          | 1100             | 2718  |
|          |                          |                  |       |
| A.D. 2000 | Central and South America | 575              | 1421  |
|          | Africa                   | 185              | 457   |
|          | Asia                     | 240              | 593   |
|          |                          | 1000             | 2471  |

### Growing stock

The total growing stock of the world's forests is estimated to be about 350,000 million cu. m (12.37 million million cu. ft). This is equivalent to a cube having sides about 7km (4½ miles) long. Of this volume roughly one-third is coniferous, or softwood, and two-thirds broadleaved or hardwood. If all this volume were utilisable it would last for about 140 years, without any further growth, at the current rate of consumption. In practice, of course, there is an annual growth of wood which sustains the growing stock, but just what the balance is between losses from cutting, fire, insect and fungal damage and old age on the one hand, and growth on the other, is not known for the world as a whole.

## Demand for wood

In 1980 the world population was roughly 4500 million and the total wood production 2500 million cu. m (88,000 million cu. ft), or 1 cu. m (3.5 cu. ft) per productive hectare (2.5 acres) per annum. More than half this wood was used as firewood and in South America and tropical Africa the proportion of fuelwood was 90 per cent.

Looking to the future the world population will inevitably rise to at least 6000 million people by the end of the century, and no matter how successful countries may be in controlling population numbers it will be many decades before the world's population is stabilised or reduced. The world demand for wood is expected to rise to over 4000 million cu. m (140,000 million cu. ft) by the year 2000. This implies an increasing pressure upon the available productive land for both food and wood production. At the same time there is a growing interest in conservation and recreation, which act as constraints on the conversion of forest land to agriculture or on the commercial management of forests for timber production.

The growing demand for timber is primarily for firewood, for producing paper and board, for the manufacture of panel products, for construction and, possibly, in some regions, for conversion into chemicals and portable fuels.

The craftsman, however, is mainly interested in the high quality, broadleaved species which have been and still are obtained from natural forests in tropical regions such as the Caribbean, South America, West Africa and South East Asia and from temperate regions such as Europe, North America and Japan.

The world trends in the demand for sawlogs and veneer logs are set out in a simplified form in Table 3. This table shows the steep rise in the output of tropical hardwoods.

## Wood supply
### Historical developments

Over the centuries the number of species in

**Table 3** *Consumption of sawlogs and veneer logs (based on FAO statistics)*

| millions of cu. m | | | | | | | | |
|---|---|---|---|---|---|---|---|---|
|  | 1950 | 1954 | 1960 | 1970 | 1971 | 1975 | 1979 | 2000 (estimated) |
| total | 450 | 560 | 650 | 760 | 780 | 790 | 880 | 1180 |
| softwood | 340 | 420 | 490 | 550 | 570 | 570 | 630 | 860 |
| hardwood | 110 | 140 | 160 | 210 | 210 | 220 | 250 | 320 |
| of which tropical hardwood | 25 | 40 | 50 | 85 | 85 | 100 | 120 | 180 |

international trade has increased and the relative importance of the various sources of supply has changed. Spruce and pine have been imported from Norway and the Baltic for many centuries, but Sweden and Russia did not become exporters of softwoods until after the Napoleonic wars. White pine was first imported into Britain from America very early in the seventeenth century, and the eastern seaboard of North America was an important supplier of masts and spars by the time of Charles II.

The spruces, pines and Douglas fir of western North America first entered world trade in the first half of the nineteenth century, and the area west of the Rockies gradually replaced eastern North America as the major timber exporting region. The pitch pines from the Southern States did not appear in Europe until after the American Civil War, and Parana pine from Argentina and southern Brazil was first imported into Britain before the Second World War but was not widely used until after the war.

Few hardwoods were found in international trade before about 1700. In Europe, oak had been the dominant structural and furniture timber for many centuries and some oak was imported into Britain from the Baltic during the seventeenth century. Mahogany from Cuba and Honduras was first brought to Britain before 1700 but was not widely used until about 1730. Rosewood, ebony and satinwood were used on both sides of the Atlantic before the end of the eighteenth century.

Indian teak was used for building European ships in India towards the end of the eighteenth century and the first teak ship of the Royal Navy was launched in Bombay in 1805.

During the nineteenth century world trade developed enormously and this led to the appearance in the world's markets of many new timber species. Iroko, under the name of African oak, was introduced into Britain in about 1825, and by the second half of the century oak was being imported from central Europe and America. Walnut, ash, maple, birch and pencil cedar from North America, walnut from Italy, various new rosewoods from South America and mahoganies from West Africa, were also introduced into Britain and other importing countries in the second half of the nineteenth century. One of the later nineteenth century introductions was sapele from West Africa.

More recent twentieth century introductions have been oak from Japan, obeche, agba, and mansonia as a substitute for walnut, from Africa, myrtle beech, Australian walnut and blackbean from Australia and meranti, lauan and keruing from South East Asia. Muhuhu and afrormosia were not introduced into Britain until after the Second World War.

### The current situation

In tropical or developing countries almost all of the timber trees used for domestic or industrial purposes and for export are hardwoods, whereas most of the major natural conifer forests are in North America, central and northern Europe and Russia, and most of the wood used by the developed nations is coniferous, the principal species being pines, spruces, larches, firs, hemlocks and Douglas fir.

As a general rule the closer forests are to the equator the greater is the number of species per area of land, and since only the larger individuals of a limited number of species are marketable, the logging of tropical forests is usually very wasteful. There are exceptions to this generalisation in South East Asia where there are relatively uniform forests of a single genus such as *Dipterocarpus* or *Shorea*, many of the species of which are marketed, often under an omnibus trade name such as keruing, dark red meranti or red lauan.

*World trade in softwoods*
The USSR and North America are the major exporting regions for softwood logs while the principal sawnwood exporters are the Nordic countries. The major importers of logs are Japan and Korea and of sawnwood Europe and Japan. These net trade flows are illustrated in Tables 4 and 5 which are based upon *The Year Book of Forest Product Statistics* published by FAO in 1980. The net trade balance of each region has been rounded to the nearest million cubic metres (1cu.m = 35.3147cu.ft).

*World trade in hardwoods*
The major trade flows in tropical hardwood logs are from South East Asia and the Pacific to Japan, China, Korea and Hong Kong with a total export volume in 1978 of 36.5 million cu.m (1288 million cu.ft). Relatively few logs are exported from South East Asia to Europe but about 5 million cu.m (230 million cu.ft) were exported from Africa to Europe. This trade pattern is illustrated in Figure 27.

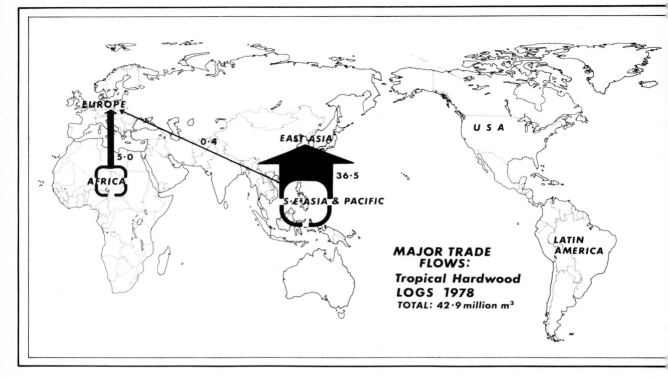

**27** World trade-flow pattern in tropical hardwood logs, 1978

**Table 4** *World trade in softwood logs*

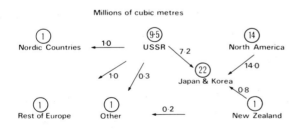

**Table 5** *World trade in sawn softwood*

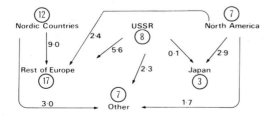

The world export market in tropical hardwood sawn timber shows a very different pattern. South East Asia is still the major exporting region with a total volume in 1978 of 2.6 million cu. m (92 million cu. ft) of which 2.0 million cu. m (70 million cu. ft) went to Europe and 0.3 million cu. m (10 million cu. ft) each to eastern Asia and the USA. Europe imported 0.4 million cu. m (14 million cu. ft) from Africa and a small quantity from South America, which also exported 0.3 million cu. m (10 million cu. ft) to the USA. this trade flow pattern is illustrated in Figure 28.

*British imports*
In 1979 Britain imported about 1 million cu. m (35 million cu. ft) of hardboard saw logs, hardwood sawn timber and hardwood veneer and about the same quantity of plywood, most of which was hardwood (Table 6).

The breakdown by major tropical species is given in Table 7 and by temperate species in Table 8.

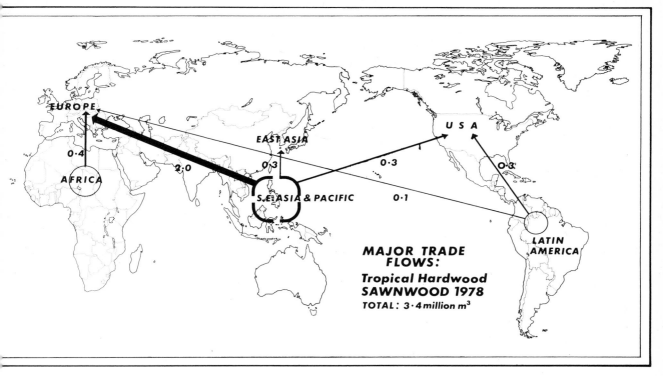

**28** World trade-flow pattern in tropical hardwood sawnwood, 1978

**Table 6** *Hardwood imports, 1979*

| | millions of cu. m | |
|---|---|---|
| *tropical* | | |
| saw and veneer logs | 0.145) | |
| sawnwood | 0.625 | |
| | 0.770 | 0.770 |
| *temperate* | | |
| saw and veneer logs | 0.020 | |
| sawnwood | 0.200 | |
| | 0.220 | 0.220 |
| *veneers* | 0.030 | 0.030 |
| *plywood* | 0.980 | 0.980 |
| | | 2.000 |

**Table 7** *Imports of tropical hardwoods by species, 1979*

| species | volume | percentage | |
|---|---|---|---|
| | cu. m millions | logs | sawn-wood |
| African walnut | 0.015 | 100 | 0 |
| afrormosia | 0.010 | 50 | 50 |
| iroko | 0.040 | 30 | 70 |
| keruing | 0.100 | 0 | 100 |
| limba | 0.001 | 0 | 100 |
| mahogany | 0.200 | 20 | 80 |
| makoré | 0.003 | 100 | 0 |
| meranti | 0.040 | 0 | 100 |
| obeche | 0.018 | 25 | 75 |
| okoumé | 0.001 | 100 | 0 |
| ramin | 0.090 | 0 | 100 |
| sapele | 0.013 | 0 | 100 |
| teak | 0.008 | 0 | 100 |
| utile | 0.016 | 25 | 75 |
| other | 0.217 | 25 | 75 |
| | 0.770 | | |

**Table 8** *Imports of temperate hardwoods by species, 1979*

| species | volume cu. m millions |
|---------|-----------------------|
| beech | 0.138 |
| birch | 0.027 |
| oak | 0.022 |
| walnut | 0.001 |
| other | 0.032 |
| | 0.220 |

The corresponding softwood imports of sawn-wood and panels were very much higher and amounted to about 7.25 million cu. m (256 million cu. ft) of sawnwood and about 1.7 million cu. m (60 million cu. ft) of panel products. The principal sources of supply are set out in Table 9.

**Table 9** *Sources of softwood sawnwood and panel products, 1979*

| region | volume cu. m millions | percentage |
|--------|-----------------------|------------|
| Nordic countries | 2.90 | 40 |
| USSR | 1.45 | 20 |
| Canada | 1.45 | 20 |
| Portugal | 0.50 | 7 |
| Poland | 0.40 | 5 |
| Other | 0.55 | 8 |
| | 7.25 | 100 |

*British timber*

With the exception of yew and, perhaps, of slow-grown Scots pine and small quantities of exotic species such as cedar, the softwoods grown in Britain are of relatively little interest to the craftsman.

Yew is highly valued for veneering, but high quality timber is scarce and expensive although it is obtainable from specialist sawmills and merchants. Hardwoods, however, are a different matter. Oak, beech, ash and sycamore are not difficult to obtain, although the quality is variable. Reasonably reliable estimates of annual consumption are available but these have been variable in recent years partly due to Dutch elm disease and partly to the economic recession. In 1978 the total consumption of home-grown hardwood timber was about 1.5 million cu. m (53 million cu. ft), of which 1.16 million cu. m (40 million cu. ft) were classified as sawn timber. The detailed breakdown by species is set out in Table 10. The average annual consumption of all home-grown hardwood timber is about 1.4 million cu. m (50 million cu. ft) of which planking quality amounts to about 1.0 million cu. m (35 million cu. ft).

**Table 10** *Estimated consumption of hardwood sawn timber in 1978*

| species | millions of cu. m volume | percentage volume |
|---------|--------------------------|-------------------|
| oak | 0.24 | 21 |
| elm | 0.48 | 41 |
| beech | 0.15 | 13 |
| ash | 0.08 | 7 |
| other species | 0.21 | 18 |
| | 1.16 | 100 |

This was a very unrepresentative year because there was a great deal of recently dead elm on the market. A more balanced picture of the potential supply of British hardwoods may be obtained by looking at the area and volume of hardwoods standing in the country in 1981. The Forestry Commission is currently engaged in making a census of the area, number and volume of trees in Britain but the results will not be available until after the publication of this book. It is, therefore, necessary to extrapolate from earlier data which are incomplete and out of date and from which only approximate estimates can be made. In order to amalgamate woodland areas with numbers or volumes of hedgerow and parkland trees the trees outside forests and woodlands have been given equivalent areas by assuming average numbers of trees or volumes of standing timber per hectare.

The total area of broadleaved forest and woodland in Britain is about 660,000 hectares (1,630,000 acres) and the equivalent area of trees in hedgerows, parks and small clumps is about 200,000 hectares (494,000 acres), making a total of about 860,000 hectares (2,125,000 acres). Of this area about 90 per cent is in England and Wales and about 10 per cent in Scotland.

The total standing volume is, very approximately, about 80 million cu. m (2800 million cu. ft), or about 60 times the annual consumption. The proportion of timber of planking quality is, however, relatively low and may not amount to more than about 25 million cu. m (880 million cu. ft).

The species breakdown by area is given in Table 11. Of the potential timber trees only four species – oak, beech, ash and sycamore – each comprise 10 per cent or more of the total and only four others more than one per cent. As can be seen in Table 11, the proportions are different if the total growing stock is taken into account.

**Table 11** *Percentages of hardwood species in Britain*

| species | percentage of total by area | |
|---|---|---|
| | potential timber trees | all trees |
| oak | 50 | 35 |
| beech | 20 | 10 |
| ash | 10 | 10 |
| sycamore | 10 | 5 |
| birch | 1.5 | 25 |
| others | 8.5 | 15 |

## Future trends

### Sources of supply-natural forests

So far as tropical hardwoods are concerned there will be major changes in the absolute and relative importance of the main exporting regions in the future.

Exports from West Africa, particularly of logs, are declining. This is due partly to heavy cutting, partly to political, economic and organisational problems, and partly to the demands upon forest land to provide wood and food for a rapidly expanding population.

South America is expected to overtake South East Asia in the early part of the next century as a source of tropical timber. Some of the South American species are of a very high quality but because they are widely scattered in the forests and occur in relatively inaccessible regions many of them have not so far been harvested and marketed on a large scale. It was estimated in 1976 that there were over 200 commercial species and over 250 lesser used species in South America. Unlike the even more numerous species of South East Asia, many of which are very similar in their timber properties, the South American species are more variable and cannot easily be grouped into a

small number of marketing categories. Nevertheless, attempts are being made to identify groups of species which are sufficiently homogeneous in the more important characteristics such as colour, density and stability, to enable any one group to be marketed for a specific purpose (page 62). Attempts are also being made to relate little-known species in South America to more familiar timbers. Table 12, for example, lists several Guyanan species which are considered to resemble familiar commercial timbers.

**Table 12** *Alternative Guyanan species*

| commercial species | Guyanan alternatives | |
|---|---|---|
| obeche | simarupa | *Simaruba amara* |
| iroko | tauroniro | *Humiria balsamifera* |
| abura | kirikana | *Iryanthera lancifolia* |
| ramin | kurokai | *Protium* species |
| rosewood | wamara | *Swartzia leiocalyuna* |
| mahogany | andiroba | *Carapa guianensis* |

### Sources of supply-plantation forests

By comparison with agriculturists, foresters are at a primitive stage of development because, over large areas of mixed hardwood forest, they gather a small proportion of wild plants from natural plant communities. There has so far been little genetic improvement of the worlds' forests, nor has there been any substantial improvement of most of the natural forests by systems of management.

Compared with the average annual yield of 1 cu. m (35 cu. ft) per hectare (2.5 acres) from natural forests, the yield from plantations generally amounts to more than 7 or 8 cu. m (250 or 280 cu. ft) and the more productive sites, particularly in the tropical and sub-tropical regions, can yield over 20 cu. m (700 cu. ft) per hectare (2.5 acres) per annum. Bearing in mind the current average annual yield quoted above it would theoretically be possible to supply the 1980 level of world demand from something like 12 per cent of the area of forest existing in 1980, provided an enormous investment were made in plantation forestry throughout the world. Plantations, however, are not likely to produce large volumes of the high quality tropical hardwoods which are obtained from natural forests.

A few of the decorative tropical timbers such as teak, iroko and some of the mahoganies are grown

**Table 13** *Percentage distribution of age classes of British hardwoods by species*

| Planting years | 1961 to 1965 | 1951 to 1960 | 1941 to 1950 | 1931 to 1940 | 1921 to 1930 | 1911 to 1920 | 1901 to 1910 | 1861 to 1900 | Pre 1861 | |
|---|---|---|---|---|---|---|---|---|---|---|
| *Species* | | | | | | | | | | *Total* |
| oak | 1 | 1 | 1 | 1 | 2 | 3 | 6 | 52 | 33 | 100 |
| beech | 4 | 4 | 2 | 2 | 2 | 2 | 6 | 38 | 40 | 100 |
| ash | 1 | 3 | 8 | 7 | 9 | 14 | 17 | 34 | 7 | 100 |
| birch | 1 | 17 | 24 | 17 | 15 | 10 | 8 | 6 | 2 | 100 |
| sweet chestnut | 3 | 3 | 1 | 7 | 9 | 14 | 9 | 31 | 23 | 100 |
| sycamore | 2 | 3 | 3 | 5 | 7 | 9 | 16 | 45 | 10 | 100 |
| elm | — | 1 | 1 | 3 | 4 | 12 | 9 | 45 | 26 | 100 |
| poplar | 20 | 46 | 14 | 3 | 3 | 1 | 2 | 1 | — | 100 |
| other species | 5 | 7 | 8 | 10 | 16 | 13 | 12 | 21 | 8 | 100 |

in plantations, although it is often not practical to grow mahogany species in pure crops because of the damage done by shoot borers. *Swietenia macrophyllum*, in particular, has been grown successfully in India and Sri Lanka. Current research, however, is likely in due course to extend the number of high quality decorative timbers which it will be possible to grow in commercial plantations.

*Sources of supply in Britain*
The principal factor determining the future supply of hardwoods in Britain in the short to medium term is the age-class structure of the present growing stock. This is because most of the trees which will be harvested during the next fifty years or so are already growing.

The distribution of age classes by species is shown in Table 13.

It can be seen from Table 13 that approximately 70 per cent of the trees were more than 70 years old in 1980, the oak being older but longer lived than the other species. Taking into account the age and specific composition of the growing stock it is reasonable to assume a current annual increment of about 1.5 per cent, or a total annual increment of about 1.2 million cu. m (42 million cu. ft). Some of this increment is going on to trees which, for a variety of reasons, will never be felled. The commercially available increment is therefore significantly less than the average annual consumption of about 1.4 to 1.5 million cu. m (50 to 53 million cu. ft). This is true of the production as a whole and is almost certainly true of good quality timber, which amounts to

something like a quarter of the total annual production. As a result there will be a gradual reduction in the stock of this material. Considering the outlook not only in Britain but in the world as a whole it is not unreasonable to predict a rise, in real terms, in the price of good quality home-grown, hardwood timber.

There are something of the order of 400,000 hectares (988,000 acres) of mediocre and poor quality broadleaved woodlands and scrub in Britain. This will be retained for a number of environmental reasons but it is possible to reconcile timber production with environmental interests. New methods of broadleaved silviculture are being developed to make it both less expensive in the short term and more profitable in the long term to grow hardwood timber. These developments, coupled with a prospect of rising prices, are stimulating a new interest in growing broadleaved trees. Oak will continue to be the major species but there is also an increasing interest in ash, cherry, sycamore, sweet chestnut, walnut and even one high quality conifer-yew.

*Prices*
It is likely that wood in general, and high quality decorative hardwoods in particular, will gradually increase in price in real terms, that is to say faster than inflation in general. There are several reasons for this. The world population and hence the demand for wood will rise, even if personal incomes remain static – which is unlikely. At the same time the area of forest will decrease as a result of cutting, overgrazing and conversion to agriculture. Harvesting and transport costs are

also expected to rise in real terms. Furthermore, there are several political developments which may lead to higher log or sawn timber prices in the importing countries. In an effort to increase industrial development and national income there is a growing tendency for timber exporting countries to export a more highly processed product. Countries which are now exporting logs will export sawn timber and the sawn timber exporters will attempt to develop a trade in processed or semi-processed wood products. As a means of achieving these objectives some of the exporting countries are forming producers' associations such as the South East Asia Log Producers' Association and the African Timber Organisation. Many developing countries are also levying export taxes, one of the objects of which is to discourage the export of unprocessed logs.

Predictions of a future wood famine or of a supply crisis at the end of the century are almost certainly unfounded. The gradual increase in price, which will vary from one timber category to another, will automatically bridge the gap between supply and demand. At the same time it will stimulate investment in forest plantations which, in the course of the twenty-first century, will almost inevitably become a major source of the world supply of timber.

As the tropical hardwoods become more scarce and expensive the temperate hardwoods such as oak, beech, walnut, cherry, sweet chestnut, ash, maple and the fruitwoods – apple, pear and plum – together with a few conifers such as yew, cedar, pencil cedar, juniper and pine, will not only retain but increase their importance as craftsmen's timbers.

# CHAPTER 8

# Hardwoods

## The nomenclature of hardwoods

Most of the decorative and specialised timbers used by craftsmen are hardwoods which are, in general, denser and stronger than softwoods and which include a greater number of species having a well-defined colour. For a number of reasons the nomenclature and the precise identification of hardwood species is often confused, particularly in tropical countries, where the range of tree species growing in a forest region is usually far greater than in temperate forests. Even today not all of the timber species harvested from a relatively underdeveloped region can be related precisely to a known tree species.

A more important reason for the uncertainly about species is the occurrence in one region of a number of closely related and similar species which cannot be identified from the timber after they have been felled and extracted as logs from the forest. A good example of this is the genus *Shorea* in South East Asia and the Philippines (page 67).

In some areas, such as the tropical forests of South America, there are so many species logged from one region that it is not practicable to create a separate market for each one. Attempts are therefore being made to market the timber not by species but by end-use categories. In this system the various species are assessed for such factors as density, strength, durability, colour, preservative permeability and stability and then given a suitability classification for a range of end uses such as general construction, pulping, furniture making, joinery, veneering and so on. This system is likely to become more widely adopted in the future when an increasing demand will necessitate the exploitation of a greater range of species than are harvested at the present time.

But the most important reason for confusion is the practice of relating as many species as possible to a well known, high quality timber such as mahogany, only some of which have been closely related to true mahogany. Over the years scores of timber species have been marketed as mahogany, some of which have little more in common with it than a pale reddish-brown colour.

Finally, many timber species or species groups have more than one name. As well as the true botanical name it may have a colloquial English and French name as well as a native name and a port of origin.

A few of the more confusing species groups are discussed in some detail below, mainly to demonstrate the need for caution when describing a timber as, say, mahogany or rosewood. The remainder of the chapter is devoted to a description, in alphabetical order of their common names, of a number of hardwood species. Alphabetical lists of botanical and common names, each cross-referenced to the other, are given in Appendix I. For the hardwoods each species or group of closely related species is illustrated by a microscopic photograph of a cross section which is intended to assist in the recognition of features visible on the end grain with a hand lens or by the naked eye. The more important species are also illustrated by a colour plate of a radial or tangential surface (Plates 1 to 31).

It should be noted that these microscopic magnifications are given in linear units whereas those of a hand lens are by area. Therefore a x10 hand lens has a linear magnification of only $\sqrt{10}$ or about $\times 3$ whereas a microscopic magnification of $\times 100$ is, in area terms, an enlargement of $100^2$ or 10,000.

There is considerable variation in density, stiffness, impact strength, hardness and durability within most timber species and for this reason relative values only, in the range of 1–5, are given for the various species, where these values are available. Since these values cover the complete range of properties of all timbers most of the more commonly used species fall somewhere in the middle of the range and it may be something of a surprise to realise that the stiffness (related indirectly to the tensile strength) of oak is classified as 4 compared with beech which is, 3 and hickory which is 2. In this classification, which applies to seasoned heartwood at a moisture content of 12 per cent, 1 is the highest value and 5 is the lowest. For stability in service and blunting effect three values only are given. These are above average, average and below average.

## Ash

There are about seventy species of ash distributed throughout the northern hemisphere.

The common European ash, *Fraxinus excelsior*, occurs throughout central and northern Europe and extends eastwards to the western Himalayas. The timber properties differ somewhat according to the region or origin but it is not possible to differentiate English, French, Hungarian or Polish ash on botanical grounds because it all comes from the same species of tree.

The only Far Eastern ash of commercial importance in Europe is Japanese or Manchurian ash, *Fraxinus mandshurica*. This is very similar to English ash in properties and appearance but occasionally has a slightly rippled grain. It is sometimes imported as a constituent of plywood.

There are about twenty species of ash in North America, but most of the ash of commerce is obtained from three species, white ash, *Fraxinus americana*, black ash, *Fraxinus nigra* and green ash, *Fraxinus pennsylvanica*. North American ash timber is similar to that of the European ash. The trade names are confusing and the timber names do not always reflect their botanical origins.

As was so often the case, the familiar name was given by the early settlers to the timber of *Eucalyptus* species in Tasmania and Australia which bore a superficial resemblance to British species. The timbers of several *Eucalyptus* species are known locally as ash; for example, mountain ash, *Eucalyptus regnans* and alpine ash, *Eucalyptus delegatensis* or *Eucalyptus gigantea*. To make the picture more confusing mountain ash and alpine ash are exported as Tasmanian or Australian oak (page 68).

## Boxwood

The name boxwood is properly applied to about twenty species of the genus *Buxus* which are all small-sized trees producing pale-coloured, hard timber with a fine even texture. The wood is used in many countries for turnery, carving and inlaying and for making mathematical instruments and parts of musical instruments.

The species common in Europe, North Africa, Asia Minor, the Caucasus region and central Russia is *Buxus sempervirens* which is imported into Britain under a variety of regional names, such as Abassian, Iranian, Persian and Turkey boxwood.

Two other *Buxus* species are East London or Cape boxwood, *Buxus macowani*, from South Africa, which is a larger tree producing lower quality timber, and Balearic boxwood, *Buxus balearica*, which, as its name implies, grows in the Balearic islands. There are several *Buxus* species in India which are used locally but which are not exported.

A number of other genera produce timbers which bear a general resemblance to true box and which are therefore given the name boxwood. These include West Indian or Maracaibo boxwood, *Gossypiospernum praecox*, which is found in Venezuela, San Domingo boxwood, *Phyllostylon brasiliensis*, and Kamassi or Knysna boxwood, *Gonioma kamassi*, from South Africa.

There are several *Gardenia* species in Siam known as Siamese boxwood and one in India, *Gardenia latifolia*. These produce a poorer quality, greyish-white timber used for making tool handles.

Cornel, or American boxwood, *Cornus florida*, differs from the other boxwoods in having a pinkish or reddish-brown colour but is a hard, tough, straight-grained timber which is suitable for the traditional boxwood uses and especially for the manufacture of shuttles.

There are several Australian species which are given the name boxwood because they are hard, fine-textured timbers, although they have little resemblance to true boxwood. One of them is brush box, *Tristania conferta*, which is a tough, fine-textured, brown or reddish-brown timber with good strength properties. It differs from many box species in being available in large sizes and is used for heavy structural work as well as for mallets and tool handles.

## Cordia

There are about 200 species of the genus *Cordia* all of which occur in tropical or sub-tropical regions. A number of species produce useful local timber but only a few appear in international trade.

*Cordia* timber is variable within the genus and of the species which are found from southern Florida to the Argentine two sub-groups are recognised. One group comprises the heavier and darker-coloured species such as *Cordia sebestena* in southern Florida and the West Indies, *Cordia gerascanthus*, which is regarded as a good quality local timber in Venezuela, and *Cordia dodecandra* in Central America.

The principal species of the less dense group is *Cordia alliodora*, American light cordia, or salmwood, which extends from Mexico and the West Indies to Brazil. *Cordia allidora* is also known as laurel and two types of timber are recognised. These are laurel blanco, a pale-coloured wood and laurel negro, a darker, more variegated and more durable timber having some resemblance to walnut. It is not certain whether the differences between laurel blanco and laurel negro are genetical or due to age or site. Another species closely related to *Cordia alliodora* is *Cordia trichotoma* which is a tree of Brazil and the Argentine.

Probably the most important *Cordia* species is freijo, *Cordia goeldiana*, also known as South American walnut which occurs in the Amazon basin. This species belongs to the less dense group but has a distinctive golden brown colour reminiscent of teak.

There are about thirteen *Cordia* species in India and Burma of which *Cordia fragrantissima* and *C. vestita* are the more important, both being regarded as good quality, decorative timbers.

There are two West African cordias which were at one time commercially important. These are *Cordia millenii* and *C. platythyrsa*. Another African species which grows in the Sudan is *Cordia abyssinica*, which produces a durable timber for local use.

### Ebony

Almost all the commercial species of ebony are hard, dense, fine-grained timbers with a dark coloured heartwood belonging to the genus *Diospyros*. They are widely distributed throughout the tropics in Asia and Africa. Species which have some resemblance to the true ebonies but which belong to other genera occur in Central and South America.

Ebony timbers are divided into two main groups, those which are black or almost black and those which are streaked or mottled. They are generally difficult to season and work but are stable in service and are highly prized for turnery, musical instrument making and other specialised uses.

*Black ebony*

| | |
|---|---|
| Ceylon ebony | *Diospyros ebenum* |
| African ebony | Several species of *Diospyros*, principally *Diospyros crassiflora* and *Diospyros piscatoria* |

*Streaked or mottled ebony*

| | |
|---|---|
| Macassar ebony | *Diospyros rumphii* |
| | *Diospyros celebica* |
| Coromandel ebony | *Diospyros quaesita* |
| Borneo ebony | *Diospyros durianoides* |
| | *Diospyros melanoxylon* |
| | *Diospyros tomentosa* |
| Andaman marble or zebra wood | *Diospyros marmorata.* This is a pale greyish-brown wood with a marble-like pattern of almost black streaks |
| King marble | A Nigerian timber with black or dark brown irregular stripes |
| Queen marble | Another Nigerian timber with black and light coloured irregular stripes |

*Other 'ebony' timbers*

Cocuswood, *Brya ebenus*, which grows in Jamaica and Cuba, is also known as brown, green or Jamaican ebony. It is a fairly uniform, dark chocolate brown in colour but has little resemblance to true ebony.

Partridgewood or Maracaibo ebony, *Caesalpinia granadillo*, is a dark chocolate-brown wood with paler feather-like markings which give it its name. It is very strong and hard but has a rather coarse and irregular grain and bears little resemblance to the *Diospyros* species.

### Elm

There are about twenty species of the genus *Ulmus*, most of which grow in the temperate regions of the northern hemisphere. A few species, however, are found in the tropical regions of southern China and South East Asia where they extend below the equator.

Elm timber is generally reddish or brownish in colour and has a coarse texture, and some species have a very irregular grain which gives an attractive figure. Most species are ring-porous but a few are diffuse-porous.

The timber is tough and difficult to split but is relatively weak and has little durability. An exception is rock or hickory elm which is strong and tough and is used for sports goods and boat frames.

There are six species in North America which are subdivided into two broad groups, hard elms and soft elms. The soft elm group consists of white or grey elm, *Ulmus americana*, a widely-used general purpose timber, and slippery elm, *Ulmus fulva*, which is also a commercial timber. The hard elms comprise rock elm, *Ulmus thomasii*, a valuable commercial species, and three minor species, winged elm, *Ulmus alata*, cedar elm, *Ulmus crassifolia* and september elm, *Ulmus serotina*.

The nomenclature of some of the European elms is confusing because there are numerous synonyms and the genetic and geographical origins of some of the varieties are uncertain.

The five principal European species are the smooth-leaved elm, *Ulmus carpinifolia*, of which there are several varieties, white elm, *Ulmus laevis*, Dutch elm, *Ulmus hollandica*, wych elm, *Ulmus glabra* and English elm, *Ulmus procera*.

Apart from wych elm, which is indigenous in Britain, all the other British elms were introduced in Roman times or earlier.

The variety in East Anglia is a form of *Ulmus carpinifolia* and the western or Cornish elms are another variety, *Ulmus carpinifolia var cornubiensis*. English elm, *Ulmus procera*, was introduced into central and southern England, probably in the Iron Age, and has been almost completely destroyed by Dutch elm disease.

Of the European elms the preferred species for furniture making are English elm and Dutch elm, mainly because of their irregular grain.

There are two commercial species in India, *Ulmus wallichiana* and *Ulmus lancifolia*, the latter being one of the diffuse-porous species.

Of the remaining twelve or so species several are used commercially in China and Japan, especially *Ulmus davidiana var japonica*, *Ulmus laciniata* and *Ulmus parvifolia*.

There is one species known in India as Indian elm which belongs to the elm family but not to the genus *Ulmus*. This is *Holoptelea integrifolia* which is a yellow-coloured, general purpose timber.

## Keruing and related timbers

There are more than 70 species of the genus *Dipterocarpus* which grow in India, Sri Lanka, South East Asia, Sumatra, Borneo and the Philippines, the timbers of which are not differentiated except by region of origin as set out in the next column:

| | |
|---|---|
| keruing | Malaya, Sarawak, Sabah, Indonesia |
| gurjun | India and Burma |
| yang | Thailand |
| apitong | The Philippines |
| eng | Burma |

Although the general character of all these timbers is very similar there is some variation between species and within regions. The variation is less in the timber from Burma and Thailand because it is produced by a relatively small number of tree species. They are all used as general purpose carpentry and joinery timbers.

## Mahogany

Scores of different species of pale reddish-brown to dark red tropical hardwoods have been described as mahogany. The only species which can legitimately be regarded as mahogany belong to the family *Meliacea* and, more particularly, to the two genera *Swietenia* in Central and South America and *Khaya* in Africa. Another genus of the *Meliacea* family – *Entandrophragma* – contains several species which resemble fairly closely the true mahogany species. The other species which have at one time or another been described as mahoganies belong to various genera which, from the botanical point of view, are generally not closely related to the true mahoganies.

Within the genera *Swietenia* and *Khaya* there are a number of species each with their own characteristics, but the variation within each species is so great that it is often not easy to distinguish one from the other. For centuries mahogany timber has been named as much from its port of origin as from any particular species of tree, and even today it is not always certain from what species of tree a particular timber has been obtained.

It is convenient to think of five broad groups of mahoganies or mahogany-like timbers. These are listed below in approximate chronological order of their introduction into Europe and North America and, incidentally, of their quality.

1) *Swietenia mahagoni* from the West Indian islands (except Trinidad and Tobago) and southern Florida.
2) *Swietenia macrophylla* and, probably, some closely related species from the mainland of Central and South America.
3) Various species of *Khya* from West, Central and East Africa.
4) Several species of *Entandrophragma* from West Africa.

5) Numerous other species from South America, Africa and Asia, bearing some resemblance to mahogany.

*Swietenia mahagoni* was first imported into Europe and North America in the early years of the eighteenth century and it came principally from Puerto Rico, San Domingo and, later, from Cuba. It was known as Spanish mahogany and it was the timber used by the eighteenth century furniture makers. It is generally considered to be the finest of all the mahoganies although even within the species there are pronounced differences in colour, density and figure. *Swietenia mahagoni* became increasingly scarce throughout the nineteenth century when there was much wasteful felling to recover only the crotches of the trees which produced finely figured veneers. The species is now virtually unobtainable except from old furniture.

*Swietenia macrophylla* and some closely related species, which are not always clearly identified, occur from Southern Mexico through Central America to Colombia, Venezuela, Eastern Peru, Brazil and Bolivia, the principal exporting regions being Mexico, Honduras and Brazil. The characteristics of the timber vary with the place of origin, the colour, for example, ranging from light yellowish-brown to dark red. The density tends to be correlated with the colour, the darker-coloured wood being denser than the paler variety. Venezuelan mahogany, *Swietenia candollei*, is said to resemble Cuban mahogany and is therefore sometimes differentiated from the *Swietenia macrophylla* group. In so far as it is possible to generalise about a variable material, South American mahogany is considered to be inferior to Spanish mahogany but superior to African mahogany for fine work. It tends to work better and to be stronger weight for weight than *Khaya*.

There are many species of *Khaya*, two of which provide most of the mahogany of commerce. The most important is *Khaya ivorensis*, which grows in the coastal rain forests of West Africa. The second in importance is *Khaya anthotheca* which occurs on less humid sites in West Africa and extends into Uganda and Tanzania. This is a similar species and may be marketed with *Khaya ivorensis*. The two species are known jointly as Ghana, Ivory Coast, Takoradi or Grand Bassam mahogany.

There are a number of other species of *Khaya* occurring in Central or East Africa or in the less humid regions of West Africa. They are generally smaller trees than the two principal species and are darker in colour, denser and harder, and have a more irregular grain. The most important of them is *Khaya grandifoliola* which extends from the drier areas of West Africa to Uganda and Tanzania. It is known as Benin wood or Benin mahogany. Two other species are *Khaya senegalensis* from the drier zones of Central Africa, Uganda and the Sudan, and *Khaya nyasica* or Mozambique mahogany, also from Central and the more southerly parts of East Africa. *Khaya grandifoliola* and *K. senegalensis* are sometimes marketed as heavy African mahogany but *K. nyasica* is rarely found outside Africa.

In general, the wood of *Swietenia* species tends to be golden brown in colour whereas that of *Khaya* species has a more reddish tinge.

The fourth group of timbers sometimes referred to as mahogany comprises several species of the genus *Entandrophragma* and particularly sapele, *Entandrophragma cylindricum*, gedu nohor, *E. angolense*, and utile, *E. utile*. These three species of the mahogany family, however, have sufficiently distinctive characteristics to be differentiated from the true mahoganies and from each other, and they are rarely described as mahogany in the timber trade.

Finally, there are various species of timber having a greater or lesser resemblance to mahogany which have been or still are referred to loosely as mahogany. African species include *Aucoumea klaineana* formerly known as Gabon mahogany but now referred to as simply as gaboon or okoumé, and *Tieghemella heckelii* from the Ivory Coast and Ghana previously marketed as cherry mahogany but now known as makoré. Two South American examples are *Ocotea rubra* which is known as red louro in Brazil, determa in Guyana and wawa in Surinam, and *Carapa guianensis*, a member of the mahogany family, which is known as andiroba in Brazil and crabwood in Guyana. The groups of similar timbers belonging to the genera *Shorea*, *Parashorea* and *Pentacme* and marketed in South East Asia as dark red and light red meranti and in the Philippines as red lauan and white lauan are sometimes sold as Philippine mahoganies.

## Maple

There are over one hundred species of the maple genus, *Acer*, distributed throughout the northern hemisphere, and several species of *Eucalyptus* in Australia described as maple but having relatively little resemblance to true *Acer* species.

There are a number of European species, mostly in the Mediterranean region, of which only field maple, *Acer campestre*, is native to Britain although sycamore, *Acer pseudoplatanus*, was introduced by the Romans and has for a very long time behaved as a native. Another species which is frequently planted in Britain is Norway maple, *Acer platanoides*. The timbers of these three species are similar, although field maple is a little darker and denser and is available only in small sizes.

There are several North American species of maple which are marketed as either hard or soft maple. The hard maple group includes *Acer saccharum*, rock or sugar maple, and *Acer nigrum*, black maple, while the soft maples are red maple, *Acer rubrum*, silver maple, *Acer saccharinum* and Pacific maple, *Acer macrophyllum*. The hard maples, as their name implies, are harder, stronger and denser than the soft maples. The colour of the wood is variable but the hard maples tend to be a light reddish brown while the soft maples are pale brown. Pacific maple, which is sometimes recognised as a separate category, is a deep pinkish brown. Hard maple is the principal source of bird's-eye maple (Figure 8(a)), the figure of which is probably caused by a fungal infection in the cambium giving rise to small depressions in the tangential pattern of the grain. A somewhat similar figure known as quilted maple is sometimes found in Pacific maple.

There are several eastern species of maple which are exported from Japan. These are mainly *Acer mono* and *Acer palmatum* known, generally, as Japanese maple. This has a closer resemblance to hard maple than to sycamore, being darker in colour and harder than sycamore.

Queensland maple is also known as silkwood. It comes from the two species *Flindersia brayleyana* and *Flindersia pimenteliana* and bears no resemblance to maple at all. It is, however, one of the outstanding cabinet-making timbers of Australia and has the appearance of a cross between mahogany and walnut.

## Meranti, seraya and lauan

The three timber names, meranti, seraya and lauan are almost synonymous. Each is applied to the timber of groups of species of the genus *Shorea*, or of two closely related genera, *Parashorea* and *Pentacme*, which grow in South East Asia and the Philippines. Lauan is a Philippine name, meranti is used in Malaya and Sarawak, and seraya in Sabah.

Because there are many similar species the timbers are classified and sold by colour. Four main groups are recognised, and it is possible to relate the South East Asian merantis (or serayas), which are all species of the genus *Shorea*, to the Philippine lauans, which also include some species of the genera *Parashorea* and *Pentacme*. The four groups are:

**a)** dark red meranti or red lauan
**b)** light red meranti or white lauan
**c)** yellow meranti or yellow lauan
**d)** white meranti

A fifth group, white seraya, differs from white meranti. It is obtained from several species of *Parashorea* and comes from Sabah and the Philippines.

All the merantis and lauans are relatively featureless but serviceable general purpose timbers used principally for construction, internal and external joinery and plywood manufacture.

The name mahogany is sometimes applied to the dark and light red merantis and to the lauan equivalents which are described as Philippine mahoganies (page 66).

## Oak

There are over 200 species of oak, *Quercus*, mostly in the northern hemisphere. There are also several species described as oak which are quite unrelated to true oak.

For practical purposes four different groups of oak can be recognised:

**a)** white oaks
**b)** red oaks
**c)** evergreen oaks
**d)** species not belonging to the genus *Quercus*.

### White oaks

The European oaks, known in Britain as sessile oak, *Quercus petraea*, and pedunculate oak, *Quercus robur* are the common oaks of central and northern Europe. Their timbers are indistinguishable but they differ to some extent according to their origin. In general, oak from central and eastern Europe, known as Polish, Danzig, Austrian and Slovenian oak, is slower grown and milder to work than oak from Germany, France or Britain.

There are about ten species of closely related white oaks in North America which are exported to Europe as white oak. Owing to the range of species and origins American white oak is more variable in colour, density and toughness than

European oak and there is a tendency for timber from the southern states to be denser and harder than that from the north.

The other important white oak of commerce is Japanese oak, *Quercus mongolica*, which grows in northern China and Japan and which is imported into Britain from Japan. It is paler, less dense and less hard than European oak, which is generally preferred for high quality work.

### Red oaks

There are about ten species of red oak in North America, the timbers of which are very similar in properties and appearance. They are, therefore, all marketed under the same name of red oak. The timber of Turkey oak, *Quercus cerris*, which is naturalised in Britain, is very similar to red oak, which is considered to be much inferior to white oak for high quality work. It has a slight pinkish colour, a coarser texture and a less attractive figure than white oak. It is also less durable and more difficult to season. One Asian species which is related to *Q. cerris*, *Quercus castaneaefolia*, has been imported from Iran for making barrel staves.

### Evergreen oaks

The evergreen oaks are associated particularly with the Mediterranean region. Many are small bushes but some species grow to timber size. The timber is hard and heavy and of inferior quality. It is easily distinguished from the timber of white or red oak.

### Other genera

The early settlers in Tasmania and Australia found several tree species which produced timber having a superficial resemblance to the oak with which they were familiar in Britain. They therefore gave the familiar name to Australian silky oak which comes from two distinct species, *Cardwellia sublimis*, and a smaller tree, *Grevillea robusta*. Three species of *Eucalyptus* in Tasmania, *Eucalyptus regnans*, *Eucalyptus delegatensis* and *Eucalyptus obliqua*, also provide a timber which is not unlike flat sawn oak in colour, grain and texture, and which is exported as Tasmanian or Victorian oak. The timber is sometimes paler in colour when it resembles ash, and *Eucalyptus regnans* is known in Tasmania as mountain ash and *Eucalyptus delegatensis* as alpine ash (page 63).

### Padauk

There are several species of padauk which grow in Asia and Africa. They all belong to the genus *Pterocarpus* and are related botanically to the rosewoods.

All the padauk timbers are red to reddish-brown, usually with some darker streaking. They are all very stable and durable.

African padauk, *Pterocarpus soyauxii*, is bright red when cut and seasons to a dark purple-brown colour.

Andaman padauk, *Pterocarpus dalbergioides*, is a more decorative reddish-brown timber with darker red or black streaks.

Burma padauk, *Pterocarpus macrocarpus*, is less variable and somewhat lighter in colour than Andaman padauk and is denser and stronger.

*Pterocarpus angolensis*, muninga, occurs in South and East Africa and *Pterocarpus indicus*, amboyna, in South East Asia.

### Rosewood

All the rosewood species are members of the genus *Dalbergia* which belongs to the same sub family of the *Leguminosae* as laburnum and robinia. *Dalbergia* species which are marketed as rosewood occur in Central and South America, Africa, India, Burma and Thailand. They are all dense, strong and hard timbers and, with one exception, they are dark brown or reddish brown in colour with very dark coloured streaks or irregular stripes. They have been valued as high quality furniture timbers in Europe and America for over two hundred years.

The outstanding commercial timber is Brazilian or Rio rosewood, *Dalbergia nigra*, and closely related species. It was originally exported from the coastal regions of south east Brazil but now comes from more inland regions. The valuable, highly figured timber is obtained from the heartwood of old trees and has a pronounced orange-brown colour with very dark streaks. The heartwood of young trees lacks the rich contrasting colour and is of little value.

There are two other familiar Brazilian rosewoods. These are kingwood, *Dalbergia cearensis* and Brazilian tulipwood, *Dalbergia frutescens var. tomentosa*. Kingwood is denser, stronger and harder than Rio rosewood and has more regular black and deep violet stripes. It is a smaller tree and produces small-sized material which is used for inlays and turnery. Tulipwood resembles Rio rosewood in grain and texture but is much lighter in colour, although a denser timber. The wood is yellowish or pinkish with less obvious red or purple streaking. It is not widely used nowadays but being a small tree was formerly used for marquetry and inlay work.

Cocobolo, *Dalbergia retusa*, is a Central American species which is denser and more variable in colour than Rio rosewood. The deep orange timber is streaked or mottled with a black colouration.

Honduras rosewood, *Dalbergia stevensonii*, is another very dense and hard Central American species which is especially valued for xylophone keys.

The only important African rosewood is known as African blackwood, *Dalbergia melanoxylon*. This is a particularly hard and heavy dark-purplish timber with numerous black streaks. It is regarded as an outstanding wood for turnery and for making wood-wind instruments. There are also some rosewoods in Malagasy.

Indian rosewood, *Dalbergia latifolia*, has a long history as a high class furniture timber. It resembles Rio rosewood but is somewhat darker, stronger and harder and tends to have a more interlocked grain. It does not have the same orange tinge as Rio rosewood. It is used for high quality furniture and for musical instruments.

Three other Asian species are Burma tulip-wood, *Dalbergia oliveri*, Thailand rosewood or chin chan, *Dalbergia cochinchinensis*, and shisham, *D. sissoo*.

There is one species which belongs to the same family but to a different genus which is sometimes used in place of Rio rosewood. This is *Machaerium scleroxylon* which resembles Rio rosewood in appearance but which has the disadvantage of producing a very irritating dust. Another species which is misleadingly referred to as African rosewood is bubinga or kevazingo, which belongs to the genus *Guibourtia*, also of the pea family.

## Teak

Teak is a timber of outstanding quality and it is not surprising that the name has been given to a number of species which have in common a golden brown colour, strength and durability. Some of these species, such as iroko and afrormosia, are high quality timbers in their own right. Others can be regarded as acceptable substitutes for teak for a number of purposes, especially for construction.

Teak, *Tectona grandis*, occurs naturally in India, Burma, Thailand and Vietnam and has been introduced into Java. It is grown as a plantation tree in West Africa and parts of the Caribbean region. There is another species of *Tectona* in Burma, *Tectona hamiltoniana* or dahat. This timber is much harder and denser than teak and is not widely used.

Brunei or Borneo teak, more properly called kapur, is obtained from a number of closely related species of *Dryobalanops* belonging to the family *Dipterocarpaceae*. It is found in Malaya, Sumatra, Borneo, Sarawak and Brunei, and due to the range of species and geographical location it shows considerable variation. The trees grow to a large size and the wood is stronger but less stable than teak. It has a somewhat dull appearance. There are two other species, *Intsia palembanica* and *I. bijuga* which are known as Borneo teak or merbau and which belong to the family *Leguminosae*.

Iroko, *Chlorophora excelsa*, is sometimes known as African or Nigerian teak. It has many of the physical qualities of teak but has a coarser and more irregular grain and is a rather crude looking timber for fine work.

Another African species which is similar to teak in properties and appearance is afrormosia, *Pericopsis elata*. This species, however, is a high class furniture timber and is marketed under its own name and not as a species of teak.

Rhodesian or Zambian teak is a leguminous species, *Baikiaea plurijuga*. It is a relatively small tree and produces a reddish-coloured timber which is harder and heavier than teak and which is exported for flooring although it is used locally as a high class furniture timber.

There are two timbers described as teak which are found in South America. These are Brazilian teak or freijo, which comes from a tree *Cordia goeldiana* and several related species, and teck de la Guyane, *Dicorynia guianensis*, known locally as angélique.

## Walnut

Like mahogany, the name walnut has been given to many species which have no botanical relationship with the valuable and highly prized genuine walnut timbers of the genus *Juglans*. They are, in general, however, high quality timbers sharing at least some of the desirable characteristics of true walnut.

The most valued species is European walnut, *Juglans regia*, which is a native of eastern Europe and the temperate regions of Asia but which has been cultivated in western Europe for more than 2000 years. It varies in properties according to its country of origin. French walnut is greyer than English walnut while Ancona or Italian walnut is darker and has a more pronounced figure. European walnut is so scarce and expensive that it is used usually only as a veneer or in small sizes for turnery and musical instruments.

Black walnut, *Juglans nigra*, is a native of the eastern United States where it is almost equally prized as a high quality decorative timber. It is darker and less variable in colour than European walnut and tends to darken with age, unlike the European species, which becomes paler.

There is another North American species of lower quality known as white walnut or butternut, *Juglans cinerea*. This species is similar in grain and texture to black walnut but it is lighter in colour, less dense and softer. It is sometimes dyed and used as a cheaper substitute for black walnut.

Another North American species, which was formerly known as satin walnut, is red gum, *Liquidambar styraciflua*, which has a pleasant, light walnut colour with irregular darker streaks. The brown heartwood of the North American black willow, *Salix nigra*, is also sometimes known as swamp walnut.

Japanese walnut, or claro, *Juglans sieboldiana*, is sometimes obtainable in Europe. This is paler, lighter and softer than *Juglans regia*.

The only commercial example from South America is Brazilian walnut or imbuia, *Phoebe porosa*. This is a decorative, walnut-like timber having a variable colour and grain and regarded as a high quality furniture timber in Brazil. There are, however, some true walnuts of local significance in the mountain regions of South America. These include *Juglans colombiensis*, *J. neotropica* and *J. australis*.

African walnut, *Lovoa trichilioides*, is a good quality timber in its own right but it belongs to the mahogany family and looks more like a cross between iroko and African mahogany than a true walnut. It is yellow brown or golden brown in colour with darker stripes and has the interlocked grain of some mahoganies. It is sometimes used for the solid parts of furniture, when the flat surfaces are veneered with true mahogany. This species is known in the USA as tigerwood, congowood or lovoa and in France as noyer d'Afrique. Another African species is African black walnut or mansonia, *Mansonia altissima*.

A number of species of two Australian genera, *Endiandra* and *Beilschmiedia*, have some resemblance to walnut and are named accordingly. Queensland walnut, *Endiandra palmerstonii*, bears the closest resemblance. Other species are New South Wales walnut, *Endiandra virens*, rose walnut, *Endiandra discolor*, yellow walnut, *Beilschmiedia bancroftii* and blush walnut, *Beilschmiedia obtusifolia*.

There is a South East Asian walnut known variously as New Guinea, Pacific or Papuan walnut which comes from various species of the genus *Dracontomelum*, especially *D. mangiferum*. This wood has a figured heartwood which bears some resemblance to walnut but is less dense. An individual species of the same genus, *Dracontomelum dao*, with the local name paldao, also occurs in South East Asia and the South West Pacific region.

East Indian walnut or kokko is a leguminous species, *Albizia lebbek*. It is coarser in texture than walnut and its irregular, interlocked grain gives it an appearance intermediate between that of walnut and iroko. It is now rarely seen in commerce.

| Name | Botanical name | Geographical origin |
|---|---|---|
| ABURA; | *Mitragyna ciliata*; | West Africa |

AFARA; *Terminalia superba*; tropical Africa

Abura is a light yellowish-brown or pinkish-brown timber with a moderately fine and even texture. The grain is usually straight but is sometimes interlocked. It seasons and works well and is a useful general purpose timber which takes a good finish but is somewhat lacking in character. Abura is used for the internal components and framing of furniture and for interior joinery and mouldings and also in plywood manufacture.

| Density | *3* | Stability in service | *above average* |
|---|---|---|---|
| Bending strength | *4* | Hardness | *3* |
| Stiffness | *5* | Durability | *4* |
| Impact strength | *4* | Blunting effect | *average* |

*Identification*
Diffuse-porous.
Growth rings absent.
Vessels fairly small and numerous, solitary and in radial chains, (two to six), occasionally in small clusters.
Rays very fine, one per vessel.
Parenchyma diffuse.

Afara, also known as korina in the United States, is variable in colour but is usually a pale straw or very light oak colour. Some logs have dark greyish-brown or nearly black markings. Ambrosia beetle holes are common.

The wood has a moderately coarse and even texture and the grain is straight or slightly interlocked, giving a banded figure on radial surfaces.

Afara is a medium weight, stable timber used for the framing and internal components of furniture, interior joinery and general utility purposes. The dark-figured logs are cut for decorative veneers.

| Density | *3* | Stability in service | *above average* |
|---|---|---|---|
| Bending strength | *4* | Hardness | *3* |
| Stiffness | *4* | Durability | *4* |
| Impact strength | | Blunting effect | *below average* |

*Identification*
Diffuse-porous.
Growth rings present.
Vessels medium to moderately large, solitary and in radial chains (two to five).
Rays very fine, one to three per vessel.
Parenchyma aliform, confluent, sometimes terminal.

**29** abura ( × *50*); afara ( × *25*)

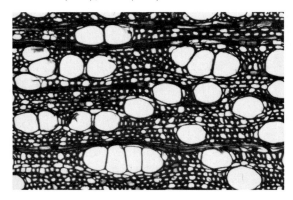 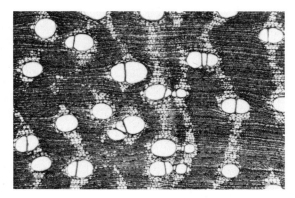

AFRORMOSIA;  *Pericopsis elata*;  West Africa

AFZELIA;  mainly *Afzelia bipindensis, A. pachyloba* and *A. africana*;  West and Central Africa and *A. quanzensis* in East Africa

Afrormosia is a medium yellow-brown in colour. It has a moderately fine texture and, very often, an interlocked grain which gives a banded figure, rather like sapele, on radial surfaces. It is similar to teak in properties but, containing less silica, does not blunt tools so quickly. It is relatively easy to work but is not a good bending timber.

Afrormosia is a high quality timber for both decorative and structural purposes and is used as solid wood and as a veneer for furniture making and high class joinery, as well as for boat building and flooring.

| Density | 2 | Stability in service | *above average* |
| Bending strength | 2 | Hardness | 2 |
| Stiffness | 3 | Durability | 1 |
| Impact strength | 3 | Blunting effect | *average* |

*Identification*
Diffuse-porous.
Growth rings visible.
Vessels small, solitary and in radial groups.
Rays very fine, one per vessel, storied.
Parenchyma aliform and confluent.
Ripple pattern on tangential surfaces.

Afzelia is a dense, reddish-brown timber with a straight to moderately interlocked grain and a rather coarse texture. It dries and works reasonably well but is difficult to glue and is variable in its bending properties.

Afzelia is strong, durable and stable and is used for high class internal and exterior joinery and flooring.

| Density | 1 | Stability in service | *above average* |
| Bending strength | 2 | Hardness | 1 |
| Stiffness | 3 | Durability | 1 |
| Impact strength | 4 | Blunting effect | *average* |

*Identification*
Diffuse-porous.
Growth rings present.
Vessels not very abundant, fairly large, solitary or in radial or tangential pairs.
Rays very fine, one per vessel, deflected by vessels.
Parenchyma vasicentric and aliform, terminal, distinct.

**30**  afrormosia ( × *50*); afzelia ( × *25*)

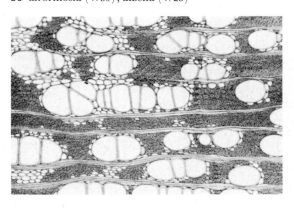
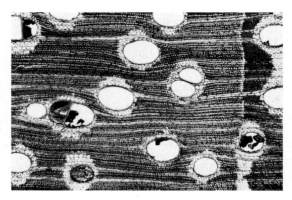

AGBA; *Gossweilerodendron balsamiferum*; West Africa

Agba is sometimes known as tola, a name also used for the species tchitola, *Oxystigma oxyphyllum*. It is a uniform pale straw or yellow-brown colour with a fine, even texture and a straight or moderately interlocked grain which gives a striped figure on radial surfaces. Brittleheart is often present in the cores of large logs.

Agba is easily seasoned and works well, apart from a tendency to gumminess, and has a slight resinous or peppery scent. It is a useful general purpose timber of moderate density and good durability and is used for furniture making, internal and external joinery and boat building.

| | | | |
|---|---|---|---|
| Density | *3* | Stability in service | *above average* |
| Bending strength | *4* | Hardness | *3* |
| Stiffness | *5* | Durability | *2* |
| Impact strength | *4* | Blunting effect | *below average* |

*Identification*

Diffuse-porous.
Growth rings distinct.
Vessels medium sized, mainly solitary, gum deposits often present.
Rays very fine, one per vessel.
Parenchyma vasicentric.
Small gum canals present.

ALBIZIA, WEST AFRICAN; *Albizia* species especially *A. ferruginea*; West and East Africa

Albizia is a hard and heavy, rich brown to deep reddish-brown timber, often with an interlocked grain giving a banded figure on radial surfaces. It has a coarse texture.

Albizia is stable and durable with quite good working characteristics and is suitable for joinery and general purpose woodwork.

| | | | |
|---|---|---|---|
| Density | *2* | Stability in service | *above average* |
| Bending strength | *3* | Hardness | *2* |
| Stiffness | *4* | Durability | *1* |
| Impact strength | *5* | Blunting effect | *average* |

*Identification*

Diffuse-porous.
Growth rings absent or indistinct.
Vessels small to moderately large, not numerous, solitary or in radial chains (two to six) and clusters.
Rays very fine, one to two per vessel.
Parenchyma aliform and confluent.

**31** agba (× *50*); albizia (and kokko) (× *25*)

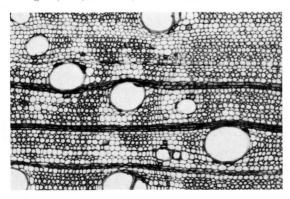
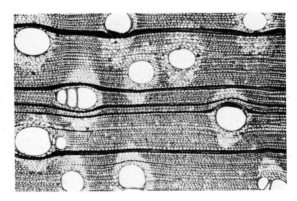

AMBOYNA; *Pterocarpus indicus*; Philippines, Borneo, New Guinea

Amboyna timber is of two types. The exported material takes the form of highly figured veneers which are cut from burrs. The unfigured wood is golden-brown to reddish-brown in colour and has a straight, interlocked or wavy grain and a rather coarse and uneven texture. The density is very variable but averages about 640kg per cu. m. (40lb per cu. ft.).

The timber dries and works well and is stable in service. It is used locally for furniture making.

| | | |
|---|---|---|
| Density *2* | Stability in service *above average* | |
| Bending strength | Hardness *2* | |
| Stiffness | Durability | |
| Impact strength | Blunting effect | |

*Identification*
Diffuse-porous.
Growth rings present.
Vessels of medium size, relatively sparse.
Rays very fine, storied, two to three per vessel.
Parenchyma vasicentric, aliform, banded and diffuse (in fine lines).
Ripple marks present.

APPLE; *Pyrus malus* and Pear, *Pyrus communis*; Europe and western Asia

Apple and pear are similar in appearance and properties, but pear is considered to be the superior timber. They are a pale to medium brown or a light reddish-brown in colour with a fine, uniform texture. Old apple often has dark streaks. Pear is straight grained but apple is sometimes irregular. They are both hard timbers which work well and take a fine polish. They are used for fine cabinet work, turnery and inlay and sometimes for making woodwind instruments. Pear is used for some of the small working parts of keyboard instruments.

| | | |
|---|---|---|
| Density *2* | Stability in service *above average* | |
| Bending strength | Hardness *2* | |
| Stiffness | Durability *4* | |
| Impact strength | Blunting effect *average* | |

*Identification*
Diffuse-porous.
Growth rings distinct to indistinct, boundaries marked by narrow bands of denser late wood.
Vessels small to very small, mostly solitary, slightly smaller and less numerous in late wood.
Rays fine, same width as vessels, two to three vessels per ray.
Parenchyma not obvious.

**32** amboyna (and muninga) ( × *25*); apple (and pear) ( × *50*)

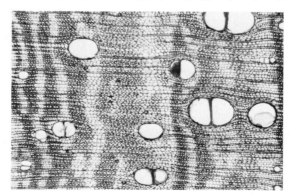 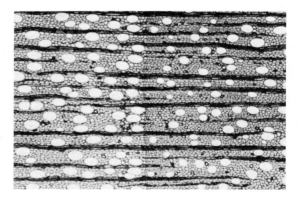

74

ASH, AMERICAN; various species of *Fraxinus* especially *Fraxinus americana*; North America

ASH, EUROPEAN; *Fraxinus excelsior*; Europe and Asia Minor

The faster grown ash is known in America as hard ash and is used where toughness is required. The slower grown ash is known as soft ash and is used for joinery and furniture making.

Hard ash is similar in properties to the faster grown European ash and both hard and soft ash closely resemble European ash from the botanical point of view.

Ash is a very pale, almost white wood which sometimes has dark streaks in the heartwood not necessarily associated with decay.

The grain is usually straight. The bands of large, early wood vessels give the timber a coarse texture and this feature produces a decorative figure on tangential surfaces. As with all ring-porous species, the faster growth is generally associated with stronger and tougher timber.

Ash is easy to work and bend and is outstanding among European species for its toughness. That is to say, it can temporarily absorb a greater strain than would break it if applied permanently. It is used wherever toughness is important as in sports equipment, tool handles, boat fittings, chair making and occasionally for cabinet making and turnery.

| | |
|---|---|
| Density  *2* | Stability in service  *average* |
| Bending strength  *3* | Hardness  *2* |
| Stiffness  *4* | Durability  *5* |
| Impact strength 2–3 | Blunting effect  *average* |

*Identification*
Ring-porous.
Growth rings distinct.
Vessels medium in early wood, small in late wood, oval.
Rays fine, one to two large vessels per ray.
Parenchyma sparse, vasicentric and diffuse, not very obvious, also terminal.

**33**  ash ( × *25*)

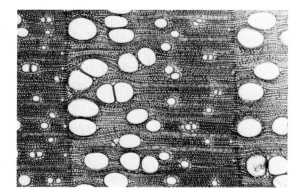

AVODIRÉ; *Turraeanthus africanus*; West Africa

AYAN; *Distemonanthus benthamianus*; West Africa

Avodiré is a pale yellow wood which darkens to a golden yellow. It is a species of the mahogany family and has the lustre and texture of mahogany. The grain is sometimes straight but often wavy, producing a mottled figure on radial surfaces.

It is used for decorative veneers, furniture making and high class interior joinery, while the straight grained logs are sometimes used for the manufacture of plywood.

| Density | 3 | Stability in service | *above average* |
|---|---|---|---|
| Bending strength | 3 | Hardness | 3–4 |
| Stiffness | 5 | Durability | 3 |
| Impact strength | 4 | Blunting effect | *below average* |

*Identification*
Diffuse-porous.
Growth rings absent.
Vessels medium sized, solitary or in pairs, moderately numerous.
Rays very fine, one to two vessels per ray.
Parenchyma not visible.

Ayan is a fine textured, yellow to yellowish-brown wood, sometimes with darker streaks. The grain is often interlocked and occasionally wavy, producing an attractive roe figure.

The timber seasons well but a varying content of silica can cause moderate to severe blunting.

Ayan is a moderately strong and heavy timber which can be used in the same way as oak for internal and external joinery, furniture making and flooring.

| Density | 2 | Stability in service | *above average* |
|---|---|---|---|
| Bending strength | 3 | Hardness | 2 |
| Stiffness | 4 | Durability | 3 |
| Impact strength | 4 | Blunting effect | *average to well above average* |

*Identification*
Diffuse-porous.
Growth rings indistinct.
Vessels not very abundant, moderately large, solitary or in short radial chains (two or three).
Rays very fine, one to two vessels per ray, storied.
Parenchyma vasicentric, aliform, confluent, sometimes banded, distinct.
Ripple marks present.

**34** avodire ( × *50*); ayan ( × *50*)

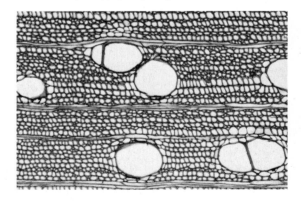
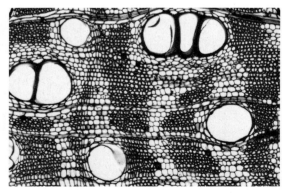

BALSA; *Ochroma lagopus*; Central and South America

BEECH, EUROPEAN; *Fagus sylvatica*; Europe and western Asia

Balsa is a pale straw-coloured, very soft and very light wood. Unlike nearly all other hardwoods the preferred commercial product is sapwood which is less dense and lighter in colour than the heartwood. It has a straight grain and an even texture.

The density can vary from 40kg per cu. m (2½lb per cu. ft) to 320kg per cu. m (20lb per cu. ft) at 12 per cent moisture content.

The very low density balsa is used for specialised purposes such as model making, insulation and for providing buoyancy, although polystyrene is increasingly being used for insulation and buoyancy.

| Density | 5 | Stability in service | *above average* |
|---|---|---|---|
| Bending strength | 5 | Hardness | 5 |
| Stiffness | 5 | Durability | 5 |
| Impact strength | 5 | Blunting effect | *below average* |

*Identification*
Diffuse-porous.
Growth rings absent.
Vessels moderately large to large, not numerous, solitary or in radial chains (two to three).
Rays fine to medium, one to two vessels per ray.
Parenchyma indistinct, predominantly diffuse.

A very pale-coloured wood sometimes showing darker reddish-brown streaks which do not necessarily indicate decay. Timber imported from Yugoslavia has usually been steamed to give it a pale pinky-brown colour.

Beech has a fine texture and is usually straight grained.

The fairly prominent rays show on tangential surfaces as closely spaced medium brown lines about 3mm (⅛in) long and on radial surfaces as medium brown flecks which change colour as the angle of the light changes.

Beech is a good timber for working and bending and is one of the most widely used general purpose timbers for utility and bentwood furniture, interior work and cabinet making, turnery, flooring and plywood manufacture. It lacks character, however, and is rarely used for fine work.

| Density | 2 | Stability in service | *below average* |
|---|---|---|---|
| Bending strength | 3 | Hardness | 2 |
| Stiffness | 3 | Durability | 5 |
| Impact strength | 3 | Blunting effect | *average* |

*Identification*
Diffuse-porous.
Growth rings fairly distinct.
Vessels small, variable in shape and gradually decreasing in size through the growth ring.
Rays distinct, large and small, many vessels per large ray.
Parenchyma not obvious.

**35** balsa ( × 25); beech ( × 50)

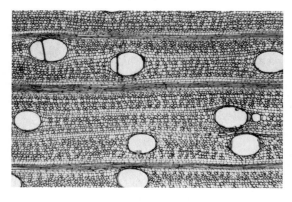
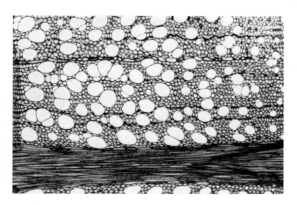

The name 'berlinia' is given to the timbers of several species of *Berlinia* including *Berlinia confusa, B. grandiflora* and *B. occidentalis*.

The wood is pinkish-brown to a medium reddish-brown with dark-coloured irregular streaks. It has a rather coarse texture with an interlocked and sometimes very irregular grain and occasionally contains dark-coloured streaks of gum.

The wood dries reasonably well but is somewhat difficult to work because of the irregular grain.

Berlinia was previously used mainly as a construction timber but is now also used for furniture making and veneering. Timber with brittleheart or exceptionally wild grain has to be rejected for structural work or for furniture construction, but a wild grain can produce decorative veneers.

| | | | |
|---|---|---|---|
| Density | 2 | Stability in service | *average* |
| Bending strength | 3 | Hardness | 2 |
| Stiffness | 4 | Durability | 4 |
| Impact strength | 4 | Blunting effect | *average* |

*Identification*
Diffuse-porous.
Growth rings present.
Vessels not very abundant, of average size, single or in short radial chains (two to three).
Rays very fine, one ray per vessel, rays deflected by vessels.
Parenchyma aliform, confluent, terminal, distinct.

Birch is an almost white to very pale fawn timber having a generally straight grain and a fine, uniform texture.

It is a strong but featureless wood, except when possessing an unusual grain pattern, and is widely used in Scandinavia for making good quality plywood. In Britain it is of limited commercial value and is used for pulping, for making items of domestic turnery such as brush backs and, sometimes, for utility or kitchen furniture and for the frames of upholstered furniture.

There are many species of birch such as North American paper birch, *Betula papyrifera*, North American yellow birch, *Betula alleghaniensis*, and Japanese birch, *Betula maximowicziana*, which are similar in appearance and properties to the European species and which are used for similar purposes.

| | | | |
|---|---|---|---|
| Density | 2 | Stability in service | *average* |
| Bending strength | 2 | Hardness | 2 |
| Stiffness | 3 | Durability | 5 |
| Impact strength | 3 | Blunting effect | *average* |

*Identification*
Diffuse-porous.
Growth rings indistinct.
Vessels small to very small, solitary or in radial chains (two to four), uniformly distributed.
Rays very fine, two to three vessels per ray.
Parenchyma terminal.

**36** berlinia ( × 25); birch ( × 50)

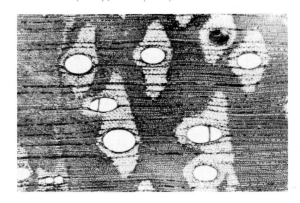 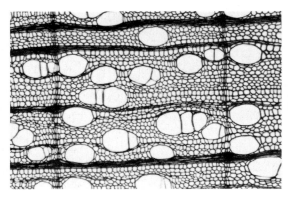

BLACK BEAN; *Castanospermum australe*; New South Wales and Queensland

Black bean is a chocolate-brown timber with paler tissue surrounding the large vessels. The grain is usually straight but may be slightly interlocked and the texture is rather coarse and uneven. It is a relatively hard and strong timber with some resemblance to walnut.

Black bean timber works reasonably well and takes a good finish. It is a high quality decorative wood used both in the solid and as a decorative veneer for furniture making, joinery, carving and turning.

| | | |
|---|---|---|
| Density *2* | Stability in service *average* | |
| Bending strength *3* | Hardness *2* | |
| Stiffness *3* | Durability *2* | |
| Impact strength *4* | Blunting effect *average* | |

*Identification*
Diffuse-porous.
Growth rings indistinct.
Vessels medium sized, not very numerous, solitary and in radial pairs.
Rays very fine, one to two vessels per ray.
Parenchyma vasicentric, aliform.

BLACKWOOD, AFRICAN; *Dalbergia melanoxylon*; East Africa

African blackwood is the only commercial African 'rosewood' species. It is a dark purplish-brown timber with dominating black streaks but because of their small size the proportion of almost white sapwood in many logs is relatively large. The trees are usually small and stunted and the wood often has a variable grain. The timber is unusually hard and heavy, with a fine even texture which takes a very fine finish. Like most very hard, dense timbers it requires careful seasoning but is stable in service and is highly valued for making woodwind musical instruments and for decorative turnery and carving.

| | | |
|---|---|---|
| Density *1* | Stability in service *above average* | |
| Bending strength | Hardness *1* | |
| Stiffness | Durability *1* | |
| Impact strength | Blunting effect *above average* | |

*Identification*
Diffuse-porous.
Growth rings not visible.
Vessels small to very small, moderately numerous, solitary or in short radial chains (two to four).
Rays very fine, one to two rays per vessel, storied.
Parenchyma vasicentric, diffuse.
Ripple marks present.

**37** black bean (×*50*); African blackwood (×*25*)

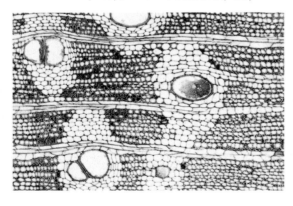
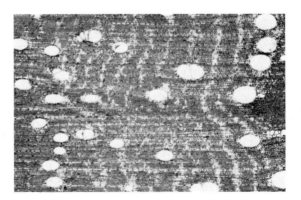

BLACKWOOD, AUSTRALIAN; *Acacia melanoxylon*;
New South Wales, Victoria, Tasmania

Australian blackwood is a golden brown to dark brown timber with fairly regular, dark, narrow lines marking the growth rings. The grain is usually straight but may be interlocked or wavy, producing a fiddle-back figure on radial surfaces. It has a medium, even texture and good working and bending properties.

Australian blackwood is one of the most decorative and valuable of Australian timbers. It is used for high class joinery, furniture making and turnery and also for bent work in boat building.

Density  *2*

Bending strength  *3*
Stiffness  *3*
Impact strength

Stability in
service  *average*
Hardness  *3*
Durability  *2*
Blunting
effect  *average*

*Identification*
Diffuse-porous.
Growth rings visible.
Vessels medium size, not very numerous, well
  distributed, round, solitary and in short radial chains
  (two to four).
Rays very fine, one ray per vessel.
Parenchyma not visible.

BOXWOOD, EUROPEAN; *Buxus sempervirens*;
Europe, North Africa, western Asia

Boxwood, *Buxus sempervirens*, is generally a small tree or shrub. The timber is a very pale yellowish colour and there is no discernible difference between the heartwood and sapwood. Home-grown box tends to be lighter in colour than imported wood. It is hard and dense with a very fine texture and a lustrous surface. The grain is variable, often somewhat curly and spiralled.

The occasional presence of a reddish colour is due to tension wood.

Like many dense, hard timbers box is difficult to season but stable in service. It is suggested that logs should be cut longitudinally with a saw down to the pith, before seasoning, to reduce radial splitting. It is highly valued for turnery, carving and inlaying and for making mathematical instruments and parts of musical instruments, tool handles, shuttles, small pulley blocks, croquet mallets and similar products.

Density  *1*

Bending strength  *3*
Stiffness  *3*
Impact strength  *3*

Stability in
service  *above average*
Hardness  *1–2*
Durability  *2*
Blunting
effect  *average*

*Identification*
Diffuse-porous.
Growth rings barely visible.
Vessels very small, solitary, evenly distributed.
Rays very fine, several vessels per ray.
Parenchyma not visible.

**38**  Australian blackwood ( × *50*); boxwood ( × *50*)

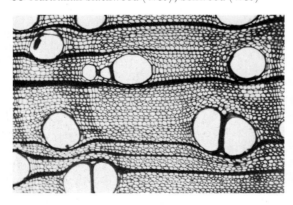
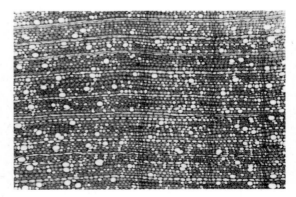

BUBINGA; *Guibourtia demeusei, G. pellegriniana* and *G. tessmannii*; West Africa

When freshly cut, bubinga has a red to reddish-brown colour with purple veining. Upon exposure the colour becomes a yellowish or chocolate-brown and the veining becomes less obvious. The timber has a moderately coarse texture and a grain which varies from straight to interlocked or very irregular.

The timber works well, apart from the usual problems with very irregular grain, and takes a fine finish.

Bubinga is a high quality decorative wood and is used for high class furniture making, turnery, carving and the manufacture of knife handles. The timber from Gabon is said to have an irregular grain and to be more highly figured. It is known as kevazingo or, misleadingly, as African rosewood, and is used as a decorative veneer.

Density *1*
Bending strength
Stiffness
Impact strength

Stability in service
Hardness *1*
Durability *3*
Blunting
effect *average*

*Identification*
Diffuse-porous.
Growth rings present.
Vessels moderately abundant, moderately large, solitary or in short radial chains (two or three).
Rays very fine to fine, one vessel per ray.
Parenchyma vasicentric, aliform.

CAMPHORWOOD, EAST AFRICAN; *Ocotea usambarensis*; East Africa

East African camphorwood is a light yellowish-brown when freshly cut but it darkens to a dark brown colour and has a characteristic smell of camphor. The grain is usually interlocked, producing a striped figure on radial surfaces, and the texture is fine and even.

The timber works well although some care is needed with the interlocked grain, and some logs with a contorted shape and twisted grain have little value.

The better shaped logs produce a good quality, medium weight timber which takes a good finish and is used for furniture making, interior and exterior joinery and flooring.

Density *3*

Bending strength *3*
Stiffness *4*
Impact strength *4*

Stability in
service *above average*
Hardness *3*
Durability *1*
Blunting effect *below average*

*Identification*
Diffuse-porous.
Growth rings absent.
Vessels of medium size, moderately abundant, solitary when oval in shape or in short radial chains when compressed (two to four)
Rays very fine, one vessel per ray.
Parenchyma not visible.

**39** bubinga (×*60*); East African camphorwood (×*50*)

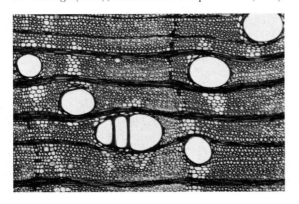
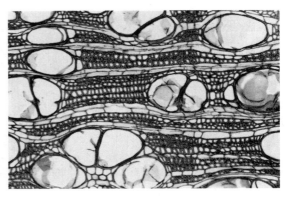

CEDAR, CENTRAL AMERICAN; principally *Cedrela odorata*; and cedar, South American; *Cedrela fissilis*; Central and South America and the West Indies

Central and South American, or cigar-box, cedar belongs to the mahogany family and has the appearance of a light weight, soft and rather coarse-textured mahogany. It is variable in appearance partly because of small species differences but mainly because the faster-grown wood is paler and lighter in weight than the darker coloured, heavier, slower grown material. The grain is straight or shallowly interlocked and it has a distinctive fragrance due to the presence of an oil which may appear as a sticky resin.

The wood works and finishes well apart from the occasional occurrence of resin. It is used for furniture making, joinery, the manufacture of cigar boxes and for the construction of light racing boats.

| | | | |
|---|---|---|---|
| Density | 3–4 | Stability in service | *above average* |
| Bending strength | 4–5 | Hardness | 4 |
| Stiffness | 5 | Durability | 2 |
| Impact strength | 5 | Blunting effect | *below average* |

*Identification*
Diffuse-porous, tending to semi ring-porous.
Growth rings visible.
Vessels large, moderately numerous, solitary or in short radial chains (two to five).
Rays very fine, one to two rays per vessel.
Parenchyma vasicentric or sparsely vasicentric and in terminal bands.

CHERRY, EUROPEAN, OR GEAN; *Prunus avium*; Europe, native to Britain

Cherry is a straight-grained, pale pinkish-brown wood with a fine grain. It is usually obtainable only in moderately small sizes and has relatively little figure, but is highly regarded as a decorative timber.

It has a pronounced tendency to warp during seasoning but is moderately stable in use. It works and bends well.

Cherry is used as a high class decorative wood in furniture making but generally only for small-scale work. It is also used for turnery, model making and for parts of musical instruments.

| | | | |
|---|---|---|---|
| Density | 3 | Stability in service | *average* |
| Bending strength | 3 | Hardness | 3 |
| Stiffness | 4 | Durability | 3 |
| Impact strength | 3 | Blunting effect | *average* |

*Identification*
Diffuse-porous.
Growth rings usually distinct.
Vessels small, concentrated more in the early than in the late wood, usually solitary or in radial chains or groups.
Rays fine, several vessels per ray.
Parenchyma not visible.

**40** Central American cedar ( × 25); European cherry ( × 60)

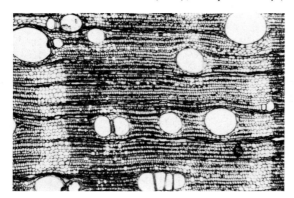
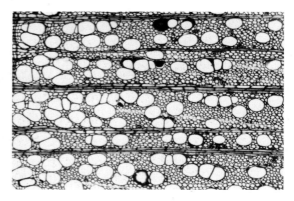

CHESTNUT, SWEET; *Castanea sativa*; Europe, introduced to Britain by the Romans

Sweet chestnut resembles flat-sawn oak but has no obvious rays. It is the same pale fawn colour with a fairly coarse texture and, normally, a straight grain. The wood from old trees may, however, have a pronounced spiral grain which is probably, in part at least, genetic. It is also liable to ring shake.

The timber needs to be dried slowly but is stable in service. It has good working properties but does not bend so well as oak or beech.

Chestnut is generally regarded as a slightly inferior timber to oak for most purposes but is coming to be more highly regarded than in the past for furniture making and high class joinery. Chestnut coppice is used for hop poles and cleft paling and, if cut at two or three years of age, for walking sticks.

| | | | |
|---|---|---|---|
| Density | *3* | Stability in service | *above average* |
| Bending strength | *4* | Hardness | *3* |
| Stiffness | *5* | Durability | *2* |
| Impact strength | *5* | Blunting effect | *below average* |

*Identification*
Ring-porous
Growth rings distinct.
Vessels oval in shape, early wood large, late wood small and arranged in a wave-like pattern.
Rays very fine and numerous, not a major feature as in oak; one to two rays per large vessel.
Parenchyma not obvious with a hand lens.

COCUSWOOD; *Brya ebenus*; West Indies

Cocuswood comes from a small tree and is available, therefore, only in small sizes. It is a rich brown colour when fresh, darkening to a dark chocolate-brown or almost black colour on exposure. The small logs have a narrow band of yellowish sapwood. The wood has a straight grain and a fine, even texture and is hard and dense. It requires careful seasoning but is stable in use and, considering its hardness, is relatively easy to work. It takes a fine finish.

Cocuswood is used for musical instrument making and for decorative turning and carving.

| | | | |
|---|---|---|---|
| Density | *1* | Stability in service | *above average* |
| Bending strength | *2* | Hardness | *1* |
| Stiffness | *2* | Durability | *2* |
| Impact strength | *2* | Blunting effect | *above average* |

*Identification*
Diffuse-porous.
Growth rings not visible.
Vessels very small, numerous, solitary or in short radial chains.
Rays very fine, one to two rays per vessel.
Parenchyma vasicentric, aliform or confluent.

**41** sweet chestnut ( × *25*) ; cocuswood ( × *50*)

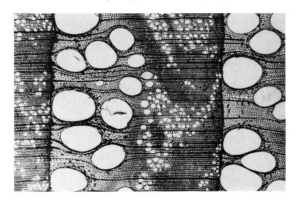
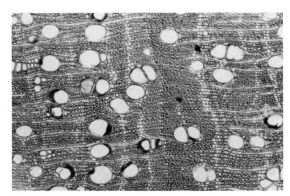

DANTA; *Nesogordonia papaverifera*; West Africa

DEGAME; *Calycophyllum candidissimum*; central and tropical South America

Danta is a reddish-brown, fine-textured timber not unlike a dark-coloured mahogany in appearance. The grain is narrowly interlocked producing a stripe figure on radial surfaces.

The timber dries well but slowly and the working properties are good, apart from the difficulty of planing the interlocked grain. It is a moderately good bending timber.

Danta is a dense, fairly strong timber which is suitable for general construction, furniture making, turnery, bench tops, gun butts and for the bent frames and planking of boats.

Density  2

Bending strength  2
Stiffness  4
Impact strength  3

Stability in
service  *average*
Hardness  2
Durability  2
Blunting
effect  *average*

*Identification*
Diffuse-porous.
Growth rings absent
Vessels fairly numerous, small, solitary or in radial chains (two to five).
Rays very fine, one to two vessels per ray, storied.
Parenchyma diffuse, not very obvious.
Ripple marks present.

Degame, which is known as lemonwood in the United States, is a somewhat variegated brownish-yellow colour with a pale sapwood. The grain varies from straight to very irregular and the texture is fine and even. Degame is a dense, hard and tough timber which works well and takes a fine finish. It is used for archery bows, fishing rods and turnery.

Density  2
Bending strength  2
Stiffness  3
Impact strength

Stability in service
Hardness  2
Durability  3
Blunting
effect  *average*

*Identification*
Diffuse-porous.
Growth rings indistinct.
Vessels small or very small, numerous, solitary or in short radial chains (two to four).
Rays very fine, moderately numerous, one to two vessels per ray.
Parenchyma not visible.

**42**  danta ( × *50*) ; degame ( × *50*)

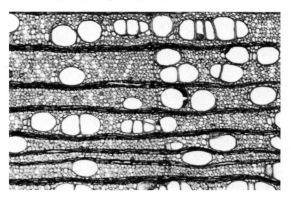 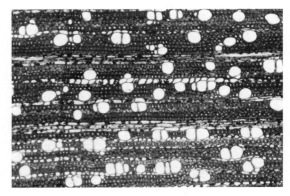

EBONY, AFRICAN; *Diospyros* species, principally *Diospyros crassiflora*; tropical Africa

EBONY, CEYLON; *Diospyros ebenum*; Sri Lanka

The colour of African ebony is variable. Some selected pieces have a uniform black colour while others are a greyish-black or grey with black stripes. In the complete log there may be a large band of pale sapwood.

The grain is straight or slightly interlocked and the wood has a fine, even texture. It seasons well but is difficult to work and, like Ceylon ebony, is used for purposes requiring hardness, a fine finish and a dark colour, such as knife handles, decorative turnery and carving and parts of musical instruments.

Ceylon ebony is an almost completely black wood with, occasionally, a few lighter coloured streaks. It differs in this respect from the other ebonies, which characteristically have a more well-defined streaky appearance and only occasionally produce completely black specimens.

The wood has a fine texture and the grain is variable, being sometimes straight and sometimes wavy.

The wood is hard to work and rather brittle and is used principally for various decorative and specialised purposes in turnery, inlaying, carving and musical instrument making.

| | | | |
|---|---|---|---|
| Density | *1* | Stability in service | |
| Bending strength | *1* | Hardness | *1* |
| Stiffness | *2* | Durability | *1* |
| Impact strength | *2* | Blunting effect | *well above average* |

*Identification*
as for Ceylon ebony

| | | | |
|---|---|---|---|
| Density | *1* | Stability in service | *above average* |
| Bending strength | | Hardness | *1* |
| Stiffness | | Durability | *1* |
| Impact strength | | Blunting effect | *well above average* |

*Identification*
Diffuse-porous.
Growth rings absent.
Vessels small to very small, moderately numerous, solitary and in short radial chains (two to four).
Rays very fine, moderately numerous, one ray per vessel.
Parenchyma abundant, diffuse, in fine concentric lines but not easily seen.

**43** African (and Ceylon) ebony ( × *50*)

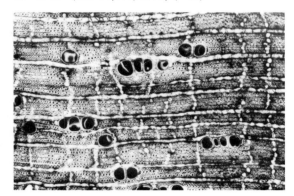

EKKI;  *Lophira alata*;  West Africa

ELM, ENGLISH;  *Ulmus procera*;  Great Britain

Ekki is a very dark red or reddish-brown colour and has white deposits in the vessels which are clearly visible on longitudinal surfaces. The grain is usually interlocked and the texture is coarse and uneven.

Ekki is a hard, dense timber which is difficult both to season and work. It is used almost exclusively for heavy construction work and heavy duty flooring in much the same way as greenheart.

| Density | *1(exceptionally heavy)* | Stability in service | *average* |
|---|---|---|---|
| Bending strength | *1* | Hardness | *1 (exceptionally hard)* |
| Stiffness | *2* | Durability | *1* |
| Impact strength | *2* | Blunting effect | *well above average* |

*Identification*
Diffuse-porous.
Growth rings absent.
Vessels moderately large, not very numerous, solitary or in radial pairs.
Rays very fine, several rays per vessel.
Parenchyma in broad, conspicuous bands.

Elm is a dull brown-coloured, cross-grained timber with a coarse texture. It has a strongly defined, attractive figure on tangential surfaces and has good working and bending properties, but it requires careful seasoning.

It is used for cottage and rustic furniture, and good quality logs, if carefully treated, are used for the manufacture of high quality furniture. Other species of elm, such as wych elm, *Ulmus glabra*, have better inherent qualities but are less valued for furniture making because they lack the characteristic figure of English elm. It is possible that the supply of European and North American elm timber will ultimately come to an end as a result of the aggressive strain of Dutch elm disease which is devastating the elm populations in the two continents.

| Density | *3* | Stability in service | *average* |
|---|---|---|---|
| Bending strength | *4* | Hardness | *3* |
| Stiffness | *5* | Durability | *4* |
| Impact strength | *5* | Blunting effect | *average* |

*Identification*
Ring-porous.
Growth rings distinct.
Vessels of early wood large, forming a closely defined band about two to three vessels wide, changing abruptly to wavy, tangential bands of small vessels.
Rays fine, one to two large vessels per ray.
Parenchyma indistinct.

**44** ekki ( ×.*50*) ; English elm ( × *25*)

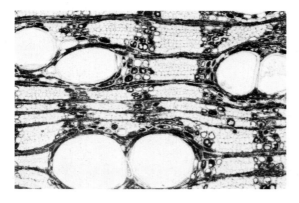
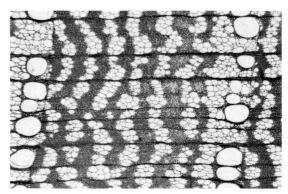

ELM, ROCK; *Ulmus thomasii*; eastern Canada and the United States

FREIJO; *Cordia goeldiana*; the Amazon Basin

Rock elm is similar in appearance to the other elms but is considerably denser and stronger. It is a light brown timber with a straight grain and a moderately fine texture. It requires careful seasoning and is rather more difficult to work than the other elms.

Rock elm is a tough timber and bends well. It is therefore used for the frames of boats and for some sports equipment. (Imports of rock elm were responsible for the introduction of the aggressive strain of Dutch Elm disease into Britain in the late 1960s. This went unnoticed for a short time because the aggressive strain had not previously been identified as distinct from the non-aggressive fungus until it was isolated by British pathologists in 1970, by which time it was too late to control the disease.)

| | | | |
|---|---|---|---|
| Density | *1* | Stability in service | |
| Bending strength | *3* | Hardness | *2* |
| Stiffness | *5* | Durability | *4* |
| Impact strength | *1* | Blunting effect | *average* |

*Identification*
Ring-porous.
Growth rings distinct.
Vessels of early wood of only moderate size, in a single row and sparsely distributed. Abrupt change to tangential band of very small vessels, later vessels also very small in irregular transverse or slanting bands.
Rays very fine, one to two larger vessels per ray.
Parenchyma not obvious.

Freijo resembles teak in colour and has a straight grain and a fine, even texture. It seasons and works well and is used for boat building, furniture making and joinery.

| | | | |
|---|---|---|---|
| Density | *3* | Stability in service | *above average* |
| Bending strength | *3* | Hardness | *3* |
| Stiffness | *3* | Durability | *2* |
| Impact strength | *3* | Blunting effect | *average* |

*Identification*
Diffuse-porous.
Growth rings present.
Vessels moderately abundant, fairly large, solitary or in radial pairs or small clusters.
Rays moderately fine, two to three vessels per ray.
Parenchyma vasicentric.

**45** Rock elm ( × *25*); freijo ( × *50*)

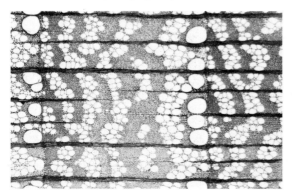
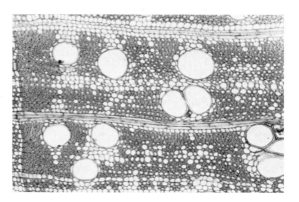

GABOON; *Aucoumea klaineana*; tropical Africa

GEDU NOHOR; *Entandrophragma angolense*; West Africa

When freshly cut, gaboon is a pinkish colour darkening on exposure to a pinkish-brown which is paler than *Khaya*. It has a medium texture and the grain is usually shallowly interlocked and occasionally slightly wavy.

The timber is not difficult to season. Sharp tools are needed to obtain a good finish and these require frequent sharpening because the wood contains silica.

Gaboon is a general purpose timber used primarily for the manufacture of facing veneers for plywood and blockboard. It is also used for joinery and the framing of furniture and, sometimes, for making cigar boxes.

| | |
|---|---|
| Density *4* | Stability in service *average* |
| Bending strength *4* | Hardness *4* |
| Stiffness *5* | Durability *4* |
| Impact strength | Blunting effect *above average* |

*Identification*
Diffuse-porous.
Growth rings absent.
Vessels of moderate size and moderately numerous, solitary or in short radial chains (two to four).
Rays very fine, one vessel per ray.
Parenchyma not visible.

Gedu nohor is a dull reddish-brown timber closely related to sapele but with a less attractive appearance.

It has a moderately coarse texture and a highly interlocked grain which does not produce the characteristic banded effect of sapele. It works reasonably well and takes a good finish.

Gedu nohor is one of the lower quality mahogany-type timbers and is used for furniture making, interior and exterior joinery, boat building and plywood manufacture.

| | |
|---|---|
| Density *3* | Stability in service *above average* |
| Bending strength *4* | Hardness *3–4* |
| Stiffness *5* | Durability *3* |
| Impact strength *4* | Blunting effect *average* |

*Identification*
Diffuse-porous.
Growth rings distinct.
Vessels medium-sized, evenly distributed, solitary and in radial chains (two to three).
Rays fine to medium, one vessel per ray.
Parenchyma terminal, vasicentric, aliform and confluent.

**46** gaboon ( × *50*); gedu nohor ( × *25*)

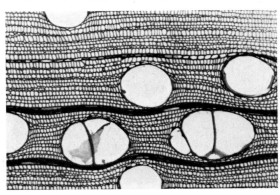
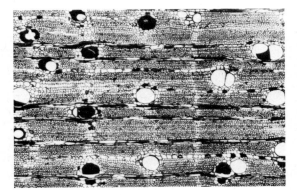

GREENHEART; *Ocotea rodiaei*; Guyana

GUAREA; *Guarea cedrata* and *G. thompsonii*; West Africa

Greenheart is a pale to dark greenish-brown wood sometimes marked with brown or black streaks. The grain is usually very straight but is sometimes interlocked and the texture is fine and even.

Greenheart is very strong, durable and resistant to marine borers. It is also available in large sizes and is therefore widely used for marine works such as piers and docks and for other construction where exceptional strength, hardness and durability are required. At the craftsman's level it is used for making fishing rods and laminated archery bows.

| | | | |
|---|---|---|---|
| Density | *1* | Stability in service | *average* |
| Bending strength | *1* | Hardness | *1* |
| Stiffness | *1* | Durability | *1* |
| Impact strength | *2* | Blunting effect | *average* |

*Identification*
Diffuse-porous.
Growth rings absent.
Vessels small, oval, solitary or in radial pairs, moderately numerous.
Rays very fine, one vessel per ray.
Parenchyma vasicentric.

The two species of guarea are similar in appearance and properties but the differences between them are sufficient to be significant.

Guarea is a pale pinkish-brown wood which darkens less than the mahoganies on exposure. The grain of *Guarea thompsonii* tends to be straighter than that of *Guarea cedrata*, which sometimes has a mottled figure. They both have a fine texture. *Guarea cedrata*, which is the principal commercial species, has an ephemeral cedar-like scent when freshly cut. Both species produce a rather irritating dust and *Guarea cedrata* contains silica which has a blunting effect upon tools. *Guarea thompsonii* is somewhat denser and stronger than *Guarea cedrata*.

Both species have average working properties and are good quality, general purpose timbers for furniture making, joinery and plywood manufacture. They should not be used where resin exudation is likely to be a problem.

| | | | |
|---|---|---|---|
| Density | *3* | Stability in service | *above average* |
| Bending strength | *3* | Hardness | *3* |
| Stiffness | *4–5* | Durability | *1* |
| Impact strength | *4* | Blunting effect | *average to less than average* |

*Identification*
Diffuse-porous.
Growth rings absent in *Guarea cedrata*, indistinct in *Guarea thompsonii*.
Vessels oval, of moderate size and frequency, mostly solitary or in radial chains (two to four).
Rays very fine, less obvious than in sapele, one vessel per ray.
Parenchyma banded, more regular and conspicuous in *Guarea thompsonii* than in *Guarea cedrata*.
Ripple marks absent, unlike sapele and American mahogany.

**47** greenheart ( × *50*) ; guarea ( × *25*)
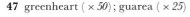

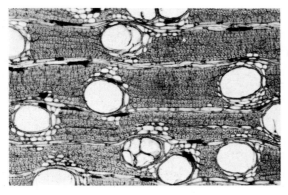
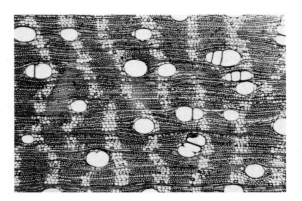

HICKORY; *Carya glabra, C. tomentosa, C. laciniosa and C. ovata*; eastern United States and south eastern Canada

HOLLY; *Ilex aquifolium*; Europe

The heartwood of hickory is a brown or reddish-brown colour and is known as red hickory, while the sapwood, which is very pale, is known as white hickory. The strength properties of each type are similar.

The grain is usually straight but is sometimes wavy and the texture is relatively coarse. Hickory works and bends well and has an unusually good impact strength, which makes it an exceptionally good timber for sports goods, handles and archery bows. It is used in America in much the same way that fast-grown ash is used in Britain.

| Density | 2 | Stability in service | |
| Bending strength | 2 | Hardness | 2 |
| Stiffness | 2 | Durability | 4 |
| Impact strength | 1 | Blunting effect | *average to above average* |

*Identification*
Ring-porous.
Growth rings visible.
Vessels, early wood vessels moderately large, late wood vessels small, mostly solitary. Some short radial chains (two to three).
Rays very fine, one to two rays per vessel.
Parenchyma diffuse in fine lines, only in the late wood.

Holly is a pale, greyish-white wood with a very fine, even texture and a somewhat irregular grain. It is a good carving and turnery wood and is used also for inlaying. It is sometimes stained black and used as a substitute for ebony. The strength properties of holly are hardly relevant because it is used only in very small sizes and never structurally.

| Density | 2 | Stability in service | *above average* |
| Bending strength | | Hardness | 2 |
| Stiffness | | Durability | 5 |
| Impact strength | | Blunting effect | *average* |

*Identification*
Diffuse-porous.
Growth rings indistinct.
Vessels very small in longish radial lines.
Rays fine, four or five times wider than the vessels, several lines of vessels per ray.
Parenchyma not visible.

**48** hickory ( × 25); holly ( × 50)

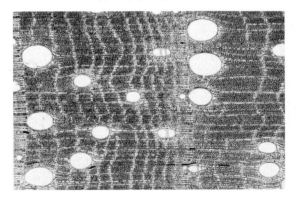
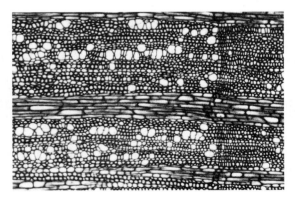

HORNBEAM; *Carpinus betulus*; Europe and Asia Minor

Hornbeam is a whitish-coloured timber with greyish streaks and flecks and may easily be identified before conversion owing to the beech-like bark with deep fluting in the stem. Hornbeam is often cross grained, has a fine, even texture and is difficult to split. It works cleanly and takes a very smooth finish.

Because of its hardness and toughness hornbeam has a number of specialist uses in the action of keyboard instruments, for turnery, carving, mallet heads and pegs. It is also sometimes used for flooring.

Density  *2*

Bending strength  *3*
Stiffness  *3*
Impact strength  *3*

Stability in service  *above average*
Hardness  *2*
Durability  *5*
Blunting effect  *average*

*Identification*
Diffuse-porous.
Growth rings visible.
Vessels small to very small, solitary or in radial chains (two to seven), uniformly distributed.
Rays both fine and large, the larger rays being easily visible, one vessel per ray.
Parenchyma diffuse, in fine, broken tangential lines, also terminal.

IDIGBO; *Terminalia ivorensis*; West Africa

Idigbo is a light yellowish or yellowish-brown wood. The grain is usually fairly straight but is sometimes slightly interlocked, giving an irregular banded figure on radial surfaces. The texture is medium to fairly coarse and the growth rings very sharply defined for a tropical timber. Brittleheart is not uncommon in the centre of the log. Idigbo seasons will and is moderately easy to work except where brittleheart occurs. It produces a yellow stain in contact with water.

Idigbo is a good quality durable and stable timber and is used for furniture making and high class joinery.

Density  *medium but variable*

Bending strength  *4*
Stiffness  *5*
Impact strength  *5*

Stability in service  *above average*
Hardness  *3–4*
Durability  *2*
Blunting effect  *below average*

*Identification*
Diffuse-porous.
Growth rings visible.
Vessels fairly large, solitary or in short radial chains.
Rays very fine, one to two vessels per ray.
Parenchyma vasicentric.

**49** hornbeam ( × *50*); idigbo ( × *50*)

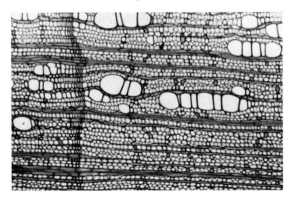
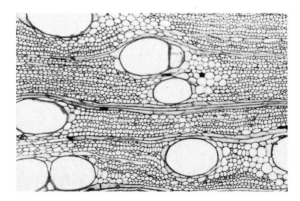

Ilomba is a rather plain looking wood, greyish-white to pale pinky-brown in colour. It has a straight grain and a moderately coarse, even texture.

It requires careful drying but appears to work reasonably well.

Ilomba is used as a general utility wood for interior joinery, the inside components of furniture and for plywood manufacture.

Density  *3*

Bending strength 3–4

Stiffness  *4*

Impact strength  *4*

Stability in service

Hardness  *3*

Durability  *5*

Blunting effect

*Identification*

Diffuse-porous.

Growth rings absent.

Vessels not very abundant, fairly large, solitary or in short radial pairs.

Rays fine, one ray per vessel.

Parenchyma not visible.

Imbuia, or embuia, which belongs to the same family as Queensland walnut, is also known as Brazilian walnut. The heartwood is yellowish to chocolate brown and is often well figured. When freshly cut the wood has a spicy, resinous scent. Imbuia has a straight, curly or wavy grain and a fine texture. It dries and works well.

Imbuia is used in Brazil for furniture making, high grade flooring and interior joinery. It is exported as a decorative veneer and is also used locally for plywood manufacture.

Density  *3*

Bending strength  *3–4*

Stiffness  *3–4*

Impact strength  *3–4*

Stability in service  *average*

Hardness  *3*

Durability  *3*

Blunting effect  *below average*

*Identification*

Diffuse-porous.

Growth rings distinct, (c.f. Queensland walnut).

Vessels small or very small, moderately numerous, solitary or in short radial chains (two to four).

Rays very fine, one to two vessels per ray.

Parenchyma vasicentric but not obvious.

Oil cells larger than fibres but smaller than vessels, close to vessels.

**50** ilomba (×*50*); imbuia (×*50*)

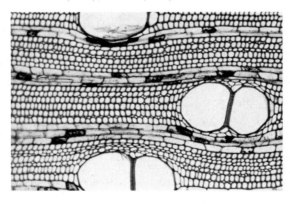

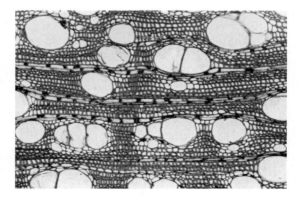

IROKO; *Chlorophora excelsa, C. regia*; East and West Africa

IRONBARK; *Eucalyptus paniculata, E. drepanophylla, E. siderophloia* (grey ironbarks), and *E. crebra and E. sideroxylon* (red ironbarks); eastern Australia

*Chlorophora excelsa* extends from East to West Africa but *C. regia*, a similar but somewhat smaller tree, is restricted to West Africa. Iroko is a dark brown, relatively coarse-textured timber with some irregular and interlocked grain. It has many of the desirable characteristics of teak, which it superficially resembles, but it is darker and has a coarser appearance and is not a high grade furniture timber.

Iroko is used for many purposes where strength, durability and stability are required, such as boat building and heavy duty joinery, both indoors and out.

The dust from iroko can be a mild irritant and it is desirable to use a mask when working the timber.

| | | | |
|---|---|---|---|
| Density | *3* | Stability in service | *above average* |
| Bending strength | *3* | Hardness | *3* |
| Stiffness | *5* | Durability | *1* |
| Impact strength | *5* | Blunting effect | *average or above average* |

*Identification*
Diffuse-porous.
Growth rings indistinct.
Vessels moderately large, oval, solitary or in small radial chains (two or three) containing whitish deposits.
Rays fine, one to two vessels per ray.
Parenchyma vasicentric, usually aliform or confluent.

The grey ironbarks are greyish-brown and the red ironbarks dark red or reddish-brown. They are all hard and heavy timbers with a fine, compact texture and, usually, an interlocked grain. Ironbark, like many dense timbers, has to be seasoned with care, and it tends to blunt tools owing to the presence of silica. It is used for heavy structural work where strength and durability are important.

| | | | |
|---|---|---|---|
| Density | *1* | Stability in service | *above average* |
| Bending strength | *1* | Hardness | *1* |
| Stiffness | *1* | Durability | *1* |
| Impact strength | | Blunting effect | *well above average* |

*Identification*
Diffuse-porous.
Growth rings indistinct.
Vessels small to very small, mostly solitary in an oblique pattern.
Rays very fine, one vessel per ray.
Parenchyma vasicentric, indistinct.

**51** iroko (× *50*); ironbark (× *25*)

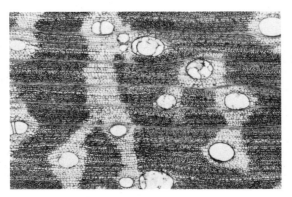
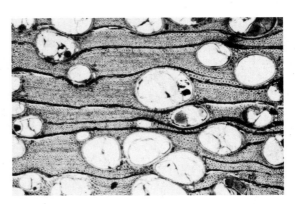

JARRAH; *Eucalyptus marginata*; south western Australia

Jarrah is a pinkish or reddish timber which turns a deep reddish-brown with age. It is sometimes marked with darker flecks caused by short tangential lenses of darker wood which have no effect upon the timber properties. The grain is usually fairly straight but may be interlocked and the texture is moderately coarse.

Jarrah requires careful seasoning but is reasonably easy to work and bend and takes a good finish. It is not normally regarded as a craftsman's timber but, being dense and durable and reasonably strong, it is widely used for heavy structural and marine work.

Density *1*

Bending strength *3*
Stiffness *3*
Impact strength

Stability in service *average*
Hardness *1*
Durability *1*
Blunting effect *average*

*Identification*
Diffuse-porous.
Growth rings not very distinct.
Vessels of medium size and moderate abundance, solitary or in oblique chains.
Rays very fine, one to three per vessel.
Parenchyma vasicentric.

JELUTONG; *Dyera costulata* and *D. lowii*; South East Asia

Jelutong is an almost white or pale straw-coloured wood, sometimes discoloured by fungi which invade latex-tapping wounds. The grain is almost straight and the texture is fine and even.

It is a somewhat featureless but stable and easily worked general purpose timber which seasons well and which is especially suitable for such uses as drawing boards, carving and pattern making.

Density *4*

Bending strength *4*
Stiffness *5*
Impact strength

Stability in service *above average*
Hardness *4*
Durability *4*
Blunting effect *below average*

*Identification*
Diffuse-porous.
Growth rings visible.
Vessels small to medium in size, not very numerous, solitary or in radial pairs.
Rays very fine, one to three vessels per ray.
Parenchyma diffuse, fine tangential lines.

**52** jarrah ( × *50*); jelutong ( × *25*)

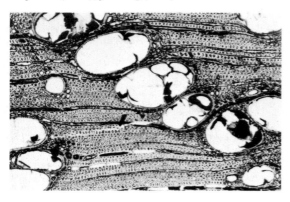 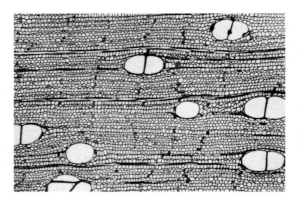

KAPUR or BORNEO CAMPHORWOOD; *Dryobalanops* species; Malaysia and Indonesia

Several species of *Dryobalanops* are marketed as kapur. Malayan timber is mainly *Dryobalanops aromatica* while that from Sabah and Sarawak is *Dryobalanops lanceolata*, *D. beccarii* and *D. aromatica*.

Kapur is a uniform reddish-brown colour. It has a straight or shallowly interlocked grain and a fairly coarse but even texture. The wood has an ephemeral camphor-like scent when freshly cut.

The timber seasons slowly and without much degrade, but owing to its hardness and interlocked grain is moderately difficult to work. It is a strong durable timber not unlike keruing but more uniform and more stable. It is used for general construction and both indoor and exterior joinery.

| | | | |
|---|---|---|---|
| Density | 2 | Stability in service | *average* |
| Bending strength | .2 | Hardness | 2 |
| Stiffness | 3 | Durability | 1 |
| Impact strength | 3 | Blunting effect | *well above average* |

*Identification (Dryobalanops aromatica)*
Diffuse-porous.
Growth rings present.
Vessels moderately abundant, of moderate size, solitary, occasional tangential pairs.
Rays very fine, one vessel, or occasionally two, per ray.
Parenchyma vasicentric, aliform.
Resin canals in tangential lines.

KERUING; *Dipterocarpus* species; South East Asia

Keruing is a plain looking pinkish-brown to dark brown timber, a little denser than oak and with a coarse texture. The grain is straight or slightly interlocked.

It lacks decorative quality and is not used for fine work, but its strength and moderate durability make it a useful general purpose carpentry and joinery timber.

| | | | |
|---|---|---|---|
| Density | 2 | Stability in service | *below average* |
| Bending strength | 2 | Hardness | 2 |
| Stiffness | 2 | Durability | 3 |
| Impact strength | 3 | Blunting effect | *average to above average* |

*Identification*
Diffuse-porous.
Growth rings absent.
Vessels medium to large, mainly solitary, tending to be arranged in an oblique pattern, gum ducts sometimes present in tangential lines.
Rays small and medium, one vessel per ray.
Parenchyma diffuse, associated with gum ducts, sometimes aliform and confluent.

Closely related species groups are known as gurjun in India and Burma, yang in Thailand, apitong in the Philippines and eng in Burma.

**53** kapur ( × *25*); keruing ( × *25*)

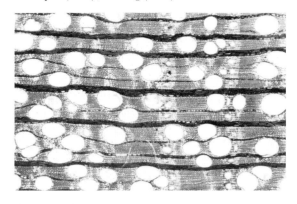
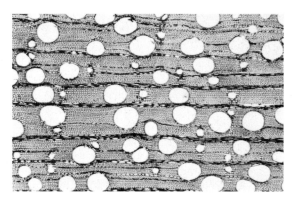

Kingwood has well defined concentric bands of brownish-violet and black or blackish-violet wood, which resemble growth rings and which are far more regular than the streaky pattern of Rio rosewood, *Dalbergia nigra*.

The dark bands are generally narrower and denser than the lighter bands. The wood has a fine texture and the grain is straight to finely mottled.

The timber is available only in small sizes and is used for fine work such as inlaying, marquetry and turnery.

| | |
|---|---|
| Density *2* | Stability in service *above average* |
| Bending strength *2* | Hardness *2* |
| Stiffness *3–4* | Durability *2* |
| Impact strength *4* | Blunting effect *above average* |

*Identification*
Diffuse-porous.
Growth rings indistinct.
Vessels small to medium, solitary or in short radial chains (two to six), sometimes containing dark deposits.
Rays very fine, one vessel per ray, storied.
Parenchyma vasicentric but indistinct.
Ripple marks present.

There is another timber from Brazil known as kingwood or kingswood which comes from the tree *Astronium fraxinifolium*. This bears some resemblance to *Dalbergia cearensis* and is used for much the same purposes.

Kokko is a rich, medium brown in colour often with irregular dark markings which give it some resemblance to walnut.

It has an irregular and interlocked grain and a coarse, even texture. Care is needed in drying and working owing to the interlocked grain and the presence of alternate bands of hard and soft material.

The colour and irregular grain make kokko a handsome timber which is used as a decorative veneer and for solid furniture and joinery. It is also used in India for structural purposes.

| | |
|---|---|
| Density *3* | Stability in service *average* |
| Bending strength *3* | Hardness *3* |
| Stiffness *3* | Durability *3* |
| Impact strength *3* | Blunting effect *average* |

*Identification*
Diffuse-porous.
Growth rings absent.
Vessels large, moderately abundant, solitary or in short radial chains (two to four).
Rays very fine, one or sometimes two per vessel.
Parenchyma vasicentric, aliform.

**54** kingwood ( × *60*); (for kokko see albizia)

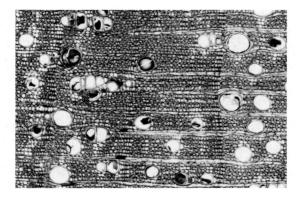

LABURNUM; *Laburnum anagyroides*; central and southern Europe, frequently grown in Britain

Laburnum may be regarded as a temperate rosewood because it belongs to the same sub family as the genus *Dalbergia*. It is golden brown when freshly cut and darkens on exposure to a dark brown colour with darker brown or black stripes. The wood has a fine texture and surface lustre and a straight grain. The decorative coloured figure is enhanced by fine zigzag lines of pale-coloured parenchyma and, on radial surfaces, by the dark flecks of the rays.

The wood is hard and durable, seasons without difficulty and works well.

Laburnum is rarely available in large sizes but is a high quality timber for small-scale cabinet work, inlay, carving and turnery and for the manufacture of woodwind instruments.

| | |
|---|---|
| Density *2–3* | Stability in service |
| Bending strength | Hardness *2–3* |
| Stiffness | Durability *2* |
| Impact strength | Blunting effect *average* |

*Identification*
Ring-porous.
Growth rings distinct.
Vessels of spring wood small to moderate in size in compact rings several rows wide. Summer vessels smaller, in wavy tangential chains.
Rays narrow to medium, wider rays approximately equal in width to the diameter of larger vessels, several large vessels per ray.
Parenchyma terminal and vasicentric; since the vessels are in lines the parenchyma appears confluent.

LANCEWOOD; *Oxandra lanceolata*; West Indies

Lancewood is unusual because the valuable part of the tree is the pale yellow sapwood and not the dark heartwood.

The timber has a straight grain and a fine texture and is dense, hard and resilient. It is tough to work but turns well and takes a fine finish.

Lancewood is used for making archery bows, fishing rods and small wooden articles for which exceptional hardness is required.

| | |
|---|---|
| Density *1* | Stability in service |
| Bending strength *2* | Hardness *1* |
| Stiffness | Durability *4* |
| Impact strength *2* | Blunting effect *average* |

*Identification*
Diffuse-porous.
Growth rings absent.
Vessels very small and frequent, solitary or in radial chains (two to four).
Rays fine, variable in width, the wider ones almost equal to the diameter of the vessels, one to two vessels per ray.
Parenchyma diffuse, forming a fine grid pattern between the rays.

**55** laburnum ( × *60*); lancewood ( × *60*)

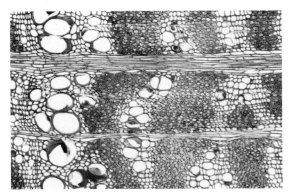
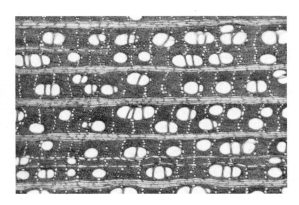

LAUREL, INDIAN; *Terminalia alata, T. crenulata* and *T. coriacea*; India and Burma

LIGNUM VITAE; *Guaiacum* species, principally *G. officinale*; West Indies, Central America, tropical South America

The colour of Indian laurel is very variable and ranges from light brown to dark brown with irregular dark streaks. The variability is partly due to specific differences and the species having the best figure is probably *Terminalia crenulata*.

The grain varies from fairly straight to irregular and the texture is rather coarse.

Indian laurel is a high class decorative timber and is used in the solid and as a veneer for furniture making and good quality joinery. It is also used in India for general structural purposes.

| | | | |
|---|---|---|---|
| Density | *1* | Stability in service | |
| Bending strength | *3* | Hardness | *1* |
| Stiffness | *3* | Durability | *3* |
| Impact strength | | Blunting effect | *average* |

*Identification*
Diffuse-porous.
Growth rings visible.
Vessels of medium size, not very abundant, solitary or short radial chains (two to four).
Rays very fine, fairly abundant, two to three rays per vessel.
Parenchyma vasicentric, aliform.

Lignum vitae is a small tree and the billets of timber often contain a band of yellowish sapwood which is sharply differentiated from the dark brown or blackish heartwood.

The wood has an interlocked grain and a fine even texture which takes a fine polish.

Lignum vitae is exceptionally hard and heavy and it contains a natural oil which acts as a lubricant. It is, therefore, particularly suitable for marine propeller bearings and also for rigging blocks, mallet heads and woods for bowling.

| | | | |
|---|---|---|---|
| Density | *1* *(exceptional)* | Stability in service | *average* |
| Bending strength | | Hardness | *1* *(exceptional)* |
| Stiffness | | Durability | *1* |
| Impact strength | | Blunting effect | *average (but hard to cut)* |

*Identification*
Diffuse-porous.
Growth rings absent.
Vessels very small, exclusively solitary.
Rays very fine, one per vessel.
Parenchyma not very obvious, very fine irregular bands, storied.
Ripple marks.

**56** Indian laurel ( × *25*); lignum vitae ( × *50*)

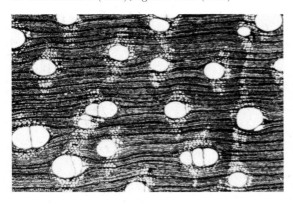 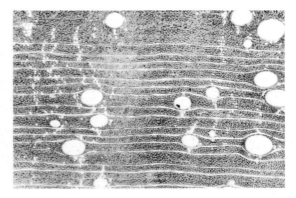

LIME, EUROPEAN;  *Tilia vulgaris, T. cordata, T. platyphyllos*;  Europe

The various species of lime are all whitish or pale coloured yellowish-brown timbers with a straight grain and a fine, even texture. They have no distinctive features but are valued for their ease of working and are used for turnery, carving and model making.

Density  *3*

Bending strength  *3*
Stiffness  *4*
Impact strength  *4*

Stability in
service  *average*
Hardness  *4*
Durability  *5*
Blunting effect  *below average*

*Identification*
Diffuse-porous.
Growth rings fairly distinct.
Vessels very small, solitary or more often clustered, rather irregular in shape.
Rays fine and medium fine, the wider ones being noded at the boundaries of the growth rings, one to two vessels per ray.
Parenchyma diffuse, fine tangential lines one cell wide, the cells being very narrow in the radial direction, not very obvious with a lens, storied.
Ripple marks are sometimes present.

Japanese lime, *Tilia japonica*, basswood, *Tilia americana*, and other species of lime are very similar in properties and appearance.

LOURO, RED;  *Ocotea rubra*;  the Guyanas, Surinam, northern Brazil

Red louro is a pale reddish-brown wood with a lustrous surface. It has a straight to irregular grain and a rather coarse texture.

Red louro seasons and works reasonably well and is used as a medium quality furniture and joinery timber. It is used locally for boat building and general construction work.

Density  *3*

Bending strength  *4*
Stiffness  *4*
Impact strength

Stability in
service  *average*
Hardness  *3*
Durability  *2*
Blunting effect  *below average*

*Identification*
Diffuse-porous.
Growth rings absent.
Vessels of moderate size, in oblique lines.
Rays very fine, one per vessel.
Parenchyma vasicentric, aliform.

**57**  European lime ( × *60*); red louro ( × *50*)

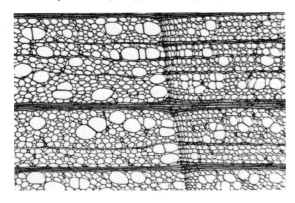 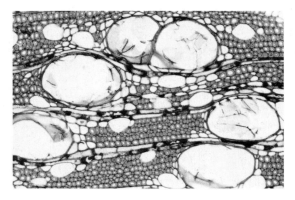

MAHOGANY, AFRICAN; *Khaya ivorensis*, occasionally *Khaya anthotheca*; West Africa

MAHOGANY, AMERICAN; *Swietenia* species, principally *Swietenia macrophylla*; Central America and parts of northern South America

*Khaya grandifoliola, K. nyasica* and *K. senegalensis* are also known as African mahogany but they rarely appear in commerce. African mahogany is a pale-coloured pinky-red wood when freshly cut, but it darkens on exposure to a reddish-brown.

The texture is fairly coarse. The grain is sometimes straight, but more often interlocked, giving a stripe or roe figure on radial surfaces. Brittleheart is not uncommon especially in the centre of large logs.

The working properties are reasonable good but it cannot be bent without severe damage.

Khaya is a good quality, all-purpose timber and is widely used for furniture making, joinery, boat building and plywood manufacture.

| | | | |
|---|---|---|---|
| Density | *3* | Stability in service | *above average* |
| Bending strength | *4* | Hardness | *3* |
| Stiffness | *5* | Durability | *3* |
| Impact strength | *5* | Blunting effect | *average* |

*Identification*
Diffuse-porous.
Growth rings rarely visible.
Vessels medium-sized, solitary or in short radial chains (two to four), deposits present.
Rays fine to medium, one vessel per ray, sometimes storied.
Parenchyma sparse, vasicentric, sometimes ill-defined terminal.
Ripple marks occasionally present.

African mahogany differs from American mahogany as follows:
a) coarser texture
b) vessels somewhat larger
c) terminal parenchyma absent or less clearly defined
d) parenchyma pinkish brown and not buff coloured as in American mahogany
e) ripple pattern on tangential surfaces less likely to be present.

*Khaya ivorensis* is occasionally marketed with *Khaya grandifoliola*, which is darker, heavier, harder, more durable and has a more distorted grain. The terminal parenchyma is more developed than in *Khaya ivorensis* but less than in *Swietenia macrophylla*.

American mahogany is somewhat variable in colour and ranges from a light reddish or yellowish brown to dark reddish brown with a natural surface lustre.

The texture is moderately coarse; the grain is often straight but sometimes irregular, giving rise to a striped or fiddle-back figure on radial surfaces or, where these two patterns are superimposed on one another, to a row figure.

American mahogany works well but is not a particularly good bending timber. It is one of the very high quality furniture timbers and is considered to be superior to the other commercial mahoganies due to its stability, appearance and ability to take a fine finish. It is used for high class cabinet making and especially for reproduction work, both in the solid and as a veneer. It is also used for very high quality joinery, as well as for boat building and model making.

| | | | |
|---|---|---|---|
| Density | *3* | Stability in service | *above average* |
| Bending strength | *4* | Hardness | *3* |
| Stiffness | *5* | Durability | *2* |
| Impact strength | *5* | Blunting effect | *below average* |

*Identification*
Diffuse-porous.
Growth rings visible.
Vessels medium-sized, solitary or in small groups, usually short radial chains (two to five), containing whitish deposits.
Rays fine, one vessel per ray, often storied.
Parenchyma indistinct vasicentric, also well-defined terminal bands or lines.
Ripple pattern on tangential surfaces.

American mahogany differs from African mahogany as follows:
a) finer texture
b) vessels somewhat smaller
c) terminal parenchyma more clearly defined
d) parenchyma buff coloured in *Swietenia*, pinkish brown in *Khaya*
e) ripple pattern common on tangential surfaces.

**58** African mahogany (×25); American mahogany (×25)

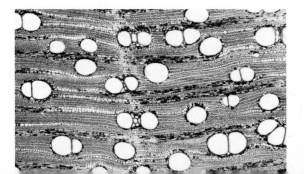

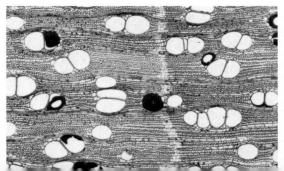

Makoré varies from pinkish to purplish or reddish-brown in colour. It has a fine texture and a variable grain which is often straight but sometimes combines an irregular interlocked and wavy pattern giving a figure which is reminiscent of watered silk. The wood is sometimes marked with darker streaks.

Makoré is a handsome timber having some similarity to a close-grained mahogany and is used in the solid and as a veneer for furniture making, internal and external joinery and boat building. The dust produced by makoré is an irritant and a mask is advisable when working with the wood.

| | |
|---|---|
| Density *3* | Stability in service *above average* |
| Bending strength *3* | Hardness *3* |
| Stiffness *4* | Durability *1* |
| Impact strength *4* | Blunting effect *above average* |

*Identification*
Diffuse-porous.
Growth rings indistinct.
Vessels small, sometimes solitary but mostly in short radial chains (two to five).
Rays very fine, one vessel per ray, sometimes storied.
Parenchyma abundant, diffuse in fine tangential lines.
Sometimes a ripple pattern on tangential surfaces.

Mansonia is also known as African black walnut. It has the variable yellowish or greyish-brown colour with paler and darker streaks and the faint purplish tinge of American black walnut, but is a finer textured wood with smaller, clustered vessels. The grain is usually straight.

Seasoning and working qualities are good but the dust produced by the wood is irritating to the nose and throat and can cause dermatitis. It is advisable to wear a mask when working with the species.

Mansonia is a high quality timber sometimes used in place of walnut. It is suitable for furniture making, joinery and turnery.

| | |
|---|---|
| Density *3* | Stability in service *average* |
| Bending strength *2* | Hardness *3* |
| Stiffness *4* | Durability *1* |
| Impact strength *3* | Blunting effect *average* |

*Identification*
Diffuse-porous.
Growth rings visible.
Vessels small, fairly numerous, solitary or in short radial chains (two to four) or small clusters.
Rays very fine, storied, one to two vessels per ray.
Parenchyma not very distinct, diffuse in fine radial lines.
Ripple marks present.

**59** makore ( × *25*); mansonia ( × *50*)

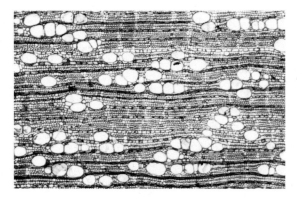
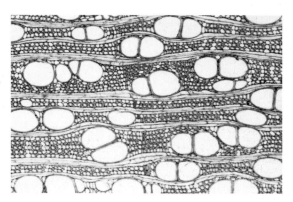

MAPLE, QUEENSLAND; *Flindersia brayleyana* and
*F. pimenteliana*; northern Queensland

MAPLE, ROCK; *Acer saccharum* and *A. nigrum*;
Canada and north eastern United States

Queensland maple has little relationship to the true
maples either botanically or in appearance. The
heartwood is a brownish-pink colour when freshly cut,
becoming a pale brown on exposure. The wood has a
natural lustre and, very often, an interlocked grain
which may also be wavy, thus producing a roe figure on
radial surfaces. The texture is medium and even. Some
care is needed in seasoning and, owing to the
interlocked grain, in working the timber.

The wood often has an attractive figure and is used
for furniture making, interior joinery and decorative
veneers.

Density  *3*

Bending strength 3–4
Stiffness  *3–4*
Impact strength  *3–4*

Stability in
service  *average*
Hardness  *3*
Durability  *3*
Blunting effect  *above average*

*Identification*
Diffuse-porous.
Growth rings visible.
Vessels of medium size, moderately abundant, solitary
  or in short radial chains (two or three).
Rays very fine, one to several vessels per ray.
Parenchyma not visible.

Rock maple is also known as hard maple and sugar
maple, and the sapwood as white maple.

The timber is rather variable in colour but is
typically a very pale reddish brown. The centre of some
large logs may be dark brown.

The grain is usually straight but may be wavy, and
the growth rings are marked by fine brown lines which
give a pronounced figure on tangential surfaces. The
rays are fairly distinctive on radial surfaces, more so
than in the soft maples.

Rock maple seasons and works well and is a good
bending wood. It has good strength properties and is
resistent to abrasion. Its main uses are for furniture
making, joinery, flooring, some working parts of
musical instruments, electric guitars and sports goods.

Density  *2*

Bending strength  *2*
Stiffness  *3*
Impact strength  *2*

Stability in
service  *average*
Hardness  *2*
Durability  *4*
Blunting
effect  *average*

*Identification*
Diffuse-porous.
Growth rings visible.
Vessels small or very small, numerous, mostly solitary,
  some short radial chains (two to three) or small
  clusters.
Rays of varying size, moderate to very small, like
  sycamore but unlike the soft maples, some rays are
  wider than the vessels, less conspicuous on end grain
  than in sycamore.
Parenchyma terminal.

**60** Queensland maple ( × *50*); rock maple (and sycamore) ( × *60*)

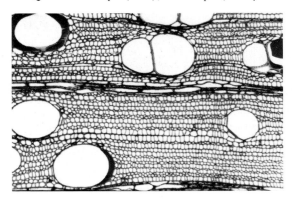
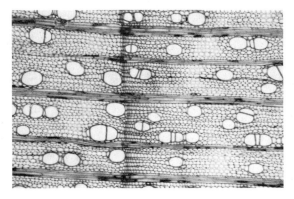

MERANTI, DARK RED;  *Shorea* species, mostly
*Shorea pauciflora*;  South East Asia

Dark red meranti is a medium to dark reddish-brown
timber with a rather coarse texture and has an
interlocked grain which gives a broad banded figure on
radial surfaces.

Dark red meranti is not used for high class joinery or
decorative work but is a good general purpose timber
which works well and is widely used for plywood
manufacture and for general purpose interior and
exterior joinery.

| | |
|---|---|
| Density  *2* | Stability in service  *below average* |
| Bending strength  *3* | Hardness  *2* |
| Stiffness  *4* | Durability  *3* |
| Impact strength  *4* | Blunting effect  *below average* |

*Identification*
Diffuse-porous.
Growth rings indistinct.
Vessels medium sized, solitary or in short radial chains
  (two to three).
Rays moderately fine, one vessel per ray, sometimes
  storied.
Parenchyma in some species is sparsely vasicentric,
  sometimes tending to aliform, also fine, diffuse; in
  other species there is no visible parenchyma.
Ripple pattern sometimes indistinct on tangential
  surfaces
Resin canals in tangential lines.

MERANTI, LIGHT RED;  about twelve *Shorea*
species;  South East Asia

Light red meranti varies from very pale pink to a
medium red colour. It has coarse, even texture and the
grain is shallowly interlocked, giving a broad stripey
effect on radial surfaces.

Light red meranti is a major export timber from
Malaya and Sabah. It is used as a general purpose
plywood and joinery timber and for the inside
structural components of furniture. It is not a high class
decorative or furniture wood.

| | |
|---|---|
| Density  *3* | Stability in service  *above average* |
| Bending strength  *3–4* | Hardness  *3* |
| Stiffness  *4* | Durability  *3–4* |
| Impact strength  *4* | Blunting effect  *below average* |

*Identification*
as for dark red meranti

**61** meranti ( *× 25*)

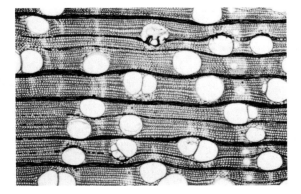

MERBAU; *Intsia palembanica* and *I. bijuga*; South East Asia and islands of the South West Pacific

MUHUHU; *Brachylaena hutchinsii*; East Africa

Merbau is a dark reddish-brown wood with a variable and often interlocked grain which produces a banded figure on radial surfaces. It has a medium-coarse texture and some vessels contain a yellowish dye.

Merbau is not a very easy timber to work but has some teak-like properties and is known as Borneo teak. It has a range of uses which include structural work, good class joinery, furniture making and flooring.

Density  *2*

Bending strength *3-4*
Stiffness  *3-4*
Impact strength  *3-4*

Stability in
service  *above average*
Hardness  *2*
Durability  *2*
Blunting
effect  *average*

*Identification*
Diffuse-porous.
Growth rings distinct.
Vessels moderate to large, not numerous, solitary and in radial chains (two to four), containing deposits.
Rays very fine, one to two rays per vessel.
Parenchyma terminal, vasicentric, aliform and confluent.

Muhuhu is yellowish brown when freshly cut, darkening on exposure to medium brown. The grain is closely interlocked or sometimes wavy, and the texture is very fine and even. Owing to its hardness, the irregular grain and the presence of gum, the timber is not very easy to work and requires care in seasoning. It has a sandalwood scent when worked.

Muhuhu is an attractive decorative timber having a particularly high resistance to abrasion. It is usually only available as flooring blocks but is suitable for turnery and carving.

Density  *1*

Bending strength  *3*
Stiffness  *4*
Impact strength  *5*

Stability in
service  *above average*
Hardness  *1*
Durability  *1*
Blunting
effect  *average*

*Identification*
Diffuse-porous.
Growth rings visible.
Vessels very small and numerous, in long radial chains and occasional clusters.
Rays very fine, one to several vessels per ray, storied.
Parenchyma not obvious.
Ripple marks present.

**62** merbau ( *× 50*); muhuhu ( *× 50*)

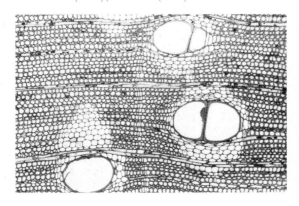
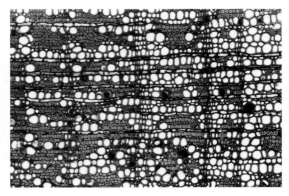

MUNINGA; *Pterocarpus angolensis*; East and South Africa

MYRTLE, TASMANIAN; *Nothofagus cunninghamii*; Tasmania and Victoria

Muninga is a rich-brown timber in colour with irregular darker markings. The grain is irregular and interlocked, giving a characteristic figure. The texture is medium to fairly coarse.

Although care is needed in working the very irregular grain the working properties are good and the timber seasons without difficulty.

Muninga is a high quality decorative wood and is used for furniture making, high class joinery and as a decorative veneer.

| | | | |
|---|---|---|---|
| Density | 3 | Stability in service | *above average* |
| Bending strength | 3 | Hardness | 3 |
| Stiffness | 5 | Durability | 1 |
| Impact strength | 4 | Blunting effect | *average* |

*Identification*
Semi ring-porous, early wood vessels considerably larger than late wood vessels.
Growth rings present.
Vessels small to moderately large, sparse to moderately numerous, solitary or in radial pairs.
Rays very fine, one to two rays per vessel, storied.
Parenchyma vasicentric, confluent and banded.
Ripple marks present.

Tasmanian myrtle or myrtle beech is a moderately dense, rather plain looking wood. It resembles European beech but does not have its prominent rays and is a pinkish or pinkish-brown in colour. The grain is straight or slightly interlocked and the texture is fine and even.

The relatively wide sapwood is known as white myrtle beech and the darker heartwood as red myrtle beech. The white beech is somewhat easier to season and work.

The timber is used in much the same way as European beech.

| | | | |
|---|---|---|---|
| Density | 2 | Stability in service | |
| Bending strength | 3 | Hardness | 2 |
| Stiffness | 3 | Durability | 4 |
| Impact strength | | Blunting effect | |

*Identification*
Diffuse-porous.
Growth rings visible.
Vessels very small, variable in size, moderately numerous.
Rays very fine, several vessels per ray.
Parenchyma terminal only.

The cross section of muninga is similar to that of amboyna

**63** Tasmanian myrtle ( × *60*)

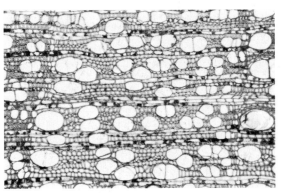

NIANGON; *Tarrietia utilis*; West Africa

NYATOH; *Palaquium* species and *Payena* species; Malaya and South East Asia

Niangon is a pale pinkish to reddish-brown timber which darkens in colour on exposure. The grain is usually interlocked and wavy producing an irregular stripe or roe figure on radial surfaces. The texture is fairly coarse and the rays are quite conspicuous on radial surfaces.

The interlocked grain makes the wood rather difficult to work but it is a useful general purpose timber for carpentry, joinery and plywood manufacture. It is sometimes used for boat building and the construction of greenhouses.

Nyatoh timber is variable because it comes from two genera and a number of different species. It is a pale purplish- to reddish-brown, sometimes with darker streaks. The grain is straight or shallowly interlocked and sometimes a little wavy. The texture is fairly fine.

Nyatoh is variable not only in colour and weight but also in working properties because it contains a variable quantity of silica. It often has an attractive roe-like figure and is suitable for furniture making and joinery. The more highly figured logs could be used for decorative veneers.

| | |
|---|---|
| Density  *3* | Stability in service  *average* |
| Bending strength  *3* | Hardness  *3* |
| Stiffness  *5* | Durability  *2* |
| Impact strength  *5* | Blunting effect  *average* |

| | |
|---|---|
| Density  *2–3* | Stability in service |
| Bending strength  *3* | Hardness  *2–3* |
| Stiffness  *3* | Durability  *3–4* |
| Impact strength  *3* | Blunting effect  *above average* |

*Identification*
Diffuse-porous.
Growth rings not very distinct.
Vessels not very abundant, fairly large, solitary or in radial pairs.
Rays medium and variable in size, one vessel per ray.
Parenchyma vasicentric, sometimes aliform or in fine lines but never very obvious.

*Identification*
Diffuse-porous.
Growth rings indistinct.
Vessels of average size, moderately numerous, mostly in radial chains (two to five).
Rays very fine, one per vessel.
Parenchyma diffuse.

**64** niangon ( × *25*); nyatoh ( × *25*)

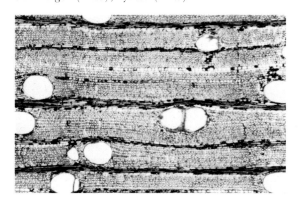
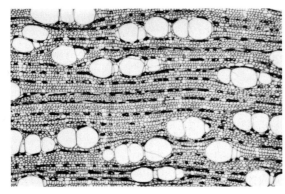

**OAK, AMERICAN RED;** *Quercus rubra, Q. falcata* and several other similar species; North America

**OAK, AMERICAN WHITE;** *Quercus alba* and about ten similar species; North America

The red oaks are not very different from the white oaks in appearance. They are a pinkish or light reddish colour and are heavy, hard and strong but much less durable and a little more difficult to work than the white oaks. They have a coarser texture and a less attractive figure due to the smaller rays.

As with the white oaks the individual timbers are not distinguishable from one another but the more southerly group are faster grown and therefore harder and stronger than the northern species.

The red oaks are considered to be inferior to the white oaks for fine work and they are not suitable for tight cooperage because of their porosity.

Density  *2*

Bending strength  *3*
Stiffness  *3*
Impact strength  *3*

Stability in
service  *average*
Hardness  *3*
Durability  *4*
Blunting
effect  *average*

*Identification*
Ring-porous.
Growth rings distinct.
Vessels, more gradual change in size between early and late wood vessels than in white oak. Also late wood vessels rather larger and less numerous than in white oak and arranged in a flame-like pattern, more oval in shape than in white oak.
Rays of two sizes. The large rays bulge slightly where they cross the growth rings and, unlike white oak, rarely exceed 40mm (1.5in) in height. The other rays are very fine but clearly visible, one vessel per narrow ray, many vessels per large ray.
Parenchyma diffuse and forming fine tangential lines.

**65** American red oak ( × *25*) ; (for white oak see European oak)

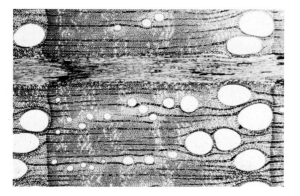

The timbers of the various American white oaks cannot be distinguished from one another although there are some regional differences. In the southern species, for example, there is a more gradual change in the size of vessels from the early to the late wood and the faster rate of growth produces a harder and tougher timber than that from the slower grown, more northerly species.

The timber is very similar in appearance to European oak and is used for much the same purposes, but is generally milder to work. It is particularly valued for the manufacture of whisky casks and oak timber is imported into Britain for this purpose.

Properties and identification as for European oak.

OAK, EUROPEAN or PEDUNCULATE; *Quercus robur*; and oak, European or sessile; *Quercus petraea*; Europe

The timbers of the two European oaks are indistinguishable and they closely resemble the American white oaks and Japanese oak in appearance and properties, although they are harder and stronger.

Timber from Central Europe generally has a slower and more even growth than that from northern Europe. British oak tends to be harder and tougher than the timber imported from continental Europe.

Oak is a pale fawn wood with a straight grain and a fairly coarse texture. Its most distinctive feature is the presence of very deep, silvery-coloured rays on radial surfaces.

Care has to be taken in drying oak and many craftsmen prefer air seasoning to kiln drying. Oak is a good bending species if the moisture content is reduced below fibre saturation point and provided the wood is dried slowly after bending.

Oak is not particularly difficult to work but the slower grown, straight-grained timber is easier than the faster grown wood which is harder and tougher and often has some irregular grain. It has the property of retaining its character no matter how badly or roughly it is treated.

The highest quality oak is valued for furniture making, interior joinery, cooperage and carving. Medium quality oak is suitable for high grade constructional work and exterior joinery, while the poorer quality material is widely used for fencing and gates.

| | | | |
|---|---|---|---|
| Density | 2 | Stability in service | average |
| Bending strength | 3 | Hardness | 2 |
| Stiffness | 4 | Durability | 2 |
| Impact strength | 4 | Blunting effect | average |

*Identification*
Ring-porous.
Growth rings distinct.
Vessels: early wood large, late wood small.
Rays large and small, a feature on radial and tangential surfaces, many vessels per large ray.
Parenchyma diffuse and forming fine tangential lines.

**66** European oak ( × *25*); Tasmanian oak ( × *50*)

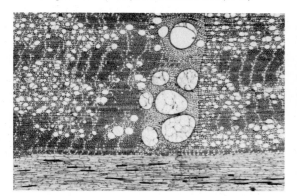

OAK, TASMANIAN; *Eucalyptus delegatensis, E. obliqua* and *E. regnans*; south eastern Australia and Tasmania

The colour of Tasmanian oak is similar to that of European oak, varying from pale to light brown but often with a pinkish tint.

The grain is usually straight but is sometimes interlocked or wavy and the texture is coarse. The general appearance is similar to that of sweet chestnut or tangentially cut European oak.

The timber dries fairly quickly but is liable to collapse and internal checking. It works well and takes a good finish.

Tasmanian oak, coming from several species of tree, is somewhat variable in its properties, but is generally a good quality, general purpose timber suitable for construction, joinery, furniture making and, if carefully selected for density, flooring.

| | | | |
|---|---|---|---|
| Density | 3–4 | Stability in service | average |
| Bending strength | 3 | Hardness | 3–4 |
| Stiffness | 3 | Durability | 3 |
| Impact strength | | Blunting effect | average |

*Identification*
Diffuse-porous but with some differentiation between early and late wood.
Growth rings present.
Vessels of medium size, solitary.
Rays very fine, one to two per vessel.
Parenchyma vasicentric but not obvious.

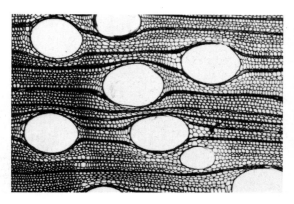

Obeche, which is sometimes known as wawa, is a very pale straw-coloured or almost white timber. The grain is almost always interlocked, giving a faintly striped figure on radial surfaces. It has a fairly coarse but even texture.

Obeche seasons and works well and can be used for bentwood work. It is a general purpose timber used where strength or appearance are of little importance.

It is suitable for utility furniture, the frames and drawer sides of higher quality furniture, interior joinery and plywood manufacture.

Density *4*

Bending strength *4*
Stiffness *5*
Impact strength *5*

Stability in
service *above average*
Hardness *4*
Durability *4*
Blunting effect *below average*

*Identification*
Diffuse-porous.
Growth rings present.
Vessels medium sized, not very numerous, mostly solitary or in radial pairs.
Rays very fine, one vessel per ray, wider rays half diameter of larger vessels.
Parenchyma diffuse, not very obvious.

Okwen timber is produced from four *Brachystegia* species. These are *B. nigerica*, *B. eurycoma*, *B. kennedyi* and *B. leonensis*. Of these, *Brachystegia nigerica* is denser and stronger than the other species. The information below refers mainly to *Brachystegia nigerica*.

Okwen is a pale whitish or yellowish-coloured timber which generally has a deeply interlocked and, sometimes also, a wavy grain giving a stripe or roe figure on radial surfaces. The texture is fairly coarse.

The timber seasons without undue difficulty but the irregular grain makes planing and moulding difficult, especially with *Brachystegia nigerica*.

The range of properties found in this commercial timber make it suitable for a range of uses from general construction to internal joinery and general utility work.

Density *2–3*

Bending strength *3*
Stiffness *4*
Impact strength *4*

Stability in
service *average*
Hardness *2–3*
Durability *3*
Blunting
effect *average*

*Identification*
Diffuse-porous.
Growth rings absent.
Vessesl not very abundant, moderately large, solitary or in short radial chains (two to five), some very small vessels in the chains.
Rays very fine, one to two rays per vessel.
Parenchyma vasicentric, aliform, confluent, terminal, distinct.

**67** obeche ( × *50*); okwen ( × *25*)

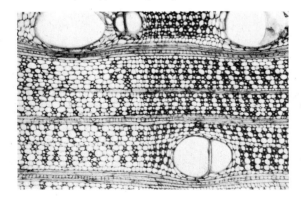
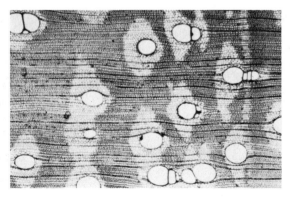

OLIVE, EAST AFRICAN; *Olea hochstetteri*; East Africa

OMU; *Entandrophragma candollei*; West Africa

East African olive is a pale brown or pinkish-brown colour with darker streaks. It has a straight or shallowly interlocked grain and a fine and even texture.

The timber is hard and heavy and has an attractive figure. It is used for good quality furniture, joinery and turnery and also as a decorative flooring timber in public buildings.

| | | | |
|---|---|---|---|
| Density | *1* | Stability in service | *below average* |
| Bending strength | *2* | Hardness | *2* |
| Stiffness | *2* | Durability | *3* |
| Impact strength | *2* | Blunting effect | *average* |

*Identification*
Diffuse-porous.
Growth rings indistinct or absent.
Vessels small, numerous, evenly distributed, mostly in radial chains (two to ten).
Rays very fine, one to two vessels per ray.
Parenchyma paratracheal but not clearly visible.

Omu is known as heavy sapele or heavy mahogany because, before seasoning, the logs will not float. It can be regarded as a coarse type of sapele or utile, being darker in colour and coarser in texture than those species.

Omu requires care in seasoning and is not particularly easy to work. It is used as an inferior type of sapele or utile.

| | | | |
|---|---|---|---|
| Density | *3* | Stability in service | *average* |
| Bending strength | *3* | Hardness | *3* |
| Stiffness | *4* | Durability | *3* |
| Impact strength | | Blunting effect | *average* |

*Identification*
Diffuse-porous.
Growth rings indistinct.
Vessels not very abundant, moderately large, solitary or in radial pairs of one normal and one very small vessel.
Rays fine to very fine, one vessel per ray.
Parenchyma in conspicuous bands.

**68** East African olive ( × *50*); omu ( × *25*)

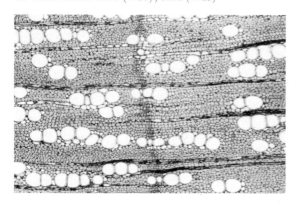
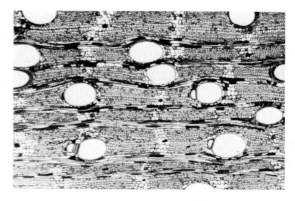

OPEPE; *Nauclea diderrichii*; West Africa

PADAUK, AFRICAN; *Pterocarpus soyauxii*; central and west tropical Africa

Opepe is a yellow or orange-yellow timber with, usually, an interlocked or irregular grain and a rather coarse texture.

Tangentially sawn timber requires care in seasoning, especially in thicker sizes, but it works reasonably well.

Opepe is strong and durable and is used mainly for heavy construction work, boat building, external joinery and flooring.

| | |
|---|---|
| Density *2* | Stability in service *above average* |
| Bending strength *3* | Hardness *2* |
| Stiffness *3* | Durability *1* |
| Impact strength *4* | Blunting effect *average* |

*Identification*
Diffuse-porous.
Growth rings absent.
Vessels moderately abundant, fairly large, all solitary.
Rays fine to very fine, one ray per vessel deflected by the vessels.
Parenchyma diffuse, not very obvious.

The heartwood of African padauk is bright red when freshly cut but it fades to a dark purplish-brown on exposure. It has a very coarse texture and the grain is straight or somewhat interlocked. The very coarse texture helps to distinguish padauk from rosewood species.

African padauk is a strong, stable timber which seasons well. It is a highly decorative wood and is used for high class joinery, furniture making, turnery, decorative veneers, carving and for small wooden articles requiring a high degree of stability, such as knife handles and spirit-level blocks. It is also suitable for heavy duty flooring, especially if under-floor heating is used.

| | |
|---|---|
| Density *2* | Stability in service *well above average* |
| Bending strength *2* | Hardness *2* |
| Stiffness | Durability *1* |
| Impact strength | Blunting effect *average* |

*Identification*
Diffuse-porous.
Growth rings absent.
Vessels round, of varying size, small to moderately large, not very numerous, solitary or in short radial chains (two to three).
Rays very fine, storied, several rays per vessel.
Parenchyma vasicentric, aliform, confluent and banded.
Ripple marks not very clearly defined.

**69** opepe (× *25*); African padauk (× *25*)

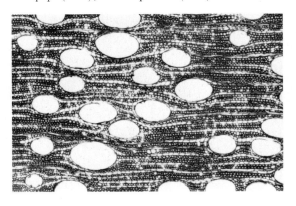 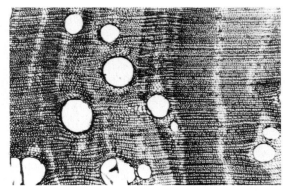

PADAUK, ANDAMAN; *Pterocarpus dalbergioides*;
Andaman Islands

PERSIMMON; *Diospyros virginiana*; central and
southern states of the USA

Andaman padauk is a rich reddish-brown wood often
with darker red and black streaks.

It usually has an interlocked grain and a medium to
coarse texture. Padauk can be confused with a
rosewood but it has a noticeably coarser texture.

Paduak is used for furniture making, high class
joinery subject to hard wear, turnery and, in Asia, for
boatbuilding and constructional work.

| Density | 2 | Stability in service | *above average* |
|---|---|---|---|
| Bending strength | 3 | Hardness | 2 |
| Stiffness | 4 | Durability | 1 |
| Impact strength | 4 | Blunting effect | *average* |

*Identification*
Diffuse-porous but early wood vessels larger.
Growth rings indistinct.
Vessels sparse, medium to large, solitary or in small
  radial chains (two to three).
Rays barely visible, several rays per vessel, storied.
Parenchyma in well defined narrow tangential bands.
Ripple pattern on tangential surface.

There is a small central core of dark-coloured
heartwood in the tree but the commercial timber is the
very pale-coloured sapwood which has a straight grain
and a fine, even texture.

Persimmon is a member of the ebony family and is a
hard, dense timber which is used for a few specialised
purposes and, in particular, for making golf club heads.

| Density | 1 | Stability in service | *above average* |
|---|---|---|---|
| Bending strength | 2 | Hardness | 1 |
| Stiffness | 3 | Durability | |
| Impact strength | | Blunting effect | |

*Identification*
Intermediate between diffuse-porous and ring-porous;
  early wood vessels are larger than late wood vessels.
Growth rings visible.
Vessels small to medium, moderately numerous,
  solitary or in short radial chains (two to four).
Rays very fine, one vessel per ray, storied.
Parenchyma terminal, diffuse in fine tangential lines,
  not always very obvious.
Ripple marks indistinct.

**70** Andaman padauk ( × 25); persimmon ( × 25)

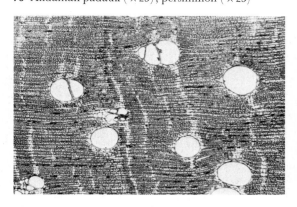
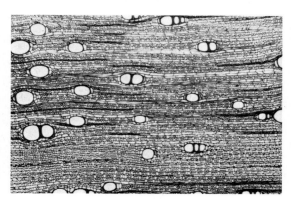

PLANE; *Platanus* species; North America, eastern Europe, western Asia and Britain

London plane is a hybrid between oriental plane, *Platanus orientalis* and American plane, *Platanus occidentalis*, which is known as sycamore in North America.

Plane has some resemblance to beech but is darker in colour and the dark flecks of the rays give it a more pronounced figure on radial surfaces. For this reason the radially cut wood is known as lacewood.

Plane is softer, less dense and less strong than beech but is easy to work and is used for decorative work in furniture making and for turnery and carving.

Density   *3–4*        Stability in service
Bending strength   *4*        Hardness   *3–4*
Stiffness   *4*        Durability   *5*
Impact strength   *3*        Blunting
effect   *average*

*Identification*
Diffuse-porous.
Rings distinct, boundary marked by lighter-coloured band of summer wood.
Vessels very small and very numerous, solitary or in small groups (two to four).
Rays fairly wide, wider than the vessels, four to five vessels per ray.
Parenchyma not visible.

PTERYGOTA, AFRICAN; *Pterygota bequaertii* and *P. macrocarpa*; West Africa

Pterygota is a pale straw-coloured wood with a shallowly interlocked grain and a moderately coarse texture. The deep rays, which are almost white, produce a flecked figure on radial surfaces.

The timber seasons well but a sharp plane is needed to produce a smooth finish.

Pterygota can be used as an alternative to ramin or beech for utility furniture, interior joinery and the inside components of higher quality furniture.

Density   *3*        Stability in
service   *average*
Bending strength   *3*        Hardness   *3*
Stiffness   *4*        Durability   *5*
Impact strength   *3–4*        Blunting
effect   *average*

*Identification*
Diffuse-porous.
Growth rings not present.
Vessels not very abundant, fairly large, solitary or in short radial chains (two to four).
Rays fine to medium, one vessel per ray.
Parenchyma vasicentric and banded, distinct.

**71** plane ( × *50*); African pterygota ( × *25*)

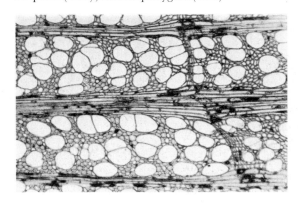
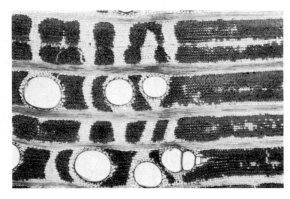

RAMIN; *Gonostylus* species, principally *Gonostylus bancanus*; Malaya

A very pale, yellowish-buff coloured wood with a moderately fine texture and a straight or sometimes slightly interlocked grain. It has virtually no figure.

Ramin is not suitable for the exterior parts of furniture or joinery because it entirely lacks character, but it is strong and hard, works well and is a useful utility timber for the interior components of furniture as well as for painted joinery and mouldings.

Density  *2*

Bending strength  *2*
Stiffness  *3*
Impact strength  *4*

Stability in
service  *average*
Hardness  *2*
Durability  *4*
Blunting effect  *above average*

*Identification*
Diffuse-porous.
Growth rings not present.
Vessels small, solitary or in short radial chains (two to three).
Rays very fine, one vessel per ray.
Parenchyma vasicentric, aliform to confluent in short, fine lines.

RAULI; *Nothofagus procera*; Chile and Argentina

The genus *Nothofagus* is closely related to beech and the wood of rauli resembles it but is purplish or light reddish-brown in colour and does not have the very conspicuous rays of beech. It is also lighter and softer. The grain is straight and the texture fine and even.

Rauli seasons and works well and takes a good finish, but is not as good a bending timber as beech.

It is used in Chile as a general purpose timber for furniture making, internal joinery and flooring. It can be regarded as a substitute for beech where strength and hardness are not of particular importance.

Density  *3–4*

Bending strength  *3*
Stiffness  *5*
Impact strength  *4*

Stability in
service  *above average*
Hardness  *3–4*
Durability  *2*
Blunting effect  *below average*

*Identification*
Diffuse-porous but early wood vessels larger than late wood vessels.
Growth rings visible.
Vessels small to very small, fairly abundant, solitary or in radial pairs, sometimes in small transverse clusters.
Rays very fine, one to three vessels per ray.
Parenchyma terminal only.

**72**  ramin ( × *25*) ; rauli ( × *50*)

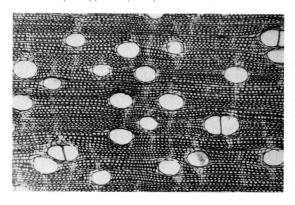
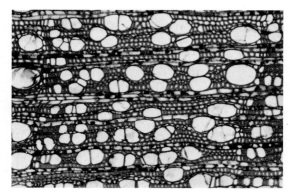

ROBINIA OR FALSE ACACIA; *Robinia pseudoacacia*; North America but widely planted in Europe since the seventeenth century

ROSEWOOD, BRAZILIAN OR RIO; *Dalbergia nigra*; Brazil

When freshly cut, robinia has a greenish colour which turns to a golden brown on exposure. The contrasting bands of lighter-coloured spring wood and darker-coloured summer wood give it an interesting figure. The wood is usually straight grained and has a moderately coarse texture.

Robinia works well, is a good bending timber, takes a good finish and is durable. It is not often available but is a high quality timber and can be used for furniture making, joinery and turnery. It is sometimes used in America in place of ash for jobs requiring strength and toughness.

| Density | *2* | Stability in service | *average* |
|---|---|---|---|
| Bending strength | *3* | Hardness | *2* |
| Stiffness | *3* | Durability | *2* |
| Impact strength | *3* | Blunting effect | *average* |

*Identification*
Ring-porous.
Growth rings present.
Vessels of early wood medium but variable in size, late wood vessels very small and fairly sparse, large vessels mostly solitary or in radial or oblique pairs.
Rays very fine, one to three large vessels per ray.
Parenchyma vasicentric or aliform.

Rosewood from young trees is not particularly attractive but that from older trees is one of the most decorative of all timbers. The colour is variable but is typically a rich orange brown with very dark or almost black irregular streaks. Indian rosewood, *Dalbergia latifolia*, is somewhat darker in colour.

Rosewood generally has a straight grain and a medium texture. It works well, can easily be bent, and takes a fine finish. It is a very high quality furniture timber both in the solid and as a veneer, and is also used for turnery and for the manufacture of decorative knife handles.

| Density | *1* | Stability in service | *above average* |
|---|---|---|---|
| Bending strength | *3* | Hardness | *1* |
| Stiffness | *4* | Durability | *2* |
| Impact strength | | Blunting effect | *average* |

*Identification*
Diffuse-porous.
Growth rings sometimes visible.
Vessels sparse, large, solitary or in small radial chains (two to three).
Rays very fine, several rays per vessel, storied.
Parenchyma terminal, otherwise sparse and not obvious.
Ripple pattern on tangential surfaces.

**73** robinia (× *25*); Brazilian rosewood (× *25*)

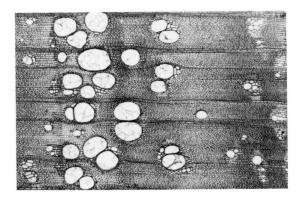
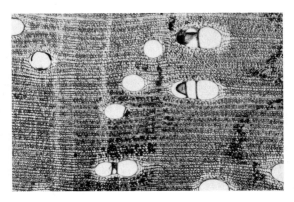

ROSEWOOD, INDIAN; *Dalbergia latifolia*; India

SAPELE; *Entandrophragma cylindricum*; West Africa

Indian rosewood is a medium to dark brown wood with a slight purplish tinge and darker streaks which give it a rich, decorative appearance. The streakiness is less pronounced than in the American rosewoods. The grain is interlocked, giving an inconspicuous narrow-banded pattern on radial surfaces. It has a moderately coarse and even texture.

The timber seasons and works well despite its hardness and interlocked grain, and also takes a fine finish.

Indian rosewood is a very high quality decorative timber used for fine furniture and joinery, parts of musical instruments, turnery and carving.

Density  *1*

Bending strength  *2*
Stiffness  *4*
Impact strength

Stability in
service  *above average*
Hardness  *1*
Durability  *1*
Blunting
effect  *average*

*Identification*
Diffuse-porous.
Growth rings sometimes visible.
Vessels medium to moderately large, fairly numerous, solitary or in short radial or tangential chains (two to four).
Rays very fine, one to two rays per vessel, storied.
Parenchyma vasicentric, aliform, confluent and finely diffuse.
Ripple marks present.

Sapele was formerly regarded as a mahogany and shipped together with several related species from the port of Sapele in Nigeria, but since the early years of this century it has been recognised as a distinct timber species. It is a fairly dark, reddish-brown wood, darker in colour than most mahoganies, and is finer textured than African mahogany, *Khaya* species. Its most characteristic feature is a pronounced and regular stripe or banded figure on radial surfaces caused by the interlocked grain. Some logs also have a roe and others a fiddle-back figure.

Sapele is used in much the same way as other mahogany or mahogany-type timbers for furniture making, joinery and as a decorative veneer. Care has to be taken in planing and finishing because the regular banding means that a plane of scraper is often working, to some extent, against a steeply angled grain. Sapele has very poor bending qualities.

Density  *3*

Bending strength  *3*
Stiffness  *4*
Impact strength  *3*

Stability in
service  *average*
Hardness  *3*
Durability  *3*
Blunting
effect  *average*

*Identification*
Diffuse-porous.
Growth rings visible.
Vessels medium-sized, moderately numerous, uniformly distributed, solitary or in short radial chains (one to four) (occasionally small groups), sometimes containing dark deposits.
Rays fine, fairly obvious, one vessel per ray, sometimes storied.
Parenchyma vasicentric and confluent, sometimes forming quite broad bands, also terminal lines.
Ripple marking sometimes clearly defined.

**74** Indian rosewood ( × *25*); sapele ( × *25*)

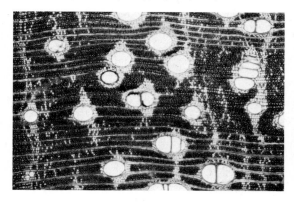 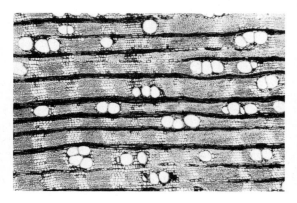

SATINWOOD, CEYLON; *Chloroxylon swietenia*; central and southern India and Sri Lanka

When freshly cut, Ceylon satinwood is a pale yellowish colour darkening on exposure to a pale lustrous brown. The grain is interlocked and wavy producing a narrow, striped and mottled or roe figure on radial surfaces. The texture is fine and even.

The timber requires some care in seasoning. It is dense and hard but is used almost entirely for decorative purposes where its strength properties are of little importance. Ceylon satinwood is an expensive timber and used principally as a decorative veneer and for specialised furniture work, joinery and turnery.

Density  *1*                Stability in service
Bending strength  *2*       Hardness  *1*
Stiffness  *3*              Durability  *2*
Impact strength  *4*        Blunting
                            effect  *average*

*Identification*
Diffuse-porous.
Growth rings visible.
Vessels very small, numerous, solitary or in radial chains (two to six) and small clusters.
Rays very fine, two to three vessels per ray, storied.
Parenchyma fairly obvious, terminal only.
Ripple marks ill-defined.

SATINWOOD, WEST INDIAN; *Fagara flava*; West Indies, Burmuda, the Bahamas, southern Florida

West Indian satinwood is a pale creamy or honey-coloured wood which darkens on exposure. It has a fine, even texture and an irregularly interlocked grain which gives a roe or mottled figure. The range of figure and colour is somewhat less than that of Ceylon satinwood.

Apart from the usual difficulties encountered with an irregular grain the timber works and turns well and takes a fine finish. It is used for high class cabinet making, turnery and decorative work.

Density  *1–2*             Stability in service
Bending strength          Hardness  *1–2*
Stiffness                 Durability  *4*
Impact strength           Blunting
                          effect  *average*

*Identification*
Diffuse-porous.
Growth rings present.
Vessels abundant, very small, solitary and in radial chains (two to four) and occasional small clumps.
Rays fine but variable in width, some rays as wide as diameter of vessels, several vessels per ray.
Parenchyma terminal, prominent.

**75**  Ceylon satinwood ( × *50*) ; West Indian satinwood ( × *50*)

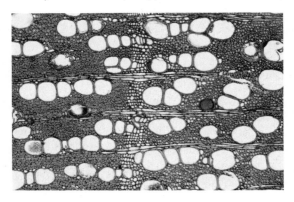
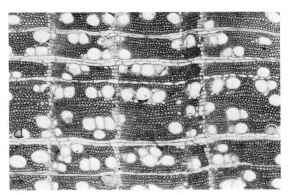

SEPETIR; *Sindora* species; South East Asia

SILKY-OAK, AUSTRALIAN; *Cardwellia sublimis*; North Queensland

The timber marketed as sepetir comes from several species of the genus *Sindora*.

The wood is golden to dark brown in colour sometimes with darker brown or black streaks producing a decorative figure. The grain is straight and shallowly interlocked and the texture moderately fine and even. Sepetir seasons and works well and gives a good finish.

Timber of average quality is used for light construction and joinery work but the more highly figured material is suitable for decorative veneers and furniture making.

| | | | |
|---|---|---|---|
| Density | 2 | Stability in service | above average |
| Bending strength | 2 | Hardness | 2 |
| Stiffness | 3 | Durability | 2 |
| Impact strength | 4 | Blunting effect | average |

*Identification*
Diffuse-porous.
Growth rings visible.
Vessels of medium size and abundance, solitary or in radial chains (two to four).
Rays very fine, one vessel per ray.
Parenchyma terminal, vasicentric, sometimes aliform.

Australian silky-oak when freshly cut has a pinkish or reddish-brown colour reminiscent of American red oak. This colour darkens with age to a mid-brown. Like the true oaks it has deep rays giving a silvery figure on radial surfaces.

The grain is usually straight and the texture is coarse and even.

The timber seasons and works well and is widely used in Australia for furniture making, joinery and decorative flooring.

| | | | |
|---|---|---|---|
| Density | 3 | Stability in service | |
| Bending strength | | Hardness | 3 |
| Stiffness | | Durability | 3 |
| Impact strength | | Blunting effect | below average |

*Identification*
Diffuse-porous.
Growth rings not visible.
Vessels medium to moderately large, solitary or in tangential or oblique pairs.
Rays very wide, twice diameter of the vessels, many vessels per ray.
Parenchyma almost entirely vasicentric, aliform and confluent.

**76**  sepetir ( × 50); Australian silky oak ( × 25)

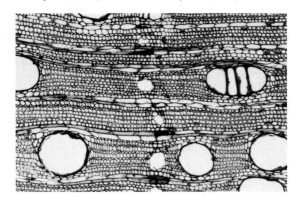 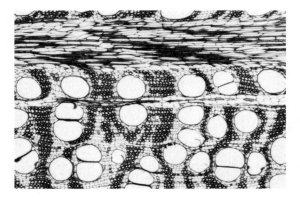

STRAWBERRY TREE; *Arbutus unedo*; Europe, including Eire but not the United Kingdom

Arbutus wood is a soft, reddish-brown colour with a fine texture and a variable grain which sometimes gives an interesting figure.

It is not available in large sizes but is fairly strong and hard and is a good turnery timber.

| | | |
|---|---|---|
| Density | *3* | Stability in service |
| Bending strength | *3* | Hardness *3* |
| Stiffness | | Durability |
| Impact strength | *3* | Blunting effect |

*Identification*
Diffuse-porous.
Growth rings distinct.
Vessels small, numerous, solitary and in radial chains (two to four) with some clusters.
Rays very fine.
Parenchyma very sparse, paratracheal, not obvious.

SYCAMORE; *Acer pseudoplatanus*; Europe, introduced into Britain by the Romans

Sycamore timber is very similar to the other common European maples, field maple and Norway maple.

It is a very pale, almost white wood with a fine, lustrous surface. Generally, there is virtually no figure but some trees have a wavy or fiddle-back grain which is visible on radial surfaces.

Sycamore is easily air or kiln dried, but very slow drying or a high temperature cause staining.

Straight grained, knot-free timber can easily be bent.

Sycamore can be given a very fine, smooth surface and it is widely used for turnery work. Figured logs are sometimes cut for veneer and they are the traditional wood for the backs of violins, hence the name fiddle-back maple.

| | | |
|---|---|---|
| Density | *3* | Stability in service *average* |
| Bending strength | *3* | Hardness *3* |
| Stiffness | *5* | Durability *5* |
| Impact strength | *4* | Blunting effect *average* |

*Identification*
Diffuse-porous.
Growth rings distinct.
Vessels small, regularly spaced, round, solitary or in small radial chains (two to five).
Rays small to medium, large rays nearly as wide as the vessels, one to three vessels per ray.
Parenchyma terminal.

**77** strawberry tree ( × *50*); (for sycamore see rock maple)

TCHITOLA OR TOLA; *Oxystigma oxyphyllum*; Congo and West Africa

TEAK; *Tectona grandis*; India, Burma, Thailand, Indo China, Java, planted in East and West Africa and the West Indies

Tchitola has a brown heartwood with darker markings which give it some resemblance to walnut. It has a moderately coarse texture and a straight or slightly interlocked grain. Agba is also known as tola but it is a paler and more uniformly coloured wood and bears no particular resemblance to tchitola.

The timber seasons and works well but contains gum which is liable to accumulate on tools.

Tchitola is used mainly as a decorative veneer.

| | |
|---|---|
| Density *3* | Stability in service |
| Bending strength *3* | Hardness *3* |
| Stiffness *4* | Durability *4* |
| Impact strength *3* | Blunting effect *average* |

*Identification*
Diffuse-porous.
Growth rings indistinct.
Vessels moderate to relatively large, not very numerous, solitary or in radial pairs.
Rays fine, one to two per vessel.
Parenchyma terminal, vasicentric, banded, obvious.

Teak is generally a fairly pale golden-brown timber but wood from dry zone forests in India may be darker and less uniform in colour. The texture is coarse and the grain usually straight. It works well but owing to the silica in the wood it blunts tools very quickly and the dust can irritate the nose and throat. It is therefore advisable to wear a face mask when working with teak. The timber contains oil which inhibits some glues and surfaces should, therefore, be washed in a solvent such as methylated spirits before gluing.

Teak has a combination of good qualities which make it one of the world's outstanding timbers for decorative and structural work. It is an exceptional timber for boat building, garden furniture and exterior joinery and is also highly regarded as a furniture and turnery timber.

| | |
|---|---|
| Density *3* | Stability in service *above average* |
| Bending strength *3* | Hardness *3* |
| Stiffness *4* | Durability *1* |
| Impact strength *4* | Blunting effect *above average* |

*Identification*
Ring-porous.
Growth rings visible.
Vessels variable-sized, some quite large, solitary and in radial chains (two to six).
Rays very fine, one vessel per ray.
Parenchyma: band of initial paratracheal in each growth ring plus some sparse and insignificant diffuse.

**78** tchitola (×50); teak (×50)

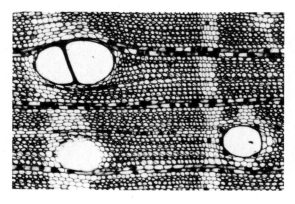
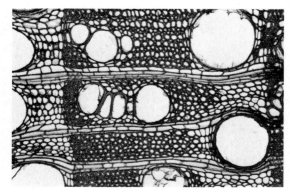

UTILE; *Entandrophragma utile*; West Africa

Utile is a fairly uniform reddish-coloured wood with a shallowly interlocked and rather irregular grain. It shows some banding on radial surfaces but does not have the regular striped figure of sapele. It lacks the character of mahogany or sapele and although it is widely used for internal and external joinery and for furniture making it cannot be regarded as a high quality decorative timber.

Density *2*

Bending strength *3*
Stiffness *4*
Impact strength *4*

Stability in service *average*
Hardness *2*
Durability *2*
Blunting effect *average*

*Identification*
Diffuse-porous.
Growth rings visible.
Vessels slightly larger and less numerous than sapele, solitary or in short radial chains (two to three), sometimes containing dark deposits.
Rays very fine, generally one vessel per ray, sometimes storied.
Parenchyma terminal, vasicentric, aliform and confluent often in somewhat wavy bands, less distinct than in sapele.
Ripple marks sometimes present.

VIROLA; *Virola* species and *Dialyanthera* species; Brazil, central and tropical South America

The timber marketed as virola is obtained from a number of different, but related, tree species. It is therefore somewhat variable in properties and appearance.

The wood is a pale pinkish-brown and the grain is usually straight. The texture varies to some extent according to origin, the Brazilian timber being denser and darker and having a finer texture than that from Colombia. The denser and darker-coloured wood is known as heavy virola and the paler, less dense wood as light virola.

Virola has to be seasoned with care but the working properties are good. It has no particular decorative value but is a useful, easily worked, general purpose timber for utility joinery and mouldings.

Density *4*
Bending strength *4*
Stiffness *3–4*
Impact strength

Stability in service
Hardness *4*
Durability *4*
Blunting effect *below average*

*Identification*
Diffuse-porous.
Growth rings absent.
Vessels of moderate size and frequency, solitary or in short radial chains (two to three).
Rays very fine, one vessel per ray.
Parenchyma: terminal sometimes present.

**79** utile ( × *25*); Virola ( × *60*)

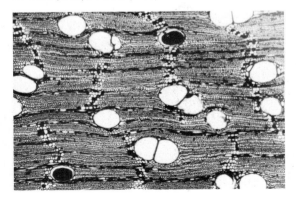
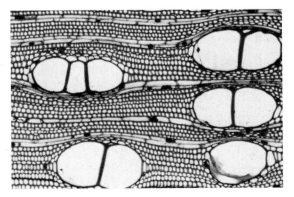

WALNUT, AFRICAN; *Lovoa trichilioides*; West Africa

WALNUT, AMERICAN; *Juglans nigra*; eastern United States and Canada

African walnut is a rich, yellowish-brown timber which is sometimes marked with darker streaks, which presumably suggested the name walnut. It is unrelated to the true walnut but belongs to the mahogany family and bears some resemblance to African mahogany, *Khaya ivorensis*.

It has a moderately fine texture and often has interlocked grain which gives a banded figure on radial surfaces.

The interlocked grain makes it a rather difficult timber to work and finish and it is classified as moderate in its bending qualities.

African walnut is a decorative timber widely used both in the solid and as a veneer for furniture making and good class joinery work.

| | |
|---|---|
| Density  *3* | Stability in service  *above average* |
| Bending strength  *4* | Hardness  *3* |
| Stiffness  *5* | Durability  *3* |
| Impact strength  *4* | Blunting effect  *below average* |

*Identification*
Diffuse-porous.
Growth rings indistinct.
Vessels medium-sized, fairly evenly distributed, solitary or in small radial chains (two to five) or groups; some contain dark deposits.
Rays very fine, one to two vessels per ray.
Parenchyma not very obvious with a hand lens, vasicentric and aliform or confluent, sometimes diffuse.

American walnut is a rich brown timber, darker and more uniform in colour than European walnut.

The grain is usually straight but sometimes wavy and the texture is rather coarse. The structure of American walnut is, therefore, very similar to that of the European species. The timber works well and is highly regarded for furniture making and for good quality rifle and gun stocks. It is also used as a decorative veneer.

| | |
|---|---|
| Density  *3* | Stability in service  *average* |
| Bending strength  *3* | Hardness  *3* |
| Stiffness  *4* | Durability  *1* |
| Impact strength  *3* | Blunting effect  *average* |

*Identification*
Diffuse-porous but tending towards ring-porous.
Growth rings usually distinct.
Vessels medium-sized, oval, solitary or in small radial chains (two to three).
Rays very fine, generally one vessel per ray.
Parenchyma not obvious.

**80** African walnut ( × *50*); American walnut ( × *25*)

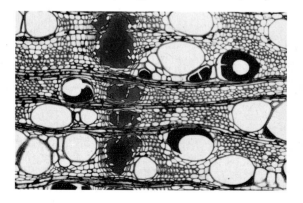
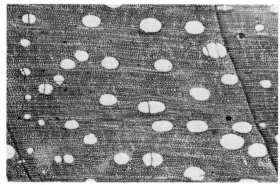

WALNUT, EUROPEAN; *Juglans regia*; Europe

Walnut is a greyish-brown wood with irregular streaks but the appearance is variable and depends upon its place of origin.

The wood has a rather coarse texture and is usually straight grained apart from the stumps, burrs and forks of a small proportion of the total number of trees harvested. These provide highly decorative veneers. The timber works and bends well and is regarded as one of the highest quality furniture timbers both in the solid and as a veneer. It is also used for turnery and for making stocks of high quality guns and rifles. Walnut has to be seasoned with care and there is somtimess a high proportion of defective timber in a log.

| Density | 3 | Stability in service | *average* |
|---|---|---|---|
| Bending strength | 3 | Hardness | 3 |
| Stiffness | 4 | Durability | 3 |
| Impact strength | 3 | Blunting effect | *average* |

*Identification*
Diffuse but tending towards ring-porous.
Growth rings usually distinct.
Vessels medium-sized, oval, solitary or in small radial chains (two to four).
Rays variable in size but fine, generally one vessel per ray.
Parenchyma terminal and diffuse.

WALNUT, QUEENSLAND; *Endiandra palmerstonii*; northern Queensland

Queensland walnut is not unlike European walnut in appearance except that the figure is more regular. The colour varies from pale to dark brown with dark or blackish streaks, and the wood has a natural lustre.

The grain is interlocked and also often wavy, giving a roe figure on radial surfaces. The texture is medium and even.

The timber requires careful seasoning and the combination of irregular grain with silica deposits makes working somewhat difficult. When freshly sawn it has an unpleasant sour smell.

Queensland walnut is a high quality decorative timber which is used for good quality furniture and joinery and as a decorative veneer. It is also suitable for relatively heavy-duty flooring.

| Density | 2 | Stability in service | |
|---|---|---|---|
| Bending strength | 3 | Hardness | 2 |
| Stiffness | 4 | Durability | 4 |
| Impact strength | | Blunting effect | *above average* |

*Identification*
Diffuse-porous.
Growth rings absent or indistinct (cf. imbuia).
Vessels of medium size, solitary or in short radial chains (two to four).
Rays very fine, about one vessel per ray.
Parenchyma: conspicuous bands at irregular intervals, vasicentric, sometimes terminal.

**81** European walnut ( × 25); Queensland walnut ( × 50)

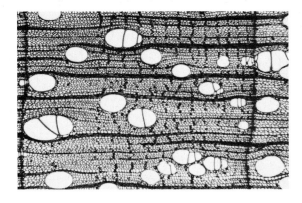

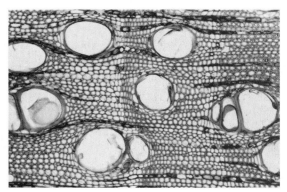

# CHAPTER 9
# Softwoods

The timber of conifers is usually referred to as softwood although some softwood timbers are harder than many hardwoods.

Conifers occur naturally in many parts of the world but most genera are confined to the northern hemisphere and, in particular, to the north temperate region. The only southern hemisphere genera are those belonging to the families *Podocarpaceae* and *Araucariaceae*, plus the genus *Callitris*, belonging to the family *Cupressaceae*. Many northern hemisphere species are, however, planted in South America and Australasia.

There are six conifer families. These are shown in Table 14 together with their more important genera.

### Table 14 Conifer families and principal genera

| Family | Genus |
|---|---|
| *Taxaceae* | *Taxus* (yew) |
| *Podocarpaceae* | *Podocarpus* |
| *Araucariaceae* | *Araucaria, Agathis* (kauri) |
| *Pinaceae* | *Abies* (fir), *Pseudotsuga* (Douglas fir), *Tsuga* (hemlock), *Picea* (spruce), *Larix* (larch), *Cedrus* (cedar), *Pinus* (pine) |
| *Taxodiaceae* | *Sequoia, Taxodium* (swamp cypress), *Cryptomeria* |
| *Cupressaceae* | *Thuja, Cupressus* (cypress), *Chamaecyparis* (false cypress), *Juniperus* (juniper, pencil cedar). |

For a number of reasons conifers provide the greater part of the industrial wood used in the more developed parts of the world. This is due partly to the geographical location of the natural coniferous forests but also because of the form of growth of softwood timber. The trees generally grow straighter and with a more pronounced central stem than most hardwoods, and the relatively small number of species in the northern forests make logging and utilisation easier; tropical forests often contain many species in intimate mixture, only a few of which in any one location have an economic value.

In plantations, conifers generally grow faster and are more profitable than hardwoods. For these reasons they make up the greater part of the 100 million hectares (247 million acres) or so of artificial plantations in the temperate and sub-tropical or upland tropical regions of the world.

The most widely used softwood species in Britain are redwood or Scots pine, *Pinus sylvestris*, and whitewood or Norway spruce, *Picea abies*, from Scandinavia and Russia, and Douglas fir, *Pseudotsuga menziesii*, western hemlock, *Tsuga heterophylla* snd Sitka spruce, *Picea sitchensis*, from Canada.

Many other spruce and pine species are used in various regions of the world and other genera in common use are larch, *Larix*, and fir, *Abies*. Some other genera or species of more limited commercial importance are western red cedar, *Thuja plicata*, cypress, *Cupressus*, false cypress, *Chamaecyparis*, pencil cedar, *Juniperus*, true cedar, *Cedrus*, sugi, *Cryptomeria japonica* and, in the southern hemisphere, *Podocarpus*, *Araucaria* and kauri, *Agathis*.

The properties of all timbers depend not only upon specific characteristics but also upon the conditions of growth. This is probably more true of most softwoods than of most hardwoods. Two factors in particular influence wood quality. These are rate of growth and the age of the wood. As with hardwoods, juvenile wood (page 9) is inferior in most characteristics to the more mature wood. As well as being less dense and less strong the cells are shorter and there is more likelihood not only of spiral grain but also of large knots, because the juvenile wood is laid down in the living crown of the tree. The more mature wood is produced below the crown after the branches have been suppressed by mutal competition between neighbouring trees for light and space. The timber from very young trees is therefore not suitable for high grade work.

The faster the growth the wider the growth rings and, usually, the larger the knots. Although fast-grown timber is likely to be less dense, and therefore less strong than slower-grown wood, the rate of growth is not generally a major factor determining the strength of timber. Faster-grown wood, other than juvenile wood, is therefore likely to be suitable for most general purposes including construction. For high grade work, however, timber with a relatively slow and even growth is required. For example, the Sitka spruce used formerly for making aeroplane spars was obtained from the mature wood of slow-growing trees. The juvenile wood, or even the mature wood from very fast-grown trees, would be unsuitable for such an exacting purpose. The resonance wood used for making the sound boards of musical instruments comes from the mountains of Central Europe and especially from Romania, where the growth of Norway spruce is slow and regular. Relatively slow-grown wood is also superior for furniture making and joinery because it works better and takes a finer finish than faster-grown material.

Softwood timber with narrow, regular growth rings is gradually becoming more difficult to obtain as the old trees from the more accessible natural forests are felled and replaced, either with natural regeneration or with plantations which will never reach the uneconomic age of the original stands.

Selected softwood timber is widely used for internal joinery and utility or cottage-style furniture, and also for a variety of specialised products such as masts and oars where straightness and a high strength to weight ratio are necessary. There are, however, very few softwood timbers which equal high quality hardwoods in their decorative value, strength and resistance to decay.

A notable exception is yew, *Taxus baccata*, which has been highly prized for centuries as a furniture timber and before that for making long bows. Some other softwood timbers which are used for high quality work are various species of cedar, alerce or *Fitzroya cupressoides*, which is rarely grown outside South America, Virginian pencil cedar, *Juniperus virginiana* and Queensland kauri pine, *Agathis robusta*. Scots pine, *Pinus sylvestris*, although a general purpose industrial timber, is also used for cottage-style furniture. It has a pleasing texture and colour which fall between the dullness of spruce or fir and the coarseness of pitch pine.

The contrast between heartwood and sapwood is usually much less pronounced in softwoods than in hardwoods. This is true not only of the visual appearance but also of the physical properties, although there are physiological differences even if there is little or no difference in appearance. The heartwood tends to be more resistant to decay and, especially with spruce, to impregnation by preservatives. A notable exception to this generalisation is yew, which has a golden-brown, highly durable heartwood and an almost white, perishable sapwood.

### Cedar

There are three true species of cedar. These are cedar of Lebanon, *Cedrus libani*, from the Middle East, Atlantic cedar, *Cedrus atlantica*, from North Africa and deodar cedar, *Cedrus deodora*, from the Himalayas, all of which have timber with a pleasing aromatic scent.

Western red cedar, *Thuja plicata*, grows in western North America. It is a very durable, lightweight, easily-worked timber which is widely used for making roof shingles, for the framing of glass houses and for weather-boarding.

White cedar, *Thuja occidentalis*, is another North American species which is less dense and less strong than western red cedar but which otherwise has similar properties and is used for similar purposes.

Incense cedar, *Libocedrus decurrens*, also occurs in the western United States and since it resembles western red cedar in appearance and properties it is used for much the same purposes and for making pencils. Two species of juniper are known as pencil cedars. These are Virginian pencil cedar, *Juniperus virginiana*, from North America, and East African pencil cedar, *Juniperus procera*, from East Africa. These two 'cedars' owe their names to their characteristic cedar-like scent and to their fine, even grain and good working properties which make them suitable for the manufacture of pencils.

*Chamaecyparis* is another genus to which the name 'cedar' has been given, again on account of its aromatic properties. Lawson's cypress or Port Orford cedar, *Chamaecyparis lawsoniana*, is a native of Oregon and California but is widely planted as an ornamental in Britain. Yellow cedar, *Chamaeacyparis nootkatensis*, occurs in the north western region of the United States and western Canada and, like Port Orford cedar, is a fine textured, easily worked and relatively strong timber used for a variety of general purposes.

### Cypress

The common name 'cypress' is applied to two genera and one hybrid of the family *Cupressaceae* and to one genus of the family *Taxodiaceae*.

The true cypresses are species of the genus *Cupressus* and include Monterey cypress, *Cupressus macrocarpa*, which is a native of California, and *Cupressus lusitanica*, which grows in Central America. Monterey cypress has been widely planted in Australia, New Zealand and East Africa and, on a small scale, in Europe. The timber of *Cupressus sempervirens* is used locally in southern Europe.

Cypress timber is strong and durable and the heartwood is a pleasant yellowish-brown to pinkish-brown colour. When freshly cut the timber has a cedar-like scent.

The timber species of *Chamaecyparis* are Lawson's cypress, *Chamaecyparis lawsoniana*, and Nootka false cypress, *Chamaecyparis nootkatensis*. These two species are also known as Port Orford cedar and yellow cedar respectively and are mentioned above under the heading 'cedar'. They are not very different from the true cypresses and are used for similar purposes.

There is a recent hybrid between Monterey cypress and yellow cypress called Leyland cypress, *Cupressocyparis leylandii*. There are few trees large enough yet to provide timber for testing but the indications are that it will produce a good quality general purpose and joinery timber similar to that of its parents.

Swamp cypress or southern cypress, *Taxodium distichum*, grows in damp and swampy situations in the United States and is planted throughout the world on similar sites. The timber ranges greatly in colour from a pale yellowish-brown on inland sites to a dark reddish-brown on coastal swamps. The darker coloured wood is associated with a better development of summer wood and also with greater durability. The timber works well and is used for general purposes and for joinery.

### Fir

There are about fifty species of the true firs or *Abies* species, all of which grow in the temperate regions of the northern hemisphere.

The timber is generally very pale in colour, ranging from almost white to a pale yellowish- or reddish-brown. The growth rings are easily visible but there is no sharp boundary between early and late wood. Fir timber is very similar in appearance and properties to spruce although it has a somewhat coarser texture and is less lustrous. For commercial purposes fir is often not distinguished from spruce, the two species being marketed as whitewood. Thus in Europe, silver fir, *Abies alba*, is marketed with Norway spruce, *Picea abies*, and in North America balsam fir, *Abies balsamea*, grand fir, *Abies grandis*, and noble fir, *Abies nobilis*, may be included in consignments of spruce or hemlock.

Fir is used for the same purposes as spruce, that is for general carpentry work, packing cases, plywood manufacture and paper making.

The common name of *Pseudotsuga menziesii* (page 128) is Douglas fir but the species is not a true fir.

### Kauri

Kauri, or *Agathis*, is one of the southern hemisphere genera. One commercial species, *Agathis dammara* or East Indian kauri, has a wide distribution in South East Asia. New Zealand kauri, *Agathis australis*, grows in New Zealand, and Queensland kauri, *Agathis robusta*, *A. palmerstonii* and *A. microstachya* has a restricted range in the state of Queensland.

All of the kauri species have a fine, even grain and they are usually of a pale, uniform colour. The most valuable of the group is New Zealand kauri, which is heavier and stronger and darker in colour than the others. It is almost as strong as pitch pine and is used for boat building. All the kauri species are regarded as high quality softwood timbers suitable for construction work, joinery and furniture making.

### Larch

There are about ten species of larch, or *Larix*, all of which grow in the colder regions of the northern hemisphere.

The timber is coarse grained, hard and strong and has a clearly defined heartwood which is usually reddish or brownish in colour. The distinction between spring and summer wood is well marked.

126

## Pine

The name 'pine' is applied to all the species of the genus *Pinus* and also colloquially to the species of several other genera.

The two South American species, *Araucaria angustifolia* and *A. araucana*, are known respectively as Parana pine and Chile pine, and the New Zealand species, *Araucaria cunninghamii*, is known as hoop pine. Three other New Zealand species are also referred to as pines. These are *Podocarpus spicatus*, New Zealand black pine, *Podocarpus dacrydioides*, New Zealand white pine and *Agathis australis*, kauri pine. The Australian species *Agathis robusta*, *A. palmerstonii* and *A. microstachya* are all known as Queensland kauri pine. Douglas fir is sometimes called Columbian or Oregon pine and Norway spruce is known as Swiss pine by musical instrument makers.

The genus *Pinus* is the largest conifer genus and comprises about one hundred species, all of which grow in the northern hemisphere from the extreme north to the tropical uplands. There are about thirty-three species in North America, thirty-five in Central America, twelve in the Mediterranean region, three in northern Europe and western Asia and twenty-five in eastern Asia.

From a botanical point of view the pines are broadly subdivided into hard pines, which bear their needles in bunches of two or three and, occasionally, four, and the soft pines, which bear their needles in bunches of five.

From the timber point of view it is possible to identify three broad categories. These are:

**a)** The pitch pines or three-needled pines
**b** The red deal pines or two-needled pines
**c)** The soft pines or five-needled pines.

The pitch pines from the southern United States and the Caribbean region are the strongest and hardest species of the genus. They have well developed heartwood and a marked contrast between hard, dark, summer wood and softer, paler early wood. Typical examples are *Pinus palustris*, American pitch pine, and *Pinus caribaea*, Caribbean pitch pine.

The red deal pines, which are generally two-needled, are the commonest species and provide most of the pine timber of commerce. The contrast between their heartwood and sapwood and between their spring and summer wood is intermediate between that of the pitch pines and the soft pines. Typical species are Scots pine, *Pinus sylvestris*, which is the principal commercial pine of Europe and western Asia, and Canadian red pine, *Pinus resinosa*, in North America.

The soft pines, as their name implies, generally produce a timber which is softer and paler in colour than the pitch pines or the red deal pines. There is also little difference between the pale heartwood and the sapwood and between the spring and summer wood. Examples of the soft pines are Weymouth or yellow pine, *Pinus strobus* and western white pine, *Pinus monticola*

## Podo

There are about seventy species of trees or shrubs in the genus *Podocarpus*, which is one of the few conifer genera of the southern hemisphere.

About one quarter of all the species occur in Central and South America and there are extensive areas of *Podocarpus* forests in the Andean regions of Chile, Bolivia and Colombia. The most common species in the northern countries of South America and in Central America are *Podocarpus coriaceus*, *Podocarpus montanus* and *Podocarpus oleifolius*. In Chile the name *mañio* is given to the two species *Podocarpus nubigenus* and *Podocarpus salignus*. A third Chilean species of poorer quality is *Podocarpus andenus*.

There are four species in East and southern Africa, *Podocarpus gracilior*, *Podocarpus milanjianus*, *Podocarpus usambarensis* and *Podocarpus ensiculus*, all of which are known as podo.

There are considerable similarities between all these *Podocarpus* timbers. They generally have a fine, even texture and no obvious growth rings. East African podo is a very pale, even-coloured, rather dull looking wood while *mañio*, especially *Podocarpus nubigenus*, is more variable in colour. It is valued in Chile as a timber suitable for carpentry and joinery, furniture making, co-operage and boat building. The strength of these species is similar to that of Baltic redwood.

Of the five New Zealand species of *Podocarpus*, New Zealand white pine, *Podocarpus dacrydioides*, totara, *Podocarpus totara* and *Podocarpus halii*, are typical of the genus while New Zealand black pine, *Podocarpus spicatus* and miro, *Podocarpus ferrugineus*, are harder and heavier and have clearly defined growth rings. They also have, together with totara, a more pronounced yellowish to orange-brown colour. All five species are used for house construction and joinery while totara, which is the only softwood relatively resistant to marine borers, is used for boat building and dock work.

## Spruce

Spruce is a tree of temperate regions of the northern hemisphere. There are almost forty species, nearly half of which are endemic to China.

Spruce timber is soft, odourless and white or very pale in colour. There is little difference between heartwood and sapwood and the contrast between spring and summer wood is not very obvious.

The timber of the various species is very similar, but there are considerable differences in strength and texture according to the age of the tree and the rate of growth. Spruce timber works, finishes and seasons well.

CEDAR; *Cedrus atlantica*; North Africa; *C. libani*; Middle East and *C. deodora*; western Himalayas

The timber from each of the three true cedars is very similar. It is strongly scented and the light brown heartwood is distinct from the paler sapwood. Cedar has a fairly fine, even texture and the spring wood is clearly differentiated from the darker bands of summer wood. Most cedar available in Britain comes from home-grown trees which are often very knotty.

The timber is durable and of moderate strength. Clear timber is easy to work and is traditionally used for making chests and wardrobes because the scent discourages moths. It is also suitable for garden furniture and sheds. Cedar is used in its countries of origin as a general purpose construction and joinery timber.

| | | | |
|---|---|---|---|
| Density | *3* | Stability in service | |
| Bending strength | *4* | *average* | |
| Stiffness | *4* | Hardness | *4* |
| Impact strength | *4* | Durability | *2* |
| | | Blunting effect | *below average* |

DOUGLAS FIR; *Pseudotsuga menziesii*; western North America

The pale reddish-brown heartwood of Douglas fir is easily distinguishable from the light-coloured sapwood. There is a pronounced contrast between spring and summer wood and this produces a characteristic wavy figure on tangential surfaces or rotary cut veneers (Figure 6).

Douglas fir, especially when from the Pacific coastal region, is one of the stronger softwood timbers. It is used for general construction work, interior and exterior joinery, plywood manufacture and paper making.

| | | | |
|---|---|---|---|
| Density | *3* | Stability in service | |
| Bending strength | *2–3* | *above average* | |
| Stiffness | *2* | Hardness | *3* |
| Impact strength | *3–4* | Durability | *3* |
| | | Blunting effect | *slightly above average* |

EUROPEAN LARCH; *Larix decidua* (*europaea*); central and eastern Europe and western Russia

European larch has been widely planted throughout Europe in regions where it is not indigenous. In Britain two similar species, Japanese larch, *Larix leptolepis*, (*kaempferi*) and the hybrid between Japanese and European larch, *Larix eurolepis*, have also been planted extensively.

Apart from yew, European larch is one of the hardest and toughest of the conifers. The pale reddish-brown heartwood contrasts with the light-coloured sapwood and within each growth ring the paler spring wood is clearly differentiated from the darker-coloured and harder summer wood.

The timber tends to distort during seasoning but is stable in use.

Larch is used for posts and stakes, for interwoven fencing and for general purpose industrial use. It is not suitable for pulping because of its colour but good quality larch is used for boat building.

| | | | |
|---|---|---|---|
| Density | *2–3* | Movement in service | |
| Bending strength | *2–3* | *below average* | |
| Stiffness | *3–4* | Hardness | *2* |
| Impact strength | *3–4* | Durability | *3* |
| | | Blunting effect | *average* |

NORWAY SPRUCE; *Picea abies*; Europe and western Russia

Norway spruce, the traditional Christmas tree in Britain, is also known as Baltic, Finnish, Swedish or Russian (etc.) whitewood according to its country of origin.

The timber varies from an almost white to a

pale yellowish-brown colour. The growth rings are distinct but the contrast between spring and summer wood is less abrupt and less pronounced than in pine. There is no visible difference between sapwood and heartwood although the heartwood is more resistant to impregnation.

The timber seasons and works well and is used for building, internal joinery, general carpentry, plywood manufacture and paper making. Slower-grown trees, free from knots, are used for masts, spars and oars and the slow-grown timber from central and eastern Europe, known as Romanian or Swiss pine, is used for making the resonance components of musical instruments.

Norway spruce from Britain is generally too fast grown and too knotty for the higher grade uses but is suitable for construction, general carpentry and paper making.

| | | |
|---|---|---|
| Density | *4* | |
| Bending strength | *3–4* | Stability in service |
| | | *average* |
| Stiffness | *4* | Hardness *4* |
| Impact strength | *4* | Durability *4* |
| | | Blunting effect *below average* |

### PARANA PINE; *Araucaria angustifolia*; Brazil, Paraguay and northern Argentina

Parana pine is a pale brown timber with reddish-coloured streaks. It is straight grained and has a fine, even texture with inconspicuous growth rings. The wood varies in density and quality and only the higher grades are exported.

The wood is very easy to work and takes a fine finish but, despite the variable colour, is somewhat dull in appearance and is more suitable for painting than for natural finishing. It has used in Britain primarily for internal joinery.

| | | |
|---|---|---|
| Density | *3* | |
| Bending strength | *3* | Stability in service |
| | | *average* |
| Stiffness | *4* | Hardness *3–4* |
| Impact strength | *4* | Durability *4* |
| | | Blunting effect *below average* |

### PITCH PINE, AMERICAN; principally *Pinus palustris* and *P. elliottii*; southern United States

The principal American pitch pines, *Pinus palustris* and *P. elliottii*, are known locally as longleaf yellow pine or simply as longleaf. Pitch pine is denser and harder than the other pines and has very sharply differentiated bands of paler, softer spring wood and dense, hard summer wood. The reddish-brown heartwood contrasts with the paler sapwood. The marked differences between spring and summer wood give the timber a coarse-textured appearance.

Being a dense, hard and strong timber pitch pine is used for boat planking, heavy construction work and flooring. It is occasionally used for joinery in public buildings and for furniture, but is not an attractive wood for these purposes.

The name American pitch pine or longleaf yellow pine should be used only for these two species. There are other pines of lower density which grow in the southern States of America. These include *Pinus echinata*, *P. taeda*, *P. rigida* and *P. virginiana*, which should be referred to generically as southern pine.

| | | |
|---|---|---|
| Density | *2* | |
| Bending strength | *2–3* | Stability in service |
| | | *average* |
| Stiffness | *3* | Hardness *3* |
| Impact strength | *4* | Durability *3* |
| | | Blunting effect *average* |

### SCOTS PINE OR BALTIC REDWOOD; *Pinus sylvestris*; Europe and northern Asia

Scots pine has a very wide distribution extending from Spain to northern Norway and eastwards to eastern Siberia. It is known by a variety of names in Great Britain according to the country of origin. These include Baltic, Finnish, Swedish or Polish redwood, while British timber is known as Scots pine.

The pale yellowish or reddish-brown heartwood of Scots pine is darker and more resinous than the sapwood. The paler bands of spring wood are distinct from the darker and harder bands of summer wood. The properties and, to some extent, the appearance of the timber are variable and depend upon the conditions of growth and its geographical origin.

The slow-grown, mature timber from natural forests in northern latitudes has narrow growth rings and small knots; as a consequence it is finer textured, although not necessarily stronger, than younger and faster-grown British timber.

The timber works well although dead knots are sometimes a problem because they are liable to become loose and fall out while the timber is being worked.

Scots pine is the most important general purpose timber in northern Europe. It is used for structural purposes, board and plywood manufacture, pit props, transmission poles and paper making, while the better quality material is used for interior joinery and the manufacture of cottage-style furniture.

| Density | 3 | Stability in service |
|---|---|---|
| Bending strength | 3 | *average* |
| Stiffness | 4 | Hardness 3 |
| Impact strength | 4 | Durability 4 |
| | | Blunting effect *below average* |

*Identification*
The contrast between spring and summer wood is clearly defined but the transition is gradual. Vertical resin cells are present.

## SEQUOIA or CALIFORNIAN REDWOOD; *Sequoia sempervirens*; Oregon to California

Sequois resembles western red cedar in its general properties. The timber varies in colour within the tree from a light red to a dark reddish-brown. It is easily seasoned, is stable and durable in service and is usually straight grained, but sometimes has a curly grain near the base of the tree. The texture varies according to the rate of growth, faster growth resulting in a coarser timber. The wood grown in Britain is usually found to be quite coarse.

Sequoia is not a particularly strong timber but it is durable and is valuable for weather-boarding, internal joinery, greenhouse framing, plywood manufacture, and for the construction of sheds and farm buildings.

| Density | 4 | Stability in service |
|---|---|---|
| Bending strength | 4 | *above average* |
| Stiffness | 4–5 | Hardness 4 |
| Impact strength | 4–5 | Durability 2 |
| | | Blunting effect *below average* |

## WESTERN HEMLOCK; *Tsuga heterophylla*; western North America

Western hemlock is a general purpose softwood timber having no particular characteristics. It is straight grained and has an even texture. The contrast between spring and summer wood is intermediate between that of spruce or fir on the one hand and Douglas fir or pine on the other. The colour of the wood is very pale brown.

Western hemlock is one of the major commercial timbers of North America and is exported throughout the world, the consignments, described as hem/fir, often containing a proportion of fir (*Abies*) species. It is used for general constructional work, utility joinery and pulping.

| Density | 3 | Stability in service |
|---|---|---|
| Bending strength | 3 | *above average* |
| Stiffness | 4 | Hardness 3 |
| Impact strength | 4 | Durability 4 |
| | | Blunting effect *below average* |

## YELLOW or WEYMOUTH PINE; *Pinus strobus*; eastern North America

Weymouth pine is a typical soft pine having an even-textured, soft timber with little contrast between spring and summer wood, or between the sapwood and the heartwood, which is a very pale yellowish or reddish-brown in colour.

The timber is easily worked and is used for pattern-making, the internal components of furniture and interior joinery.

| Density | 4 | Stability in service |
|---|---|---|
| Bending strength | 4 | *above average* |
| Stiffness | 5 | Hardness 4 |
| Impact strength | 5 | Durability 4 |
| | | Blunting effect *below average* |

## YEW; *Taxus baccata*; Europe, North Africa, western Asia and the Himalayas

When freshly cut, yew is a pale-coloured, somewhat streaky looking wood with some superficial resemblance to pine, but it mellows and darkens on exposure to a more uniform golden-brown colour.

The timber is stronger and tougher and more durable, not only than any other conifer, but also than most hardwoods. It has a fine, even texture and a variable grain which depends upon the growth pattern of the tree.

The spring wood merges into a narrow band of sharply defined, darker and harder summer wood. Variation in the width of individual growth rings often produces an irregular figure on tangential surfaces.

Straight-grained timber seasons well but internal stresses are likely to result in fine cracks in parts of a board, especially in areas of faster growth. This cracking, together with the frequent presence of included bark and very wild grain, results in a low recovery of high grade material from sawn planks.

The wood works and bends well, apart from some difficulty with wild grain, and takes a very fine and almost bone-like finish. Provided the grain is reasonably straight it is stable in service.

Yew is one of the finest of all decorative timbers and is used for furniture making (colour plate 31), traditional archery bows, the manufacture of decorative veneers, turnery and carving. Rougher timber is used for gate and fence posts where durability is of importance.

| | | | |
|---|---|---|---|
| Density | 2 | Stability in service | |
| Bending strength | 2 | average | |
| Stiffness | 2 | Hardness | 2 |
| Impact strength | 2 | Durability | 2 |
| | | Blunting effect | average |

# CHAPTER 10
# Panel products and veneers

## Types of panel

Although panel products are not generally associated with craftsmanship there are many uses for them in structural work, joinery and furniture making, and some knowledge of their properties is useful to the craftsman. Apart from veneers there are four main categories of panel products. These are particle board, fibre building board, veneer plywood and core plywood. There is, in addition, a product known as slicewood or presslam, which is not yet produced on a significant commercial scale. There is considerable variation and development within each category, particularly in particle board and fibreboard.

## Demand

Both nationally and internationally the relative importance of panel products in relation to solid timber and to each other is changing from year to year. These changes are likely to become even more marked as a result of technological development and varying price differentials.

At the present time the world consumption of solid structural wood is nearly nine times that of panel products but as recently as 1966 it was thirteen times as great. Table 15, in which for the sake of clarity the figures are rounded to the nearest whole number, is based upon data produced by the Food and Agriculture Organisation of the United Nations. The years between 1966 and 1977 span a period of recession in the mid-seventies but nevertheless give a general indication of current trends. These figures cannot be projected into the future with any precision but they indicate the growing relative importance of panel products and, in particular, the rapidly growing demand for various forms of particle board.

## Dimensions

The dimensions of panels are generally the metric equivalents of 4 × 8ft (1220 × 2440mm) or 5 × 10ft (1525 × 3050mm), but various other sizes are also found, such as the rounded metric sizes of 1220 × 2500mm and 1530 × 2500mm. A large number of thicknesses are available. These differ

**Table 15** *World production of panel products and sawlogs*

| Product | Millions of cubic metres | | | | | | | | | | | | Percentage increase 1966–77 | Annual percentage increase, compound |
|---|---|---|---|---|---|---|---|---|---|---|---|---|---|---|
| | 1966 | 1967 | 1968 | 1969 | 1970 | 1971 | 1972 | 1973 | 1974 | 1975 | 1976 | 1977 | | |
| Veneer sheets | 2 | 3 | 3 | 3 | 3 | 3 | 3 | 4 | 4 | 4 | 4 | 4 | 74 | 5 |
| Plywood | 26 | 27 | 30 | 31 | 33 | 36 | 40 | 42 | 36 | 34 | 39 | 40 | 57 | 4 |
| Particle board | 11 | 13 | 15 | 17 | 19 | 23 | 27 | 32 | 32 | 31 | 35 | 37 | 233 | 12 |
| Fibreboard | 12 | 13 | 14 | 14 | 14 | 16 | 117 | 18 | 17 | 16 | 18 | 18 | 46 | 4 |
| Panel products total | 51 | 56 | 62 | 65 | 69 | 78 | 87 | 96 | 89 | 85 | 96 | 99 | 93 | 6 |
| Softwood saw and veneer logs | 500 | 510 | 530 | 540 | 550 | 570 | 570 | 594 | 570 | 570 | 600 | 620 | 22 | 2 |
| Hardwood saw and veneer logs | 190 | 190 | 190 | 200 | 210 | 210 | 220 | 240 | 230 | 220 | 240 | 250 | 30 | 2 |
| Saw and veneer logs total | 690 | 700 | 720 | 740 | 760 | 780 | 790 | 830 | 800 | 790 | 840 | 870 | 25 | 2 |

from one product to another but are generally in whole millimetres (except the $\frac{1}{8}$in equivalent which is 3.2mm) and normally within the range of 3.2–30mm. If the thickness of a board is a critical factor it should be checked, because there are sometimes discrepancies between actual thickness and nominal thickness.

## Particle board

### Wood chipboard

The most familiar and readily available particle board is known as wood chipboard or simply as chipboard and it is made of small, graded wood chips mixed with an adhesive, usually urea formaldehyde, and pressed into flat sheets. The individual chips are aligned in all directions but predominantly in the same plane as the surface of the board.

Single-layer particle board is homogenous in structure, three-layer board has finer and denser surfaces with a coarser core, while graded density board has a fine texture on the surfaces which becomes progressively coarser towards the centre.

Until recently particle board was unsuitable for outside use but some manufacturers are now using phenol formaldehyde and melamine formaldehyde glues to produce a moisture resistant, exterior grade particle board. Board is also produced with a range of coatings such as resin film, metal foil, wood veneers, plastic laminates, fire resistant coats, paper foil and thin films of PVC. There is a growing use of particle board for flooring, and special tongued-and-grooved flooring panels are now being produced.

### New developments in particle board

There are several new types of particle board which have considerably greater structural strength than chipboard:

**a**) *Flakeboard*
Flakeboard is composed of randomly orientated thin wafers of wood each up to about 50mm (2in) square and up to 1mm thick, aspen being favoured for this product. Flakeboard requires less glue in its manufacture than conventional chipboard and its strength is somewhere between that of conventional chipboard and oriented strand board. This product is easily obtainable.

**b**) *Oriented strand board* (OSB)
Oriented strand board is made of wood flakes – so far of conifers – about 70mm (3in) long, 5–10mm

$(\frac{3}{16} - \frac{13}{32}$in) wide and 0.3–0.5mm $(\frac{1}{25} - \frac{1}{50}$in) thick. These are oriented electrostatically into a three-layer board, the flakes in each layer being oriented predominantly in the same direction and the layers being oriented at right angles to each other. OSB may thus be regarded as a cross between wood chipboard and plywood which approaches plywood in strength. A number of different adhesives are used according to the type of finished board. Urea formaldehyde is used for interior panels and melamine/urea or, occasionally, phenol formaldehyde for exterior board. OSB is not readily available in Britain.

**c**) *Glass fibre reinforced board*
Glass fibre reinforced chipboard is similar in principle to reinforced concrete, the glass fibre providing tensile strength in the same way that steel does in concrete. It has two major disadvantages, however: it is expensive, and it cannot easily be cut to size on site. This product is not yet commercially available in Britain.

### Properties of particle board

The properties of particle board are little affected by the species of wood used in their manufacture but they are greatly influenced by the shape, size and orientation of the individual wood particles.

All particle board is denser than most softwoods but the modulus of rupture of chipboard, which is the same in all directions, is much less than that of plywood, blockboard or wood (parallel with the grain) of comparable dimensions. Flakeboard has greater tensile strength than chipboard while orientated strand board is very much stronger than chipboard but less strong than plywood.

Chipboard is relatively stable in the plane of the board but expands considerably in thickness with increase in moisture content, and if urea formaldehyde board is subjected over a period of time to high humidity it suffers a permanent and considerable loss in strength which is not recovered after drying. Phenol and melamine/phenol boards lose very little strength as a result of increasing moisture content and they expand only about half as much in thickness as urea formaldehyde board for a given increase in moisture content.

If one side of a board is veneered it is liable to bow with changes in moisture content and unless it is held rigidly in position a backing veneer is needed to maintain stability.

Chipboard tends to creep under a sustained load. It is rather crumbly to work but it can be sawn, planed on the edge, bored and sanded. It cannot satisfactorily be planed to thickness and it does not hold nails or screws well, especially near the edge. There are, however, special particle board screws which hold relatively strongly. Cutting tools are quickly blunted by the hard adhesives. It has very good gluing characteristics and a strong edge-to-edge or face joint can be made with glue alone. The face should be lightly sanded before gluing to remove the surface glaze.

The role of osb is not yet entirely clear. It is stronger and more expensive than chipboard but weaker and less expensive than plywood. It is superior to chipboard in such load-bearing situations as flooring, shelving, large table tops and bench seats but where strength is a critical factor it is inferior to plywood and for many joinery and furniture units it is unnecessarily strong.

## Fibre building board

There are three main categories of fibre building board:

a) *Unglued, compressed board*: hardboard and medium board.
b) *Unglued, uncompressed board*: insulating (or soft) board.
c) *Glued, compressed board*: medium density fibre-board, MDF.

### Unglued, compressed board

The category of unglued, compressed board comprises tempered and standard hardboard and high and low density medium board (Figure 82).

All these types of board are made by subjecting wood fibres to steam heat and pressure to form a medium to dark brown, dense, sheet material. Normally no glue is used in the process but a water repellent, such as size, is generally added and sometimes also phenol formaldehyde to give additional strength. The fibres are usually wet pressed against a mesh and this gives the characteristic mesh pattern on the reverse side of the sheet. Some hardboard and medium board is made with dry fibres for which a mesh is unnecessary and the board is consequently smooth on both sides. This is known as duo-board.

Standard hardboard is the most widely used board and is denser than chipboard. Tempered hardboard, which is made by impregnating standard board with oils or resins during the

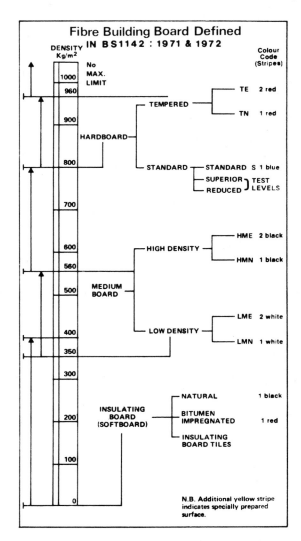

82 Categories of fibre building board

manufacturing process, is stronger and more water resistant than standard hardboard. The medium boards are less dense and weaker than the hardboards. They are also less dense than chipboard.

Hardboard and medium board can be planed on the edges, sawn, drilled and sanded. They are rather wooly to work and should be sawn from the face side and supported close to the saw cut because they tend to tear away from the lower side. The boards are flexible and are often used as panel materials supported on a wooden frame. They are stable in service but will distort if their moisture content changes to a significant degree after they are fixed in position. They should, therefore, be conditioned before use. For most internal situations this is done by leaving the board for several days in the conditions of temperature and humidity that it will experience in service. If tempered or standard hardboard is to be used in unheated buildings or in damp situations it should be conditioned with water according to the manufacturer's instructions.

## Unglued, uncompressed board

Insulating board is a soft board which, as its name implies, is used primarily for thermal insulation. It is sometimes used as a notice board because drawing pins can easily be pushed into it with the fingers.

### Variants

There are at the present time eleven variants of hardboard, medium board and insulating board:

| VARIANT | BOARD TYPE |
|---|---|
| *Pulp and ivory surfaced* <br> Having a finely ground surface layer | standard <br> medium <br> insulating |
| *Primed* <br> Primed ready for painting | standard <br> insulating |
| *Painted, enamelled and lacquered* <br> A painted surface normally heat cured | standard <br> medium <br> insulating <br> tempered |
| *Surface laminated* <br> Surface finishes include melamine laminates, PVC, paper and metal foils and fabrics. There is usually a laminate on the reverse face to prevent warping | standard <br> insulating |
| *Woodgrain effect* <br> A woodgrain effect is achieved either by painting and sealing or by gluing on a woodgrain laminate | standard |
| *Moulded and embossed* <br> A variety of surface patterns can be produced during manufacture. These include reeded, leather grain, stone and brick | standard |
| *Duo-faced* <br> Boards which are smooth on both sides | standard <br> medium <br> tempered |
| *Perforated* <br> Boards with regularly spaced holes for acoustic or decorative effects | standard <br> insulating <br> tempered |
| *Flame retardant* <br> Boards can be made flame retardant either by the addition of chemicals during manufacture or subsequently by the application of flame retardant paints | standard <br> medium <br> insulating |
| *Oil treated* <br> A surface treatment to retard, for a limited period, the absorption of water. | standard <br> medium |

## Glued, compressed board

There is a relatively new type of fibreboard known as MDF board. The initials stand for Medium Density Fibreboard, but the board is not the same thing as the medium board described above. MDF is made by a dry-forming process in which the wood fibres are dried and coated with a synthetic resin, usually urea formaldehyde, before being formed into a continuous mat and then compressed to the desired thickness in a hot press.

The density of the standard MDF board is 480–560kg per cu. m (30–35lb per cu. ft) but denser grades are available up to 880kg per cu. m (55lb per cu. ft). The board is hard and homogeneous in texture and density. The fine texture gives a very smooth surface for grain printing, laminating, staining or painting and it can be machined like wood when an edge moulding is required.

## Veneer plywood

Plywood is made by gluing wood veneers (usually an odd number) in alternate directions, almost always at right angles to each other. It can be made from a wide variety of hardwood and softwood timber species. The variables in plywood are the species composition, the number of plies or thickness, the surface quality and finish, and the type of glue.

Different countries use a variety of identification marks to differentiate the various categories and qualities of plywood. The system used by the American Plywood Association can be taken as an example, although at the time of writing (1981) the APA is planning to introduce a new classification based not upon a description of the product but upon performance standards.

In the present descriptive system five species groups are recognised, Group 1 comprising the strongest timbers and Group 5 the weakest. The surfaces are described by the letters A to D, A being the highest quality and D the lowest. Plywood classified as AA has two high quality surfaces while DD grades are used for rough work where appearance is of little importance. An AD grade is suitable for panelling if one side is permanently hidden. For interior plywood the inner plies are usually D grade while for exterior plywood, where durability is more important, the knots, knotholes and small splits which are permitted in D grade plies are not acceptable and the interior plies are usually C grade.

Apart from the decorative timbers which may be used for the A grade plies of interior quality plywood, various surface patterns are available. These include etched, streaked, grooved and lined finishes.

Interior plywood is usually glued with urea formaldehyde and exterior grades always with phenol formaldehyde.

A typical example of an APA plywood classification is shown in Figure 83.

Plywood has a greater strength to weight ratio than steel and is almost as strong laterally as longitudinally, particularly in thicker sizes. It is stable in both planes, the greater the number of plies the greater being the stability. Taking an average figure, the movement from an oven-dry condition to complete saturation is about 0.2 per cent, so that a 2m (6ft 7in) length (or width) of plywood would expand by about 4mm ($\frac{3}{16}$in).

**83** APA plywood classification

Under normal service conditions the movement of plywood is virtually negligible.

Plywood holds nails and screws well, especially in the surface faces, and is easy to glue. Thick plywood can be jointed like solid wood. It tends to tear away on the lower surface when being sawn but this can be prevented by scoring a line with a marking knife and sawing just outside it.

## Core plywood

### Blockboard

Blockboard consists of a core of wooden strips of equal width and thickness laid longitudinally, usually glued edge-to-edge with urea formaldehyde, and sandwiched between two or four sheets of veneer (Figure 84).

The sheets of veneer are usually all laid with their grain at right angles to that of the strips (Figure 84(a)) but five-ply boards can be obtained with two adjacent sheets of veneer laid with their grain at right angles to each other and with the outer sheet running parallel with or at right angles to the strips (Figure 84(b) and (c)).

The individual strips are about 25mm (1in) wide and they are usually made from softwood species. Most European blockboard is faced with birch but various surface finishes are available. These include decorative veneers of such species as oak, sapele, khaya and teak, phenolic film overlays and decorative plastic laminates.

Blockboard has properties similar to those of a solid conifer board but is more stable, particularly across the grain. It can be jointed, although not very elegantly, and it holds screws strongly in both the surfaces and edges. It is, therefore, suitable for the construction of flush doors and fitted utility furniture.

The strength of blockboard depends more upon the surface veneer than upon the core strips, so it is stronger and stiffer parallel with the veneers than parallel with the core. This feature is more marked with thinner than with thicker boards, the strength of which is more nearly equal in each direction.

The boards which are strongest parallel with the external grain, but weakest across the grain, are those with two surface veneers laid at right angles to each other. This is because the external veneer is reinforcing the longitudinal strength of the core.

Softwood of comparable thickness is generally stronger than blockboard parallel with the grain

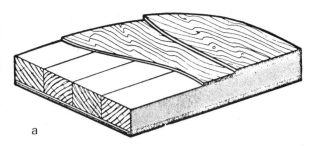

a

standard five-ply blockboard
all veneers with their grain direction at
right-angles to the length of the core
strips

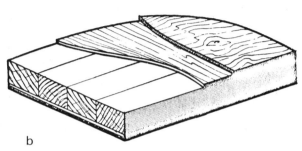

b

five-ply cross-banded blockboard with face
veneer parallel with core strips
( five-ply cross—banded laminboard similar)

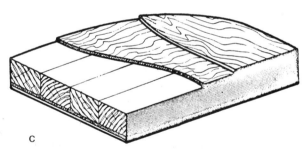

c

five-ply cross-banded blockboard with face
veneer perpendicular to core strips

84 Types of blockboard

but weaker and more liable to movement across the grain. Blockboard is stronger than chipboard but weaker and less stable than plywood. When three-ply blockboard is painted, especially with high gloss paint, the longitudinal pattern of the core material tends to show through the surface veneer. This does not happen with five-ply board.

### Laminboard

Laminboard is a form of high quality blockboard. The core strips are only about 7mm ($\frac{9}{32}$in) wide and they are more often made from hardboard species than those of blockboard (Figure 85).

The various configurations of the surface veneers are the same as for blockboard but laminboard is denser, more stable and a little stronger than blockboard. It is also appreciably more expensive and can be obtained with phenol formaldehyde glue for external use.

85 Laminboard

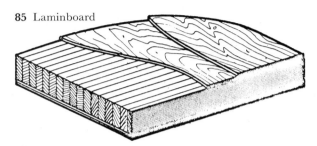

Standard five-ply laminboard all veneers
with their grain direction at right-angles to
the length of the core strips

### Plywood-faced particle board

A comparatively recent development is a five-ply composite product having a particle board core and a two-ply plywood skin on each face. This board is stronger than particle board and cheaper than plywood and has a high quality surface for painting and varnishing.

## Slicewood or presslam

New developments in peeling or slicing have made it possible to cut veneers or slices up to 25mm (1in) in thickness. Such veneers or slices can be glued together to make thick-section timber either by parallel or right-angled laminating. The object of this process, which is barely past the development stage, is to distribute any features such as large knots, over a larger area and to make it possible to manufacture large structural members from relatively small logs.

## The relative properties of panel products

There are considerable variations within each type of panel product and this makes it difficult to

137

compare them. By taking average categories of each type, however, some very broad but valid comparisons can be made and these are summarised in table 16. The values are based on the assumption that all the products are of equal thickness and data for Scandinavian fifth grade softwood are given for comparison. The relative prices of the various products are given in Table 21 (page 151).

**Table 16** *The properties of panel products*

| as panel materials | Stability* | | relative tensile strength |
|---|---|---|---|
| | Longi-tudinal | trans-verse | 1 = very low 5 = very high |
| Plywood (3mm) | 0.13 | 0.16 | 4 |
| Hardboard (3.2mm) | 0.23 | 0.25 | 2 |
| Chipboard (3.2mm) | 0.30 | 0.32 | 2 |
| 3.2mm = $\frac{1}{8}$in | | | |
| **as structural materials** (18mm, $\frac{11}{16}$in) | | | |
| Softwood (parallel with grain) | 0.15 | 2.50 | 5 |
| Plywood | 0.15 | 0.15 | 5 |
| Chipboard | 0.31 | 0.32 | 2 |
| Blockboard | 0.21 | 0.13 | 3 |
| Laminboard | 0.19 | 0.09 | 4 |

* percentage movement for a change in relative humidity from 35 per cent to 85 per cent.

There are three materials which can be used as thin panels. Of these plywood is the strongest, but it is also the most expensive. Hardboard and chipboard are comparable both in strength and price, but hardboard is the more stable. There is no reason to use plywood, therefore, unless strength and stability are important factors.

For structural purposes the choice lies between softwood timber, thick plywood, thick chipboard, blockboard or laminboard. Softwood (parallel with the grain) and plywood are comparable in strength and stability but plywood is very much stronger and more stable in the transverse plane. It is also more expensive. These two materials are considerably stronger than chipboard or blockboard and marginally stronger than laminboard, which is the most expensive. For most types of framing, softwood timber has the advantages of strength, relative cheapness and versatility. Where strength is not a particular advantage, chipboard is the most economical material. Blockboard and laminboard are particularly suitable for the construction of unframed doors.

The use of plywood is only justified where strength and stability in two planes are of particular importance.

## Veneers

Veneering has been a feature of high class cabinet making for over three hundred years and fine veneers have been used to achieve decorative effects which it would be impossible to obtain by any other means. As high class timber becomes increasingly expensive veneers are also being used for reasons of economy.

Veneers for decoration or marquetry are almost always obtained by slicing a log tangentially or radially. This is in contrast to the industrial veneers used for plywood or blockboard manufacture which are cut peripherally by rotating the veneer log against a fixed cutter.

For decorative veneers the log is sliced according to a predetermined pattern and the veneers then reassembled in their original position in the log. This enables matching sheets to be located for subsequent use. The pattern illustrated in Figure 86 is adopted for species having a more decorative figure on tangential than radial surfaces. The central core is not used at all, while the radial portion is sold separately as an inferior product having a less decorative figure.

Decorative veneers were formerly cut to a thickness of about 0.7mm. Today, partly due to rising prices and partly to technological developments, they are generally between 0.5mm and 0.6mm in thickness although American veneers

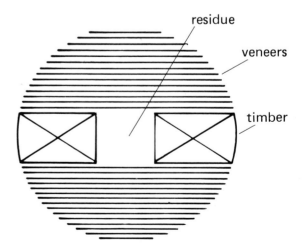

**86** Tangentially cut veneers

are usually somewhat thicker. Some veneers produced in Japan are as thin as 0.3mm. These have to be handled very carefully, both before and after gluing, because sandpapering can cut right through them.

Rotary peeled veneers for plywood cores are considerably thicker and range from 1.6–3.2mm in thickness.

Table 17 lists a range of high quality veneers currently available.

**Table 17** *Commercially available decorative veneers*

| Species | Botanical name | Trade name | Price range |
|---|---|---|---|
| abura | *Mitragyna ciliata* | | M |
| afrormosia | *Pericopsis elata* | | L |
| afzelia | *Afzelia* spp. | doussie | L |
| Agba | *Gossweilerodendron balsamiferum* | | L |
| ash | *Fraxinus excelsior* | | M |
| aspen | *Populus tremula* | | M |
| avodire | *Turraeanthus africanus* | | M |
| beech | *Fagus sylvatica* | | L |
| cedar, cigar box | *Cedrela odorata* | Honduras cedar | M |
| cherry | *Prunus* spp | fruit cherry | M |
| ebony, East Indian | *Diospyros celebica* | Macassar ebony | H |
| elm | *Ulmus* spp | | M |
| guarea | *Guarea cedrata* | Nigerian pear | L |
| idigbo | *Terminalia ivorensis* | | L |
| iroko | *Chlorophora excelsa* | | L |
| mahogany, African | *Khaya ivorensis* | | L |
| mahogany, American | *Swietenia macrophylla* | Honduras mahogany | L |
| maple | *Acer* spp | | M |
| oak | *Quercus* spp | | L |
| oak, brown | *Quercus* spp | | H |
| olive, East African | *Olea hochstetteri* | tropical olive | L |
| paldao | *Dracontomelum dao* | | M |
| rosewood, Brazilian | *Dalbergia nigra* | Rio rosewood | H |
| rosewood, Indian | *Dalbergia latifolia* | Bombay rosewood | H |
| rosewood, San Domingan | *Dalbergia retusa* | | H |
| sapele | *Entandrophragma cylindricum* | | L |
| sycamore | *Acer pseudoplatanus* | | M |
| teak | *Tectona grandis* | | M |
| walnut, African | *Lovoa trichilioides* | | L |
| walnut, American black | *Juglans nigra* | | M/H |
| walnut, European | *Juglans regia* | French walnut | M/H |
| walnut, Queensland | *Endiandra palmerstonii* | Australian walnut | M |
| zebrano | *Brachystegia fleuryana* | | M |
| cedar of Lebanon | *Cedrus libani* | | M |
| Douglas fir | *Pseudosuga menziesii* | Oregon pine | M |
| yew | *Taxus baccata* | | H |

## CHAPTER 11
# Crafts and industries

## Furniture making

It is difficult to review briefly, even for one country, the timber species used in cabinet making over the centuries because different species were used for different types of furniture, and as a wider range of timber became available fashion influenced the high quality, sophisticated furniture but not the vernacular tradition. In the middle ages, for example, oak was almost the only species used for furniture making for all classes of society in Britain, but by the end of the seventeenth century it was rarely used for fashionable work although it continued to be used in country districts.

Isolated examples of a new species may antedate its more general introduction by fifty years or more. Mahogany, for example, was not widely used in Britain until about 1730, although there are occasional examples of mahogany furniture dating from about 1670.

### Cabinet making

Cabinet making developed from the craft of coffering or chest making. The early chests were of cleft or sawn oak and were not jointed but held together by wooden pins or metal brackets. Mortice-and-tenon frames enclosing wooden panels were not generally made before the sixteenth century. The craft of cabinet making was greatly stimulated in England by the restoration court of Charles II when the King and his exiled supporters returned with new ideas from France and Holland.

It is convenient to recognise three classes of wood used for cabinet making. These are first, the major structural species, secondly, the minor structural species and thirdly, the rarer decorative species used almost entirely for inlaying and veneering.

Of the major species oak was the dominant timber until the latter part of the seventeenth century. It then declined in relative importance and became a utility or rural species until the nineteenth century when it was widely used for furnishing the churches, public buildings and houses of the gothic revival period.

The first of the important fashionable species was walnut, which is first recorded in English furniture at the end of the Tudor period although it had been introduced earlier in Italy and France. It was not widely used, however, until the latter part of the seventeenth century and it became the principal high quality furniture timber throughout the reigns of William and Mary, Queen Anne and George I. A dovetailed walnut chest has been found in the Mary Rose which sank in 1545. It seems probable that this chest was made in France or Italy.

Mahogany from Cuba and Honduras is recorded as having been used in Spain as early as 1514 but first appeared in England as a rarity in about 1670. It was not in common use until after 1730 when it rapidly succeeded walnut as the major furniture timber. Mahoganies from Central and South America have retained their high reputation, but towards the end of the nineteenth century they were supplemented by various species of *Khaya* from Africa.

A taste for lighter-coloured and more delicate furniture developed in the later decades of the eighteenth century. This fashion coincided with the availability of West Indian satinwood, which was first introduced in about 1750. Satinwood continued to be a popular furniture timber throughout the Regency period but declined in relative importance after about 1820. During the Victorian period, and later, Ceylon satinwood was also used for cabinet making.

The first rosewood furniture was made in Britain in about 1750 but this species was not in general use until towards the end of the century. It remained an important, high quality furniture species throughout the nineteenth century but in recent times has become so expensive that it is rarely used except as a veneer.

Species of major importance which were introduced during the nineteenth century include the various African mahoganies, sapele, teak and iroko. Most of the more recently introduced species have been general purpose rather than furniture timbers, but some high quality species such as afrormosia and mansonia first appeared in Britain after World War II.

A number of species, most of which are native, have been used on a relatively small scale for cabinet making for many centuries. Examples of elm, beech, ash, sweet chestnut, yew, pine, cedar, apple and pear furniture survive from the seventeenth century but some of these species, especially elm, beech, ash and yew were probably used before then.

The more unusual woods used for decoration include holly, which is found in some Tudor furniture, sycamore, kingwood, elm burr, ebony and lignum vitae from the seventeenth century and padauk, thuja, tulipwood, laburnum and amboyna from the eighteenth century. Harewood, which is sycamore stained a greyish-green colour with an iron oxide, was first used in the late seventeenth century. A jewel box made for Queen Charlotte in 1761 has a mahogany frame with padauk veneers and amboyna panels.

A most unusual early introduction was identified in a chest made in about 1630 in Holland, which was found by wood scientists of the Victoria and Albert Museum to have drawer sides made of eucalyptus. This discovery cast doubts at first upon its authenticity but the provenance of the chest was established beyond doubt. It is apparent, therefore, that the eucalyptus was a very early introduction from the Dutch East Indies. Three species of *Eucalyptus* – *E. alba*, *E. deglupta* and *E. urophylla* – occur in Timor, New Guinea and the eastern part of the Indonesian archipelago, all at sea level, and they could well have been obtained by an early Dutch trader.

The history of cabinet making followed a different pattern in the USA from that in Britain, although many of the styles were influenced by English furniture. The principal species, like mahogany and rosewood, were imported into the USA during the eighteenth and nineteenth centuries but there was also a widespread use of the rich variety of regional species, such as walnut, elm, maple, ash, cherry and white oak.

## Chair making

During the middle ages chairs were made either by cofferers or by turners and the two crafts remained quite distinct until the seventeenth century. The turned chair tradition survives to the present day in the Chilterns, which is the home of the windsor chair.

Coffered or framed chairs were almost always made of oak, until the introduction of walnut in the seventeenth century and mahogany and rosewood in the eighteenth century.

The strength of the timber is more critical for chairs than for other forms of furniture and particularly for turned chairs, the legs of which were almost always made of oak, beech or yew or sometimes of birch or ash and the seats of elm, or more rarely of oak.

## Present day requirements

The timber qualities required for furniture making are a decorative appearance, adequate strength, stability and, of course, availability. These requirements explain the long-term pre-eminence of such species as oak, walnut, mahogany, rosewood and teak. There are, however, differences between the criteria of the commercial manufacturer and the craftsman.

The commercial manufacturer is rather more influenced by public opinion than the craftsman and this explains the periodic changes in fashion from light to dark or red to brown timbers. He also depends upon an assured and regular supply of a consistent product and requires a timber which can be easily seasoned, probably in a kiln, and which is relatively easy to work, glue and finish. The craftsman, on the other hand, is more interested in decorative and unusual species and he is better able to deal with a variable product, even if it is at times somewhat refractory.

Many craftsmen today prefer native species such as ash, cherry, walnut, sycamore, oak and yew. Yew is expensive and can be difficult to work but is one of the finest of all furniture timbers. English oak is tougher and harder to work than imported European, American or Japanese oak but is considered to have more character. Fruitwoods such as mulberry, pear or apple are also highly prized. One of the finest of all British grown species is laburnum, the temperate 'rosewood', but it is very rarely obtainable in sufficient sizes for furniture making.

Of the imported timbers the current (1980) preference is for dark rather than pale timbers and brown or reddish brown rather than red. Despite their excellent intrinsic properties teak and iroko are not very popular. Rio and Indian rosewoods are highly regarded and American mahogany is preferred to African mahogany or sapele.

### Seasoning

Commercial manufacturers always kiln dry their timber to a predetermined moisture content although some adopt a two-stage process, with a preliminary period of air drying followed by a final stage in the kiln. A rule of thumb which is often followed is to allow one year of air drying for each 25mm (1in) of thickness.

Craftsmen almost invariably air dry their timber. They, too, often allow one year in the open, but under cover, for each 25mm (1in) of thickness. The timber is then stored indoors in a warm dry atmosphere followed by a period in a room having the same conditions that the finished furniture will experience in service. The yew for the desk illustrated in colour plate 31 was sawn into 32mm (1¼in) planks and stored in a dry stable for two years. It was then planed approximately to size and stored in a centrally heated room for a further year. Most craftsmen prefer their timber to be sawn initially to the approximate working thickness. If thick, partly seasoned blanks are sliced into thinner sections there is likely to be further movement and distortion (pages 27 and 30).

## Carving

As with turnery, the wood qualities needed for carving depend upon the type of work to be done. Broadly speaking, wood may be used as a medium for creating shapes, or carving may be a means of exploiting the natural beauty of wood.

If wood is used primarily as a raw material like clay or stone, rather than as a material of natural beauty, the requirement is for an even coloured, fine textured, stable timber which can be cut easily in all planes, which can be fashioned in sharp detail and which takes a fine finish. The outstanding species of this type are American lime, or basswood, and European lime, the wood used by Grinling Gibbons. Very fast-grown wood is inferior in quality but the slower-grown material fulfils all the requirements of workability. Jelutong is another easily worked timber which is often used by wood-carving students. Other species which can be cut with fine detail

and which take a good finish are pear, apple, boxwood, holly, plane, hornbeam, hawthorn and Australian blackwood. Most of them, however, are harder to work than lime.

There are several coarser-textured species which are suitable for a somewhat bolder treatment. These include oak, sweet chestnut, elm and teak.

The wood carver is as often concerned with the material he is using as with the shapes he creates from it, and in the hands of a craftsman the material and the subject are closely related.

There are many species which have a fine figure and which are sufficiently workable and stable to be used by wood carvers. Straight-grained yew cuts quite easily and takes a fine bone-like finish, but is rather brittle for very precise work. American mahogany is another handsome wood which works well. The rosewoods, despite their hardness and moderately coarse texture, can be given a fine finish and their decorative value repays the effort required to work them. The related laburnum is very hard to carve but like the rosewoods has a high decorative value and takes a beautiful polish.

## Housebuilding

The traditional timbers for housebuilding in Britain were oak and, in some regions, elm. Rather surprisingly sweet chestnut has rarely been used although it has been available since Roman times and has many of the desirable properties of oak. Elm is more often found where particularly long beams have been required. In more recent times softwoods have been the principal building timbers and a wide variety of species has been used. The principal timbers in Europe are Scots pine and Norway spruce but silver fir and a number of North American species have also been used. These include Sitka spruce, western hemlock and balsam fir and, for better quality work, Douglas fir. None of the commonly used softwood timbers has much natural durability and it is therefore desirable, and in some regions a statutory requirement, that they should be adequately impregnated with a preservative after having been cut to size.

Hardwood building components such as sills and window frames are sometimes made of teak or iroko but more often of the cheaper merantis, serayas or lauans.

## Joinery

The timbers selected for joinery, and especially for decorative panelling, doors and fittings, are usually the same as those chosen for furniture making. Owing to the quantities involved, however, the more expensive timbers have not often been used except, in more recent years, as veneers. The most widely utilised species have been oak and the mahoganies, but a very wide range of general purpose decorative hardwoods, and occasionally conifers, has been used for interior panelling and fittings. Sweet chestnut, for example, which is an undervalued species, was used very effectively for the internal joinery in the new London Museum.

For painted or utility work the requirements are consistency of product, stability and workability. This implies a straight grain, relatively few knots of small to moderate size, fairly slow growth and careful sawing and packaging. Many species are suitable, most of them being conifers. These include Scots pine, Norway spruce, silver fir, Sitka spruce, western hemlock, Douglas fir and Parana pine. In the southern hemisphere various species of *Podocarpus and Agathis* are regarded as high quality joinery species.

If there is a pronounced differentiation between spring and summer wood in a particular species, fast growth is not acceptable because the spring wood shrinks more than the summer wood and produces a corrugated surface which is visible through paint.

There is an increasing use of panel products in general purpose joinery, and decorative veneers are sometimes used in the highest quality work.

## Musical instruments

Craftsmen working in different regions and at different periods have not always chosen the same species for particular purposes, with the result that there are usually several alternatives for each purpose. On the one hand the choice has widened as more species have become available on the world markets; on the other hand the choice has sometimes been reduced as species have become less freely available as a result of scarcity, increasing cost, or political barriers to trade.

In a brief survey, therefore, it is possible to mention only the more important species and the reasons for their choice.

There are three principal types of musical instrument made of wood: stringed, keyboard and woodwind instruments.

### *Stringed instruments*

Despite their obvious differences there is much in common in the methods of construction of such stringed instruments as violins, violas, double-basses, guitars and lutes and the materials and methods have changed little over the centuries.

The belly or front of the instrument is the soundboard and requires a wood with good resonance qualities. This was traditionally Norway spruce from central Europe and is known in the trade as Swiss pine. For most of this century, however, much of the Swiss pine has been obtained from the Carpathian mountains in Romania where great attention is paid to the selection of straight trees having a slow and regular rate of growth. A Romanian forester has recently said that there are seventy-six visible characteristics which can indicate the quality of the 'resonance' timber in a tree. The favoured width of annual ring is not more than 2mm ($\frac{3}{32}$in) for the larger instruments and rather less than this for the smaller instruments such as violins.

Violin makers refer to the darker, denser summer wood as the reeds of the wood and although they choose slow-grown timber, they look for wood in which the softer, early wood is wider than the late wood. This gives a high ratio between stiffness along, as compared with that across, the grain. Experience has shown that the best violin wood has a stiffness ratio of about ten to twelve along the grain compared with one across the grain.

The bottom 2.5m (8ft) or so of the tree are regarded as inferior because they are more likely to contain compression wood or other internal stresses. Radial, wedge-shaped slices are cut or, better, cleaved from the tree, each one large enough to make one belly. The reason for cleaving is to make sure that the direction of grain is parallel, in both planes, with the long axis of the instrument. After seasoning they are cut or cleaved in half, trued, and glued back to back with a rubbed joint (Figure 87).

Although some of the subtleties of the Romanian forester's criteria may have no great practical significance, the slow and evenly-grown spruce has some particular qualities which make it supremely suitable for its purpose. The ratio of its modulus of easticity to density is high, giving it strength and stiffness without weight. Experience

143

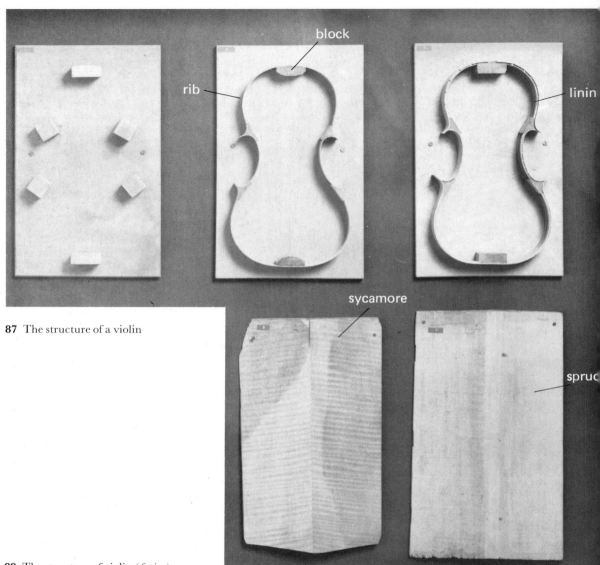

**87** The structure of a violin

**88** The structure of violin (*facing*)

has also shown that the resonance of the spruce belly of the instrument is compatible with that of the hardwood back. Some other spruce species are sometimes used, especially Sitka spruce, and it is possible that carefully selected Sitka spruce, or indeed other species of spruce, would be little different from Norway spruce.

Sycamore and Norway maple are the most favoured and commonly used species for the back and ribs (sides) of the violin type of instrument. These are chosen partly for their technical resonance qualities and partly for aesthetic reasons because some sycamore and maple trees have well-defined undulating grain in the radial plane. The wood from such trees is highly prized and is known as fiddle-back maple. Fruitwood such as apple or pear, beech and occasionally poplar and willow have been used instead of sycamore; American maples have also been used to make fine instruments, but the European maples are generally considered to be the best for the purpose.

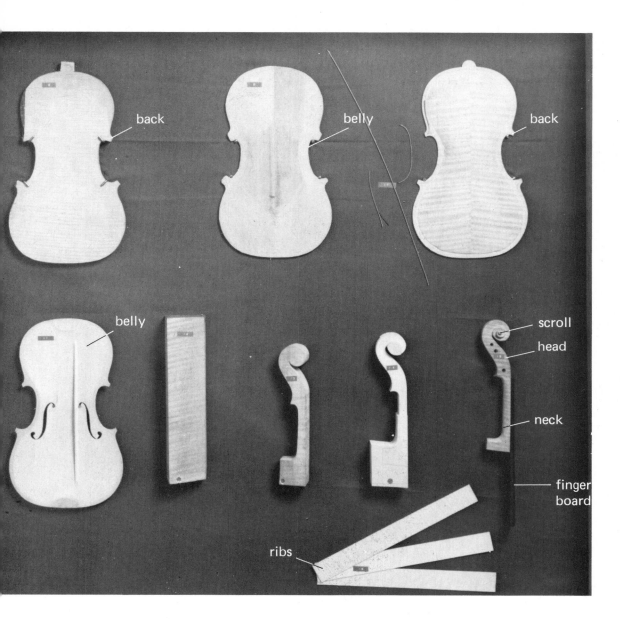

The internal blocks which are used to strengthen the two ends and the four angles of the violin are usually made of spruce, but willow or cedar are sometimes used. The sound post, which is wedged between the back and belly, is always made of spruce.

The thin ribs of the stringed instruments are strengthened along each edge by a lining of spruce, willow, lime or beech, which also provides an additional surface for gluing the belly and back to the ribs (Figure 88).

The neck, head and scroll of the violin-type of instrument are fashioned from one piece of wood, which is almost invariably sycamore or Norway maple. The finger board which lies beneath the strings has to be very hard, to resist indentation when the strings are pressed against the wood by the player. African ebony is universally used, although some makers, including Stradivarius, have used ebony veneer on a lighter wood, such as maple or beech. Stained box or holly and rosewood have also been used for the finger board.

Boxwood, ebony and rosewood are considered to be the best species for the pegs, which have to be very hard and smooth.

Guitars have traditionally been made of the same materials as violins but the backs and ribs are now usually made of Indian or, preferably, Rio rosewood. Various species, such as African mahogany, western red cedar and pencil cedar, have been used for the neck but American mahogany, *Swietenia macrophylla*, which combines stability and strength with lightness, is regarded as the best choice. The finger board is usually ebony or rosewood.

The body of an electric guitar has little effect on the tone and so stability and strength, coupled with reasonable lightness, are the principal criteria. Rock maple and mahogany are commonly used for the body and rosewood for the finger board.

Lutes and similar instruments were traditionally made with spruce sound boards and sycamore or fruitwood backs, and modern reproductions are made in the same way.

### Keyboard instruments

The early keyboard instruments are the clavicord, spinet, virginal and harpsichord, which were in use in one form or another by the early sixteenth century. The piano appeared in something like its modern form early in the eighteenth century.

A variety of species have been used for the casings of all these instruments, including poplar, lime, pine, cedar, cypress, sycamore, walnut and mahogany.

Today, some makers do not consider the casing to be an important acoustic component and various forms of veneer on a solid plywood or chipboard core are used instead of solid wood for the lower quality harpsichords. The casings of grand pianos are usually laminated into shape and then veneered.

The soundboard is almost always made of spruce, the slow grown resonance wood from central Europe being preferred, but Sitka spruce and Douglas fir (British Columbian pine) are also used for cheaper instruments.

Strength and stability are required for the main structural members. In the case of pianos, beech is the species which is the most widely used but for some purposes lime, sycamore, sweet chestnut and rock maple are also used. The structural members of harpsichords are often made of spruce or pine.

The actions of all the keyboard instruments are complex and involve the precise shaping of small parts for which stability in dimension and shape is always important. Hardness and strength are also required for some purposes. Stable woods capable of precise shaping are pear, lime and boxwood, while for hardness hornbeam and Tasmanian myrtle are widely used.

### Woodwind instruments

Woodwind instruments are turned on a lathe and for centuries the preferred species was box, but sycamore and the various fruitwood species such as apple, pear and plum were also used. The plugs were of pencil cedar.

The technical requirements of wood used for making woodwind instruments are stability and ease of working and this implies a relatively high density and fine texture. The wood must also be capable of taking a fine finish.

In recent times woodwind instruments have increasingly been made from several species of tropical hardwoods, the most popular of which is African blackwood, but rosewood is also used.

### Sources of wood

Most of the spruce used for soundboards is imported from Romania, Germany, Austria and Yugoslavia. Some sycamore is obtained from Britain but there are specialist timber dealers centred on the town of Mittlewald in Germany who export partially-prepared backs and necks of fiddle-back maple primarily for the amateur musical instrument maker.

### Seasoning

Musical instrument makers believe that air seasoning is preferable to kiln drying and the usual procedure is to buy partially-seasoned wood and to store this indoors for some time before it is used.

Billets are prepared for making woodwind instruments and before indoor seasoning starts they are hollowed out through the middle on a lathe to facilitate drying and to prevent surface tension set and consequential checking.

Most tropical hardwoods have been kiln dried before they are bought. These are stored indoors in the same way as the air seasoned timber until they are required for use.

### Gluing

Animal glue is always used for stringed instruments and for the actions of keyboard instruments, but modern resin glues are often used for the cases of keyboard instruments.

There are very good reasons for using animal glue. In the first place instruments have proved to last for several hundred years with the water soluble glue being renewed when necessary. But even more important is the fact that animal-glue seams can be opened with a thin blade without damaging the wood. This is an important characteristic because musical instruments have to be opened from time to time for repair and renovation.

## Turnery

It is not really possible to make broad generalisations about turnery timbers. Almost any timber can be turned after a fashion and the desirable qualities vary from one purpose to another.

At the risk of considerable oversimplification it is possible to recognise five types of turnery. These are:

**a**) woodwind instruments
**b**) hollow ware, such as basins, round boxes and goblets
**c**) structural members, such as chair components, handles and bannisters
**d**) solid articles, such as plinths
**e**) purely decorative objects, such as wooden eggs.

The timber for woodwind instruments has to satisfy some very exacting criteria. It has to be very stable and capable of being fashioned in precise detail. It also has to take a fine finish, to be strong and resonant and to have a good appearance. Relatively few species satisfy all these requirements but those that do are all very fine textured, strong and straight grained (see page 146).

The wood used for turning hollow articles has, above all, to be stable. Teak is preferred for larger bowls and basins but box and yew are used for goblets and egg cups, and a wide range of species is used for turned boxes which are as much objects of decoration as utility.

The prime qualities for structural members are strength and straightness of grain, and the more widely used species are beech, hickory, oak, yew and birch.

Almost any stable timber of pleasing appearance can be used for making turned plinths or frames and the same criteria apply to purely decorative objects which are intended to display the figure and texture of fine looking or unusual timbers such as Australian blackwood, Burma padauk, Indian laurel, Queensland maple, Ceylon satinwood and European walnut.

The African mahoganies, utile, sapele, guarea and afrormosia are all relatively stable and suitable for less detailed work, but their interlocked grain can make finishing and polishing difficult.

With the obvious exception of yew the majority of conifers are too soft to be carved satisfactorily and they do not take a fine finish. Scots pine is something of an exception and is suitable for bold, simple work.

Any wood used for large-scale carving has to be seasoned very carefully and because uniform drying throughout a large block of wood is almost impossible to achieve special measures may be required (see page 40). These include preliminary hollowing, if appropriate, or slicing and re-gluing after the individual slices have been seasoned and re-trued.

## Miscellaneous

There are a number of crafts which involve, or have involved in the past, the exploitation of special properties of particular species of wood. A good example is wheel making. The hub, nave or stock is made of elm, which is very tough and resistant to cleaving and therefore allows the spokes to be driven into closely spaced mortices without splitting the wood. The spokes have to be strong in tension and compression and are made of oak. In order to ensure that the grain is perfectly straight the wood is first cleaved and then shaped with a spokeshave. The rim has to withstand frequent shocks and therefore needs to be tough and resilient. Ash is the ideal wood for this purpose and to avoid too much cross-grain the rim is built up with a series of relatively short segments, or felloes, each with the grain running longitudinally or, preferably, if a curved stem is available, with the grain following the curve. The felloes are fixed together with dowels and the whole wheel bound tightly together with a heated iron band which is shrunk onto the rim.

In the days of wooden ships the keel and keelson were made of elm, partly because of its toughness and availability in large sizes and partly because elm is resistant to decay under water. The planking was of oak for some distance above the water line because oak, as well as being strong, is durable when exposed to the air under wet conditions. Pine was often used for the upper planking which is less liable to decay.

Ladder poles have to be strong but relatively light in weight and to have a perfectly straight grain. Conifers like spruce, pine and western red cedar are used for this purpose and, for heavier work, ash is sometimes employed. A high tensile strength is required for the rungs, which are usually made of oak or beech.

Beech and hornbeam were used for the moving parts, and especially the cogs and screws, of wooden machinery in mills and presses. In the Mediterranean region olive wood was used for similar purposes.

Cricket bat willow combines the qualities of lightness, toughness and the ability to resist bruising and splintering and is the only species in the world capable of producing top quality cricket bats.

Before the days of metal and plastic archery bows, the timber properties required for bow making were a high bending strength coupled with a relatively low modulus of elasticity. Of the European species wych elm and yew were preeminent, yew being superior to elm. The construction of a bow further exploited the different properties of the heartwood and sapwood of yew because the sapwood is better able to withstand tension and the heartwood to withstand compression. The bow staves were therefore made of cleft wood containing both sapwood and heartwood, the sapwood being on the outer curve of the bow. Lancewood and degame, or lemon wood, are two other straight-grained, fine-textured, resilient species used for modern wood bows.

Ash in Europe and hard ash and hickory in America are the species chosen when toughness and resilience are particularly important. They are used, for example, for tool handles and various items of sports equipment such as tennis rackets, lacrosse sticks and baseball bats. Hickory is superior to ash and was used for golf club shafts before the advent of steel clubs.

In contrast to ash and hickory the special quality of balsa is its very low density, which makes it suitable for model aircraft construction. As a consequence of its extreme lightness it is particularly easy to work and is also used for various other types of model making.

# CHAPTER 12

# The commercial product

## Conversion

In the process of converting the tree in the forest into timber for sale the volume of wood is successively reduced and the cumulative cost of conversion increased with each stage of the process which includes all or most of the following operations: felling, debranching, cross-cutting, extraction from the forest to the road, loading onto a lorry, transporting from the forest to the mill, unloading, sawing, resawing, kiln drying or air seasoning, shipping, further sawing, planing and final delivery. At several stages in the process the timber may have to be handled for temporary storage and additional transportation.

There is generally less wastage in converting softwoods and imported hardwoods than in converting home-grown hardwoods into timber. This is because the softwoods and imported hardwoods have been grown under forest conditions and are likely, therefore, to be straighter, less tapered and less knotty than the British hardwoods, many of which come from parks, hedgerows and small copses. But even when grown in plantations, species such as oak and beech tend not to have the straight, clear stems which are characteristic of conifers and tropical hardwoods. Furthermore, it is generally only the better quality logs or parcels of sawn timber which can economically be exported and which provide about 90 per cent of the timber used in Britain.

An approximate indication of the successive reduction in volume from the tree to the prepared timber is given in Tables 18(a) and 18(b).
The figures quoted in the tables are no more than rough averages but they show that less than half of the volume of well shaped logs and less than one third of the volume of more irregular logs is recovered as timber.

Although an increasing proportion of forest and mill residues are coming to be used for pulping, chipping and as a fuel, the value of these

**Table 18** *Reduction in volume from standing tree to prepared timber*

| sources of volume loss | volume loss per cent | residual volume per cent |
|---|---|---|
| **a) Softwoods and imported hardwoods** | | |
| Standing tree | | 100 |
| bark | 10 | 90 |
| sawdust and slabwood | 40 | 50 |
| planing waste | 5 | 45 |
| **b) Home-grown hardwoods** | | |
| Standing tree | | 100 |
| bark | 10 | 90 |
| cross cutting to remove major knots and defects | 10 | 80 |
| sawdust and slabwood | 45 | 35 |
| planing waste | 5 | 30 |

secondary products is relatively low in comparison with that of sawn timber. It is not surprising, therefore, when the costs of conversion are taken into account that the grower may obtain, say, £20 per cu. m (57p per cu. ft) for standing timber which costs £150 per cu. m (£4.25 per cu. ft) as prepared timber in the merchant's yard.

## Softwood timber

More than 90 per cent of the softwood timber used in Britain is imported and about 80 per cent of it comes from Scandinavia, Russia and Canada.

The European and Russian species are Scots pine, known as European redwood, and Norway spruce with some silver fir, known as European whitewood. The Canadian species are Sitka spruce, Douglas fir, western red cedar and a commercial package known as hem/fir which consists mainly of western hemlock with about ten minor species, the most important of which is balsam fir.

Some Parana pine is imported from South America and some cedar from the Lebanon. Home-grown softwoods are used as structural and general purpose timbers but are generally too fast-grown for joinery or furniture making.

In general, the quality of softwood timber is determined more by the conditions of growth and the standard of preparation and grading than by the species themselves (pages 19 and 124). Softwoods are rarely bought kiln dried although most imported timber is pre-kilned to reduce the moisture content from about 100 per cent to about 25 per cent. This is to reduce both the risk of fungal staining and the cost of transport.

Imported European red and whitewood is graded into six categories as set out in Table 19.

**Table 19** *Grades of imported European red and whitewood*

| description | grades | | relative price |
|---|---|---|---|
| | Scandinavian | Russian | |
| unsorted | 1–4 | 1–3 | 140 |
| saw-falling | | | 120 |
| fifths | 5 | 4 | 100 |
| sixths (planks) carcassing (scantlings) | 6 | 5–6 | 80 |

Whitewood is generally about 10 per cent cheaper than redwood.

The grades are mainly differentiated by the size and frequency of knots but no European red or whitewood is entirely knot free.

The categories considered suitable for furniture making or unpainted joinery are fifths or the two higher grades and redwood is preferred to whitewood. Canadian hem/fir is a good general-purpose product but is not of joinery quality. If completely knot-free timber is required it is necessary to buy imported Douglas fir, Parana pine or western red cedar, the red cedar being used for sheds and greenhouses. True cedar, for the manufacture of chests in particular, is imported from the Lebanon.

## Hardwood timber
### *Differences between home-grown and imported timber*

From the marketing point of view the principal difference between imported and home-grown hardwood timber is that the imported wood is relatively consistent in quality whereas the home-grown wood is very variable both in quality and in price. The other difference is that most imported timber is sold after being kiln dried whereas British timber is generally not kiln dried unless specifically requested. It is rare, however, for kiln dried timber to be maintained at a constant moisture content of about 12 per cent before it is sold (page 17). It is quite likely, therefore, to have a variable moisture content ranging from about 12 to 15 per cent, depending upon the season and conditions of storage.

### *Commercial species*

The more commonly available species are listed in Table 20. This table also indicates their relative prices in a range of 1 to 5 (1 being the cheapest). Some indication of their relative abundance is given in Table 7. The home-grown species are assumed to be of furniture quality.

**Table 20** *The commonly available commercial species in Britain*

| species | relative price |
|---|---|
| keruing | 1 |
| obeche | 1 |
| ramin | 1 |
| beech | 2 |
| lauan | 2 |
| meranti | 2 |
| nyatoh | 2 |
| elm | 3 |
| idigbo | 3 |
| iroko | 3 |
| mahogany, African | 3 |
| mahogany, American | 3 |
| ash, American | 4 |
| ash, English | 4 |
| cherry | 4 |
| chestnut, sweet | 4 |
| oak, Tasmanian | 4 |
| sapele | 4 |
| utile | 4 |
| yew | 4 |
| afrormosia | 5 |
| oak, English | 5 |
| teak | 5 |

Rosewood, padauk, ebony and other valuable species are in a relative price range of 6 to 7 +. For the purpose of comparison with softwoods, Scandinavian fifths, on the same price scale, are about 0.7.

## Panel products

Panel products are nearly always sold in 2440 × 1220mm (8 × 4ft) sheets but small merchants and DIY shops will cut to size for a small extra charge. Stocks of small offcuts are sold at a lower price. Specialist firms can supply 3050 × 1520mm (10 × 5ft) sheets and even larger sizes are sometimes available.

The common thicknesses are 3.2mm, which corresponds with ⅛in, 4mm, 6mm, 9mm, 12mm, 18mm and 25mm and the cost is approximately proportional to the thickness. Plywood as thin as 0.4mm is available from specialist firms for the construction of sailplanes and models.

There are various qualities and specifications for each type of panel product and this makes it difficult to generalise about price. This is illustrated in Table 21 which shows the approximate (and rounded) prices for different categories of plywood of comparable thickness.

*Table 21* *The relative prices of different categories of plywood*

| Finnish birch | Far eastern | Douglas fir sheathing grade |
|---|---|---|
| 100 | 65 | 40 |

Nevertheless, it is possible to give some indication of the relative prices per unit area of the various types of panel product. It is assumed that each product is of average quality and that they are all of the same thickness. The price of Scandinavian fifth-grade softwood is taken as a standard (Table 22).

*Table 22* *The relative prices of different types of panel product*

| | |
|---|---|
| Softwood, Scandinavian fifth grade | 100 |
| Plywood | 200 |
| Particle board | 75 |
| Blockboard | 175 |
| Laminboard | 210 |
| Medium density fibreboard (MDF) | 150 |

## Measurement

The timber trade, or more particularly its customers, have been slow to adopt metrication and both the metric and imperial units are used in the measurement and purchase of timber.

Larger quantities of timber are sold by the cubic metre or the cubic foot but smaller quantities are sold at so much per foot or per metre for a plank or scantling of particular dimensions. The very expensive woods, which are sold in small quantities for carving, turnery or inlay work, are sometimes sold by the pound or the kilogram.

Prepared wood is usually sawn or planed to a metric dimension and with planed wood the final thickness is slightly smaller than the nominal thickness. A planed 1in plank, therefore, is likely to measure about ⅞in in thickness.

Panel products are often still measured in superficial square feet but the thicknesses are all in metric units, usually in whole or half millimetres. Particle board and hardboard are, however, available in a thickness of 3.2mm which is equivalent to ⅛in.

## Sizes and definitions of sawn timber

In the United Kingdom timber sizes and quantities are now quoted in metric terms. The following are names of the sizes most commonly used and defined in BS 565 1972.

**Batten** A piece of square-sawn softwood timber, 50–100mm thick and 100–200mm wide.

**Baulk** A piece of square-sawn or hewn softwood timber, approximately square in cross-section and of greater size than 100 × 125mm.

**Board** *a) Softwood.* A piece of square-sawn timber under 50mm thick, and 100mm or more wide.
*b) Hardwood.* A piece of square-sawn or unedged timber, 50mm or less thick, and usually, 150mm or more wide.

**Deal** A piece of square-sawn softwood timber 50–100mm thick and 225–300mm wide.

**Lath** A piece of sawn or cleft timber 6–17mm thick and 22–36mm wide.

**Plank** *a) Softwood.* A piece of square-sawn timber 50–100mm thick and 250mm or more wide.
*b) Hardwood.* A piece of square-sawn or unedged timber over 50mm thick and of various widths.

**Scantling** *a) Softwood.* A piece of square-sawn timber 50–100mm thick and 50–125mm wide.
*b) Hardwood.* Timber cut to an agreed specification such as waggon oak scantling; or a square-edged piece not conforming to other standard terms, normally less than 150mm wide.

**Stave** A piece of sawn or cleft timber intended to form part of a cask.

**Strip** *a) Softwood.* A piece of square-sawn timber less than 50mm thick and under 100mm wide.
*b) Hardwood.* A piece of square-sawn timber usually 50mm or less thick and 50–140mm wide. Usually for flooring.

## Sources of wood

### Timber
Local timber merchants can generally supply most commercial softwoods and the more common imported hardwoods such as obeche, iroko and mahogany. For the more valuable or less widely used species such as afrormosia and teak it may be necessary to go to the larger timber merchants who may also be importers. The very valuable species such as rosewood or the rare carving and turnery timbers may have to be obtained from merchants who specialise in that trade.

Home-grown timber of good quality is stocked by the larger timber merchants but a wider range of qualities and species is likely to be found at local merchants or in local sawmills. Some small sawmills which specialise in fencing material occasionally have small quantities of such species as yew, cherry or walnut which are likely to be of mediocre quality but which may be worth buying at a modest price. If high quality timber of those scarce and more valuable species is required it is usually necessary to go to specialist sawmills or timber merchants.

In the process of cutting timber to size timber merchants accumulate short lengths, or offcuts, which they are often willing to sell at a very low price. It is well worthwhile for the amateur craftsman to look out for such a source of small-sized material.

Many craftsmen prefer to select a standing tree and arrange for it to be felled and planked by a local merchant. This is only practicable if the craftsman has a maturing stock of wood so that he can afford to wait for several years for the newly planked timber to season. For some species, such as apple, plum or laburnum, this is virtually the only way to obtain supplies of wood.

It is always worth keeping an eye open for second-hand wood from various sources such as demolition work, sales of solid furniture of low value or the closure of wood-working premises.

The craftsman needs to look ahead in building up a stock of timber and, if he has storage space available, to acquire potentially useful material whenever he has the opportunity. Over a period of time the price of high quality timber is more likely to increase than to decrease in real terms and the purchase of any timber and, in particular, of unseasoned but valuable species, can be regarded as a good investment.

### Panel products
The more common specifications and sizes of panel products can be obtained from craftsmen's shops and local wood merchants who are usually willing to cut to the customers requirements. For the less common specifications, sheet sizes and thicknesses it is necessary to go to the larger timber firms who will usually sell only by the whole sheet. These firms are generally willing to give technical advice on the choice and use of panel products.

# Appendix

Lists of timber species based on British
Standards 881 and 589:1974

## A. Hardwoods: common names in alphabetical order

| Common name | Botanical name | Local or trade name |
|---|---|---|
| abura | *Mitragyna ciliata* | |
| afara or limba | *Terminalia superba* | korina (USA) |
| afrormosia | *Pericopsis elata* | kokrodua (W. Africa) |
| afzelia | *Afzelia species*, inc. | |
| | *A. africana* | |
| | *A. bipindensis* | |
| | *A. pachyloba* | |
| | *A. quanzensis* | |
| agba | *Gossweilerodendron balsamiferum* | tola (France, Zaire) |
| albizia, West African | *Albizia* species, principally | |
| | *A. ferruginea* | |
| amboyna | *Pterocarpus indicus* | |
| apitong (in the Philippines) | *Dipterocarpus* species | |
| apple | *Pyrus malus* | |
| ash, American | *Fraxinus* species, principally | (1) white ash (Canada) |
| | (1) *F. americana* | (2) black ash (USA) |
| | (2) *F. nigra* | (2) brown ash (USA) |
| | (3) *F. pennsylvanica* | (3) green ash (USA) |
| | | (3) red ash (Canada) |
| | | (1) (3) hard ash (fast grown) (USA) |
| | | (1) (2) (3) soft ash (slow grown) (USA) |
| ash, European | *Fraxinus excelsior* | |
| ash, Japanese | *Fraxinus mandshurica* | |
| avodire | *Turraeanthus africanus* | |
| ayan | *Distemonanthus benthamianus* | Nigerian satinwood (UK) |
| balsa | *Ochroma lagopus* | |
| basswood | *Tilia americana* | |
| beech, European | *Fagus sylvatica* | |
| berlinia | *Berlinia* species, inc. | |
| | *B. confusa* | |
| | *B. grandiflora* | |
| | *B. occidentalis* | |
| birch, European | *Betula pendula* | |
| | *B. pubescens* | |
| birch, Japanese | *Betula maximowicziana* | |
| birch, paper | *Betula papyrifera* | |
| birch, yellow | *Betula alleghaniensis* | American birch (UK) |
| | | Canadian yellow birch (UK) |
| | | hard birch (Canada) |
| black bean | *Castanospermum australe* | |
| blackwood, African | *Dalbergia melanoxylon* | |
| blackwood, Australian | *Acacia melanoxylon* | black wattle (Australia) |

| Common name | Botanical name | Local or trade name |
|---|---|---|
| boxwood, American | *Cornus florida* | cornel (USA) |
| boxwood, Balaeric | *Buxus balaerica* | |
| boxwood, East London | *Buxus macowani* | Cape boxwood (UK) |
| boxwood, European | *Buxus sempervirens* | Iranian boxwood (UK) |
| | | Turkey boxwood (UK) etc. |
| boxwood, Knysna | *Gonioma kamassi* | Kamassi boxwood (UK) |
| boxwood, Maracaibo | *Gossypiospermum praecox* | West Indian boxwood (UK) |
| boxwood, Siamese | *Gardenia* species | |
| brush box | *Tristania conferta* | |
| bubinga | *Guibourtia demeusei* | African rosewood (UK) |
| | *G. pellegriniana* | kevazingo (Gabon) |
| | *G. tessmannii* | |
| camphorwood, East African | *Ocotea usambarensis* | |
| cedar, Central American | *Cedrela* species, principally | cigar-box cedar (UK) |
| | *C. odorata* | Honduras cedar (UK) |
| | | Mexican cedar (UK) etc. |
| cedar, South American | *Cedrela* species, principally | Brazilian cedar (UK) |
| | *C. fissilis* | cigar-box cedar (UK) |
| | | Peruvian cedar (UK) etc. |
| cherry, European | *Prunus avium* | gean (UK) |
| chestnut, sweet | *Castanea sativa* | European chestnut (UK) |
| | | Spanish chestnut (UK) |
| cocobolo | *Dalbergia retusa* | |
| cocuswood | *Brya ebenus* | brown ebony (USA) |
| | | green ebony (USA) |
| | | Jamaica ebony (USA) |
| cordia, African | *Cordia abyssinica* | omo (Nigeria) |
| | *C. millenii* | |
| | *C. platythyrsa* | |
| cordia, American dark | *Cordia dodecandra* | |
| | *C. gerascanthus* | |
| | *C. sebestena* | |
| cordia, American light | *Cordia alliodora* | laurel blanco (Brazil) |
| | *C. trichotoma* | laurel negro (Brazil) |
| | | salmwood (British Honduras) |
| cordia, Indian | *Cordia fragrantissima* | |
| | *C. vestita* | |
| danta | *Nesogordonia papaverifera* | |
| degame | *Calycophyllum candidissimum* | lemonwood (USA) |
| | | degame lancewood (UK) |
| ebony, African | *Diospyros* species, principally | Gaboon ebony (UK) |
| | *D. crassiflora* | Madagascar ebony (UK) |
| | *D. piscatoria* | Nigerian ebony (UK) etc. |
| ebony, Borneo | *Diospyros durianoides* | |
| | *D. melanoxylon* | |
| | *D. tomentosa* | |
| ebony, Ceylon | *Diospyros ebenum* | East Indian ebony (UK) |
| ebony, Macassar | *Diospyros rumphii* | |
| | *D. celebica* | |
| ekki | *Lophira alata* | |
| elm, Dutch | *Ulmus hollandica* | |
| elm, English | *Ulmus procera* | red elm (UK) |
| | | nave elm (UK) |

| Common name | Botanical name | Local or trade name | |
|---|---|---|---|
| elm, rock<br>    other hard elms | (1) *Ulmus thomasii (racemosa)*<br>(2) *U. alata*<br>(3) *U. crassifolia*<br>(4) *U. serotina* | (1) Canadian rock elm<br>    (Canada, UK)<br>(1) cork bark elm (USA)<br>(1) hickory elm (USA)<br>(2) winged elm (USA)<br>(3) cedar elm (USA)<br>(4) september elm (USA) | <br><br>hard<br>elms<br>(USA) |
| elm, smooth-leaved | *Ulmus carpinifolia* | | |
| elm, white (N. America) | (1) *Ulmus americana* | (1) American elm (in part)<br>    (Canada, UK) | soft<br>elms |
|    another soft elm | (2) *U. fulva (rubra)* | (2) slippery elm (USA) | (USA) |
| elm, white (Europe) | *Ulmus laevis* | | |
| elm, wych | *Ulmus glabra* | | |
| eng (in Burma) | *Dipterocarpus* species | | |
| freijo | *Cordia goeldiana* | | |
| gaboon | *Aucoumea klaineana* | okoumé (Gabon)<br>Gaboon mahogany (UK) | |
| gedu nohor | *Entandrophragma angolense* | | |
| greenheart | *Ocotea rodiaei* | | |
| guarea | *Guarea cedrata*<br>*G. thompsonii* | Nigerian pearwood (UK) | |
| gurjun (in India and Burma) | *Dipterocarpus* species | | |
| hickory | *Carya glabra*<br>*C. laciniosa*<br>*C. ovata*<br>*C. tomentosa* | mockernut hickory (USA)<br>pignut hickory (USA)<br>red hickory (USA)<br>shagbark hickory (USA)<br>shellbark hickory (USA)<br>white hickory (sapwood) (USA) | |
| holly | *Ilex aquifolium* | | |
| hornbeam | *Carpinus betulus* | | |
| idigbo | *Terminalia ivorensis* | | |
| ilomba | *Pycnanthus angolensis* | | |
| imbuia | *Phoebe porosa* | embuia (Brazil)<br>Brazilian walnut (UK, USA) | |
| iroko | *Chlorophora excelsa*<br>*C. regia* | mvule (East Africa) | |
| ironbark | (1) *Eucalyptus crebra*<br>(2) *E. drepanophylla*<br>(3) *E. paniculata*<br>(4) *E. siderophloia*<br>(5) *E. sideroxylon* | (1) (5) red ironbark (Australia)<br>(2) (3) (4) grey ironbark (Australia) | |
| jarrah | *Eucalyptus marginata* | | |
| jelutong | *Dyera costulata*<br>*D. lowii* | | |
| kapur | (1) *Dryobalanops* species, principally<br>(2) *D. aromatica*<br>(3) *D. beccarii*<br>(4) *D. lanceolata* | Borneo camphorwood (UK)<br>(1) (2) Malaysian kapur (UK)<br>(2) (4) Sarawak kapur (UK)<br>(3) (4) Sabah kapur (UK) | |
| keruing (in Malaya, Sarawak,<br>    Sabah, Indonesia) | *Dipterocarpus* species (numerous) | | |
| kingwood | *Dalbergia cearensis* | violetta (USA)<br>violet wood (USA) | |

| Common name | Botanical name | Local or trade name |
| --- | --- | --- |
| kokko | *Albizia lebbek* | East Indian walnut (UK) |
| laburnum | *Laburnum anagyroides* | |
| lancewood | *Oxandra lanceolata* | asta (USA) |
| lauan | *Parashorea* species | |
| | *Pentacme* species | |
| | *Shorea* species | |
| laurel, Indian | *Terminalia alata* | |
| | *T. coriacea* | |
| | *T. crenulata* | |
| lignum vitae | *Guaiacum* species, principally | |
| | *G. officinale* | |
| lime, European | *Tilia cordata* | English lime (UK) |
| | *T. platyphyllos* | |
| | *T. vulgaris* | |
| lime, Japanese | *Tilia japonica* | |
| louro, red | *Ocotea rubra* | |
| mahogany, African | (1) *Khaya anthotheca* | (1) (3) Ghana mahogany (UK) |
| | (2) *K. grandifoliola* | (1) (3) Grand Bassam mahogany (UK) |
| | (3) *K. ivorensis* | (1) (3) Ivory Coast mahogany (UK) |
| | (4) *K. nyasica* | (1) (3) Takoradi mahogany (UK) |
| | (5) *K. senegalensis* | (2) Benin mahogany (UK) ⎫ heavy |
| | | (5) Guinea mahogany (UK) ⎬ mahogany (UK) |
| | | (4) Mozambique mahogany (UK) |
| mahogany, American | *Swietenia* species, principally | |
| | (1) *S. candollei* | (1) Venezuelan mahogany (UK) |
| | (2) *S. macrophylla* | (2) Brazilian mahogany (UK) |
| | (3) *S. mahagoni* | (2) British Honduras mahogany (UK) |
| | | (2) Central American mahogany (UK) |
| | | (2) Costa Rica mahogany (UK) |
| | | (2) Honduras mahogany (UK) |
| | | (2) Peruvian mahogany (UK) |
| | | (3) Cuban mahogany (UK) |
| | | (3) Jamaica mahogany (UK) |
| | | (3) San Domingo mahogany (UK) |
| | | (3) Spanish mahogany (UK) |
| makoré | *Tieghemella heckelii* | |
| mansonia | *Mansonia altissima* | African black walnut (UK) |
| maple, field | *Acer campestre* | |
| maple, Japanese | *Acer mono* | |
| | *A. palmatum* | |
| maple, Norway | *Acer patanoides* | |
| maple, Pacific | *Acer macrophyllum* | soft maple (USA) |
| maple, Queensland | *Flindersia brayleyana* | Australian maple (UK) |
| | *F. pimenteliana* | maple silkwood (Australia) |
| maple, rock | *Acer nigrum* | hard maple (UK, Canada, USA) |
| | *A. saccharum* | white maple (sapwood) (USA) |
| | | sugar maple (Canada) |
| maple, soft | (1) *Acer rubrum* | (1) red maple (Canada, USA) |
| | (2) *A. saccharinum* | (2) silver maple (Canada, USA) |
| marblewood, Andaman | *Diospyros marmorata* | zebra wood (UK) |

| Common name | Botanical name | Local or trade name |
|---|---|---|
| meranti, dark red | *Shorea* species, principally | red lauan (UK) |
| | *S. pauciflora* | |
| meranti, light red | *Shorea* species | white lauan (UK) |
| meranti, white | *Shorea* species | |
| meranti, yellow | *Shorea* species | yellow lauan (UK) |
| merbau | *Intsia bijuga* | Borneo teak (UK) |
| | *I. palembanica* | |
| muhuhu | *Brachylaena hutchinsii* | |
| muninga | *Pterocarpus angolensis* | |
| myrtle, Tasmanian | *Nothofagus cunninghamii* | myrtle beech (Australia) |
| | | myrtle (Australia) |
| | | white myrtle beech (sapwood) (Australia) |
| | | red myrtle beech (heartwood) (Australia) |
| niangon | *Tarrietia utilis* | |
| nyatoh | *Palaquium* species | |
| | *Payena* species | |
| oak, American red | *Quercus* species, principally | |
| | (1) *Q. falcata* | (1) southern red oak (USA) |
| | (2) *Q. rubra* | (2) northern red oak (Canada, USA) |
| oak, American white | *Quercus* species, principally | |
| | (1) *Q. alba* | (1) white oak (USA) |
| | (2) *Q. lyrata* | (2) overcup oak (USA) |
| | (3) *Q. michauxii* | (3) swamp chestnut oak (USA) |
| | (4) *Q. prinus* | (4) chestnut oak (USA) |
| oak, European | (1) *Quercus petraea* | (1) sessile oak (UK) |
| | (2) *Q. robur* | (2) pedunculate oak (UK) |
| | | (1) (2) English oak (UK) |
| | | (1) (2) French oak (UK) |
| | | (1) (2) Polish oak (UK) etc. |
| oak, Japanese | *Quercus mongolica* | |
| oak, Tasmanian | (1) *Eucalyptus delegatensis* | (1) alpine ash (Australia) |
| | (2) *E. obliqua* | (2) messmate stringybark (Australia) |
| | (3) *E. regnans* | (3) mountain ash (Australia) |
| oak, Turkey | *Quercus cerris* | |
| obeche | *Triplochiton scleroxylon* | wawa (Ghana) |
| okwen | *Brachystegia eurycoma* | |
| | *B. kennedyi* | |
| | *B. leonensis* | |
| | *B. nigerica* | |
| olive, East African | *Olea hochstetteri* | |
| omu | *Entandrophragma candollei* | heavy mahogany (Nigeria) |
| | | heavy sapele (Nigeria) |
| opepe | *Nauclea diderrichii* | |
| partridge wood | *Caesalpinia granadillo* | Maracaibo ebony (UK) |
| padauk, African | *Pterocarpus soyauxii* | camwood (UK) |
| padauk, Andaman | *Pterocarpus dalbergioides* | |
| padauk, Burma | *Pterocarpus macrocarpus* | barwood (UK) |
| pear | *Pyrus communis* | |
| persimmon | *Diospyros virginiana* | |
| plane, American | *Platanus occidentalis* | sycamore (USA) |
| | | buttonwood (USA) |
| plane, London | *Platanus hybrida* | London plane is a hybrid between American and oriental planes |

| Common name | Botanical name | Local or trade name |
|---|---|---|
| plane, oriental | *Platanus orientalis* | |
| pterygota, African | *Pterygota bequaertii* | |
| | *P. macrocarpa* | |
| ramin | *Gonostylus* species, principally | |
| | *G. bancanus* | |
| rauli | *Nothofagus procera* | |
| red gum, American | *Liquidambar styraciflua* | satin walnut (USA) |
| | | sweet gum (USA) |
| robinia | *Robinia pseudoacacia* | black locust (USA) |
| | | false acacia (UK) |
| rosewood, Brazilian | *Dalbergia nigra* | Bahia rosewood (UK) |
| | | jacaranda (Brazil) |
| | | Rio rosewood (UK) |
| rosewood, Honduras | *Dalbergia stevensonii* | |
| rosewood, Indian | *Dalbergia latifolia* | Bombay blackwood (India) |
| | | East Indian rosewood (UK) |
| rosewood, Thailand | *Dalbergia cochinchinensis* | |
| sapele | *Entandrophragma cylindricum* | |
| satinwood, Ceylon | *Chloroxylon swietenia* | East Indian satinwood (UK) |
| satinwood, West Indian | *Fagara flava* | Jamaica satinwood (UK) |
| | | San Domingan satinwood (USA) |
| sepetir | *Sindora* species | |
| seraya | *Parashorea* species | |
| | *Shorea* species | |
| seraya, white | *Parashorea* species | |
| silky-oak, Australian | *Cardwellia sublimis* | Northern silky-oak (Australia) |
| strawberry tree | *Arbutus unedo* | |
| sycamore | *Acer pseudoplatanus* | plane (sometimes in Scotland) |
| tchitola | *Oxystigma oxyphyllum* | tola (Angola) |
| teak | *Tectona grandis* | |
| teak, Rhodesian | *Baikiaea plurijuga* | |
| tulip wood, Brazilian | *Dalbergia frutescens* var. *tomentosa* | |
| tulip wood, Burma | *Dalbergia oliveri* | |
| utile | *Entandrophragma utile* | |
| virola | *Virola* species | heavy virola (darker and denser |
| | *Dialyanthera* species | wood) (UK) |
| | | light virola (paler and less dense |
| | | wood) (UK) |
| walnut, African | *Lovoa trichilioides* | Benin walnut (UK) |
| | | Congo wood (USA) |
| | | lovoa wood (USA) |
| | | Nigerian walnut (UK) |
| | | noyer d'Afrique (France) |
| walnut, American | *Juglans nigra* | black walnut (UK, USA) |
| | | walnut (USA) |
| walnut, blush | *Beilschmiedia obtusifolia* | |
| walnut, European | *Juglans regia* | English walnut (UK) |
| | | French walnut (UK) |
| | | Italian walnut (UK) etc. |
| walnut, Japanese | *Juglans sieboldiana* | claro (UK) |
| walnut, New Guinea | *Dracontomelum mangiferum* | Pacific walnut (UK) |
| | | Papuan walnut (UK) |
| walnut, New South Wales | *Endiandra virens* | |
| walnut, Queensland | *Endiandra palmerstonii* | Australian walnut (Australia) |
| | | oriental wood (USA) |
| | | walnut bean (Australia) |

| Common name | Botanical name | Local or trade name |
|---|---|---|
| walnut, rose | *Endiandra discolor* | |
| walnut, white | *Juglans cinerea* | |
| walnut, yellow | *Beilschmiedia bancroftii* | |
| yang (in Thailand) | *Dipterocarpus* species | |

## B. Hardwoods: botanical names in alphabetical order

| Botanical name | Common name | Botanical name | Common name |
|---|---|---|---|
| *Acacia melanoxylon* | Australian blackwood | *Cardwellia sublimis* | Australian silky-oak |
| *Acer campestre* | field maple | *Carya glabra* ⎫ | |
| *Acer macrophyllum* | Pacific maple | *C. laciniosa* ⎬ | hickory |
| *Acer mono* | Japanese maple | *C. ovata* | |
| *Acer nigrum* | rock maple | *C. tomentosa* ⎭ | |
| *Acer palmatum* | Japanese maple | *Carpinus betulus* | hornbeam |
| *Acer platanoides* | Norway maple | *Castanea sativa* | sweet chestnut |
| *Acer pseudoplatanus* | sycamore | *Castanospermum australe* | black bean |
| *Acer rubrum* ⎫ | | *Cedrela fissilis* and related | South American cedar |
| *A. saccharinum* ⎬ | soft maple | species | |
| *Acer saccharum* | rock maple | *Cedrela odorata* and related | Central American cedar |
| *Afzelia africana* ⎫ | | species | |
| *A. bipindensis* ⎪ | | *Chlorophora excelsa* ⎫ | iroko |
| *A. pachyloba* ⎬ | afzelia | *C. regia* ⎭ | |
| *A. quanzensis* ⎭ | | *Chloroxylon swietenia* | Ceylon satinwood |
| *Albizia ferruginea* and | West African albizia | *Cordia abyssinica* | African cordia |
| related species | | *Cordia alliodora* | American light cordia |
| *Albizia lebbek* | kokko | *Cordia dodecandra* | American dark cordia |
| *Arbutus unedo* | strawberry tree | *Cordia fragrantissima* | Indian cordia |
| *Aucoumea klaineana* | gaboon | *Cordia gerascanthus* | American dark cordia |
| *Baikiaea plurijuga* | Rhodesian teak | *Cordia goeldiana* | freijo |
| *Beilschmiedia bancroftii* | yellow walnut | *Cordia millenii* ⎫ | African cordia |
| *Beilschmiedia obtusifolia* | blush walnut | *C. platythyrsa* ⎭ | |
| *Berlinia confusa* ⎫ | | *Cordia sebestena* | American dark cordia |
| *B. grandiflora* ⎬ | berlinia | *Cordia trichotoma* | American light cordia |
| *B. occidentalis* ⎭ | | *Cordia vestita* | Indian cordia |
| *Betula alleghaniensis* | yellow birch | *Cornus florida* | American boxwood |
| *Betula maximowicziana* and | Japanese birch | *Dalbergia caerensis* | kingwood |
| related species | | *Dalbergia cochinchinensis* | Thailand rosewood |
| *Betula papyrifera* | paper birch | *Dalbergia frutescens* var. | Brazilian tulipwood |
| *Betula pendula* ⎫ | European birch | tomentosa | |
| *B. pubescens* ⎭ | | *Dalbergia latifolia* | Indian rosewood |
| *Brachylaena hutchinsii* | muhuhu | *Dalbergia melanoxylon* | African blackwood |
| *Brachystegia eurycoma* ⎫ | | *Dalbergia nigra* | Brazilian rosewood |
| *B. kennedyi* ⎪ | | *Dalbergia oliveri* | Burma tulipwood |
| *B. leonensis* ⎬ | okwen | *Dalbergia retusa* | cocobolo |
| *B. nigerica* ⎭ | | *Dalbergia stevensonii* | Honduras rosewood |
| *Brya ebenus* | cocuswood | *Dialyanthera* species | virola |
| *Buxus balaerica* | Balaeric boxwood | *Diospyros celebica* | Macassar ebony |
| *Buxus macowani* | East London boxwood | *Diospyros crassiflora* | African ebony |
| *Buxus sempervirens* | European boxwood | *Diospyros durianoides* | Borneo ebony |
| *Caesalpinia granadillo* | partridgewood | *Diospyros ebenum* | Ceylon ebony |
| *Calycophyllum* | degame | *Diospyros marmorata* | Andaman marblewood |
| candidissimum | | *Diospyros melanoxylon* | Borneo ebony |

| Botanical name | Common name | Botanical name | Common name |
|---|---|---|---|
| *Diospyros piscatoria* | African ebony | *Guibourtia demeusei* ⎫ | |
| *Diospyros rumphii* | Macassar ebony | *G. pellegriniana* ⎬ | bubinga |
| *Diospyros tomentosa* | Borneo ebony | *G. tessmannii* ⎭ | |
| *Diospyros virginiana* | persimmon | *Ilex aquifolium* | holly |
| *Dipterocarpus* species | apitong (the Philippines) | *Intsia bijuga* ⎱ | merbau |
| | eng (Burma) | *I. palembanica* ⎰ | |
| | gurjun (India, Burma) | *Juglans cinerea* | white walnut |
| | keruing (Malaya, | *Juglans nigra* | American walnut |
| | Sarawak, Sabah, | *Juglans regia* | European walnut |
| | Indonesia) | *Juglans sieboldiana* | Japanese walnut |
| | yang (Thailand) | *Khaya anthotheca* ⎫ | |
| *Distemonanthus* | ayan | *K. grandifoliola* ⎪ | |
| *benthamianus* | | *K. ivorensis* ⎬ | African mahogany |
| *Dracontomelum mangiferum* | New Guinea walnut | *K. nyasica* ⎪ | |
| *Dryobalanops* ⎫ | | *K. senegalensis* ⎭ | |
| *aromatica* ⎪ | | *Laburnum anagyroides* | laburnum |
| *D. beccarii* ⎬ | kapur | *Liquidambar styraciflua* | American red gum |
| *D. lanceolata* ⎭ | | *Lophira alata* | ekki |
| *Dyera costulata* ⎱ | | *Lovoa trichilioides* | African walnut |
| *D. lowii* ⎰ | jelutong | *Mansonia altissima* | mansonia |
| *Endiandra discolor* | rose walnut | *Mitragyna ciliata* | abura |
| *Endiandra palmerstonii* | Queensland walnut | *Nauclea diderrichii* | opepe |
| *Endiandra virens* | New South Wales walnut | *Nesogordonia papaverifera* | danta |
| *Entandrophragma angolense* | gedu nohor | *Nothofagus cunninghamii* | Tasmanian myrtle |
| *Entandrophragma candollei* | omu | *Nothofagus procera* | rauli |
| *Entandrophragma* | sapele | *Ochroma lagopus* | balsa |
| *cylindricum* | | *Ocotea rodiaei* | greenheart |
| *Entandrophragma utile* | utile | *Ocotea rubra* | red louro |
| *Eucalyptus crebra* | ironbark | *Ocotea usambarensis* | East African |
| *Eucalyptus delegatensis* | Tasmanian oak | | camphorwood |
| *Eucalyptus drepanophylla* | ironbark | *Olea hochstetteri* | East African olive |
| *Eucalyptus marginata* | jarrah | *Oxandra lanceolata* | lancewood |
| *Eucalyptus obliqua* | Tasmanian oak | *Oxystigma oxyphyllum* | tchitola |
| *Eucalyptus paniculata* | ironbark | *Palaquium* species | nyatoh |
| *Eucalyptus regnans* | Tasmanian oak | *Parashorea* species | lauan |
| *Eucalyptus* ⎫ | | | meranti |
| *siderophloia* ⎬ | ironbark | | seraya |
| *E. sideroxylon* ⎭ | | *Payena* species | nyatoh |
| *Fagara flava* | West Indian satinwood | *Pentacme* species | lauan |
| *Fagus sylvatica* | European beech | *Pericopsis elata* | afrormosia |
| *Flindersia* ⎫ | | *Phoebe porosa* | imbuia |
| *brayleyana* ⎬ | Queensland maple | *Platanus hybrida* | London plane |
| *F. pimenteliana* ⎭ | | *Platanus occidentalis* | American plane |
| *Fraxinus americana* | American ash | *Platanus orientalis* | oriental plane |
| *Fraxinus excelsior* | European ash | *Prunus avium* | European cherry |
| *Fraxinus mandshurica* | Japanese ash | *Pterocarpus angolensis* | muninga |
| *Fraxinus nigra* ⎱ | American ash | *Pterocarpus dalbergioides* | Andaman padauk |
| *F. pennsylvanica* ⎰ | | *Pterocarpus indicus* | amboyna |
| *Gardenia* species | Siamese boxwood | *Pterocarpus macrocarpus* | Burma padauk |
| *Gonioma kamassi* | Knysna boxwood | *Pterocarpus soyauxii* | African padauk |
| *Gonostylus bancanus* | ramin | *Pterygota bequaertii* ⎱ | African pterygota |
| *Gossweilerodendron* | agba | *P. macrocarpa* ⎰ | |
| *balsamiferum* | | *Pycnanthus angolensis* | ilomba |
| *Gossypiospermum praecox* | Maracaibo boxwood | *Pyrus communis* | pear |
| *Guaiacum officinale* | lignum vitae | *Pyrus malus* | apple |
| *Guarea cedrata* ⎱ | guarea | *Quercus alba* | American white oak |
| *G. thompsonii* ⎰ | | *Quercus cerris* | Turkey oak |

| Botanical name | Common name | Botanical name | Common name |
|---|---|---|---|
| *Quercus falcata* | American red oak | *Terminalia ivorensis* | idigbo |
| *Quercus lyrata*⎤ | | *Terminalia superba* | afara (limba) |
| *Q. michauxii*⎦ | American white oak | *Tieghemella heckelii* | makoré |
| *Quercus mongolica* | Japanese oak | *Tilia americana* | basswood |
| *Quercus petraea* | European oak | *Tilia cordata* | European lime |
| *Quercus prinus* | American white oak | *Tilia japonica* | Japanese lime |
| *Quercus robur* | European oak | *Tilia platyphyllos*⎤ | European lime |
| *Quercus rubra* | American red oak | *T. vulgaris*⎦ | |
| *Robinia pseudoacacia* | robinia | *Triplochiton scleroxylon* | obeche |
| *Shorea* species esp. *S. pauciflora* | dark red meranti | *Tristania conferta* | brush box |
| | | *Turraeanthus africanus* | avodiré |
| *Shorea* species | light red meranti | *Ulmus alata* | (winged elm) (local name) |
| | yellow meranti | | |
| | white meranti | *Ulmus americana* | white elm |
| | seraya | *Ulmus carpinifolia* | smooth-leaved elm |
| | lauan | *Ulmus crassifolia* | (cedar elm) (local name) |
| *Sindora* species | sepetir | *Ulmus fulva (rubra)* | (slippery elm) (local name) |
| *Swietenia candollei*⎤ | | | |
| *S. macrophylla* ⎬ | American mahogany | *Ulmus glabra* | wych elm |
| *S. mahagoni* ⎦ | | *Ulmus hollandica* | Dutch elm |
| *Tarrietia utilis* | niangon | *Ulmus procera* | English elm |
| *Tectona grandis* | teak | *Ulmus serotina* | (september elm) (local name) |
| *Terminalia alata*⎤ | | | |
| *T. coriacea* ⎬ | Indian laurel | *Ulmus thomasii (racemosa)* | rock elm |
| *T. crenulata* ⎦ | | *Virola* species | virola |

## C. Softwoods: common names in alphabetical order

| Common name | Botanical name | Local or trade name |
|---|---|---|
| alerce | *Fitzroya cupressoides* | |
| cedar | (1) *Cedrus atlantica* | (1) Atlantic cedar (UK) |
| | (2) *C. deodora* | (1) Atlas cedar (UK) |
| | (3) *C. libani* | (2) deodar cedar (UK) |
| | | (3) cedar of Lebanon (UK) |
| cedar, East African pencil | *Juniperus procera* | African pencil cedar (UK) |
| cedar, incense | *Libocedrus (Calocedrus) decurrens* | Californian incense cedar (USA) |
| cedar, Port Orford | *Chamaecyparis lawsoniana* | Lawson's cypress (UK) |
| cedar, Virginian pencil | *Juniperus virginiana* | eastern red cedar (USA) |
| cedar, western red | *Thuja plicata* | British Columbia red cedar (UK) red cedar (Canada) |
| cedar, white | *Thuja occidentalis* | eastern white cedar (Canada) northern white cedar (USA) |
| cedar yellow | *Chamaecyparis nootkatensis* | Alaska yellow cedar (USA) Nootka false cypress (USA) Pacific coast yellow cedar (Canada) yellow cypress (Canada) |
| cypress species with names based on geographical origin and having no standard common names | various species e.g.: *Cupressus lusitanica* *C. sempervirens* | |
| cypress, Lawson's (see cedar, Port Orford) | | |
| cypress, Leyland | *Cupressocyparis leylandii* | |

| Common name | Botanical name | Local or trade name |
| --- | --- | --- |
| cypress, Monterey | *Cupressus macrocarpa* | |
| cypress, swamp | *Taxodium distichum* | southern cypress (USA) |
| fir, balsam | *Abies balsamea* | balsam (USA) |
| fir, Douglas | *Pseudotsuga menziesii* | Columbian pine (UK) |
| fir, grand | *Abies grandis* | lowland fir (Canada) |
| | | western balsam fir (USA) |
| | | white fir (USA) |
| fir, noble | *Abies nobilis* | |
| fir, silver | *Abies alba* | whitewood (in part, see Norway spruce) |
| hemlock, western | *Tsuga heterophylla* | British Columbia hemlock (USA) |
| | | Pacific hemlock (USA) |
| kauri, East Indian | *Agathis dammara* | Sabah kauri (UK) |
| | | Sarawak kauri (UK) etc. |
| kauri, New Zealand | *Agathis australis* | kauri pine (UK) |
| kauri, Queensland | *Agathis microstachya* | kauri pine (Australia) |
| | *A. palmerstonii* | Queensland kauri pine (UK) |
| | *A. robusta* | |
| larch, European | *Larix decidua ( europaea )* | |
| larch, hybrid | *Larix eurolepsis* | Dunkeld larch (UK) (a hybrid between European and Japanese larch) |
| larch, Japanese | *Larix leptolepis ( kaempferi )* | |
| mañio | *Podocarpus nubigenus* | |
| | *P. salignus* | |
| miro | *Podocarpus ferrugineus* | |
| pine, American pitch | *Pinus elliottii* | longleaf (USA) |
| | *P. palustris* | longleaf pitch pine (UK) |
| | | longleaf yellow pine (USA) |
| | | southern pine (in part) (USA) |
| | | southern yellow pine (in part) (USA) |
| pine, Canadian red | *Pinus resinosa* | Norway pine (USA) |
| | | red pine (Canada, USA) |
| pine, Caribbean | *Pinus caribea* | Caribbean longleaf (pitch pine) (UK) |
| | *P. oocarpa* | Nicaraguan pitch pine (UK) etc. |
| pine, Columbian (see fir, Douglas) | | |
| pine, Corsican | *Pinus nigra* var. *laricio ( maritima )* | |
| pine, Chile | *Araucaria araucana* | monkey puzzle (UK) |
| pine, hoop | *Araucaria cunninghamii* | |
| pine, kauri (see kauri, New Zealand and kauri, Queensland) | | |
| pine, lodgepole | *Pinus contorta* | contorta pine (UK) |
| pine, New Zealand black | *Podocarpus spicatus* | black pine (New Zealand) |
| | | mai (New Zealand) |
| | | matai (New Zealand) |
| pine, New Zealand white | *Podocarpus dacrydioides* | white pine (New Zealand) |
| pine, Parana | *Araucaria angustifolia* | |
| pine, Scots | *Pinus sylvestris* | Baltic redwood (UK) |
| | | Finnish redwood (UK) |
| | | red deal (UK) |
| | | redwood (UK) |
| | | Russian redwood (UK) |
| | | Swedish redwood (UK) |
| | | yellow deal (UK) |
| pine, southern | *Pinus echinata* | |
| | *P. rigida* | |
| | *P. taeda* | |
| | *P. virginiana* | |

162

| Common name | Botanical name | Local or trade name |
| --- | --- | --- |
| pine, western white | *Pinus monticola* | Idaho white pine (USA) |
| pine, yellow | *Pinus strobus* | Weymouth pine (UK) |
| podo | *Podocarpus ensiculus* | |
| | *P. gracilior* | |
| | *P. milanjianus* | |
| | *P. usambarensis* | |
| sequoia | *Sequoia sempervirens* | Californian redwood (UK, USA) |
| spruce, Norway | *Picea abies* | Baltic whitewood (UK) |
| | | Finnish whitewood (UK) |
| | | Russian whitewood (UK) |
| | | Swedish whitewood (UK) |
| | | whitewood (in part, see silver fir) |
| spruce, Sitka | *Picea sitchensis* | silver spruce (UK, Canada, USA) |
| sugi | *Cryptomeria japonica* | |
| totara | *Podocarpus totara* | |
| yew | *Taxus baccata* | |

## D. Softwoods: botanical names in alphabetical order

| Botanical name | Common name |
| --- | --- |
| *Abies alba* | silver fir |
| *Abies balsamea* | balsam fir |
| *Abies grandis* | grand fir |
| *Abies nobilis* | noble fir |
| *Agathis australis* | New Zealand kauri |
| *Agathis dammara* | East Indian kauri |
| *Agathis microstachya* *A. palmerstonii* *A. robusta* | Queensland kauri |
| *Araucaria angustifolia* | Parana pine |
| *Araucaria araucana* | Chile pine |
| *Araucaria cunninghamii* | hoop pine |
| *Cedrus atlantica* *C. deodora* *C. libani* | cedar |
| *Chamaecyparis lawsoniana* | Port Orford cedar |
| *Chamaecyparis nootkatensis* | yellow cedar |
| *Cryptomeria japonica* | sugi |
| *Cupressocyparis leylandii* | Leyland cyprus |
| *Cupressus* species, e.g, | |
| *C. lusitanica* | cypress species with |
| *C. sempervirens* | names based on geographical origins |
| *Cupressus macrocarpa* | Monterey cypress |
| *Fitzroya cupressoides* | alerce |
| *Juniperus procera* | East African pencil cedar |
| *Juniperus virginiana* | Virginian pencil cedar |
| *Larix decidua (europea)* | European larch |
| *Larex eurolepis* | hybrid larch |
| *Larix leptolepis (kaempferi)* | Japanese larch |
| *Libocedrus (Calocedrus) decurrens* | incense cedar |

| Botanical name | Common name |
| --- | --- |
| *Picea abies* | Norway spruce |
| *Picea sitchensis* | Sitka spruce |
| *Pinus caribea* | Caribbean pine |
| *Pinus contorta* | lodgepole pine |
| *Pinus echinata* | southern pine |
| *Pinus elliottii* | American pitch pine |
| *Pinus monticola* | western white pine |
| *Pinus nigra* var. *laricio (maritima)* | Corsican pine |
| *Pinus oocarpa* | Caribbean pine |
| *Pinus palustris* | American pitch pine |
| *Pinus resinosa* | Canadian red pine |
| *Pinus rigida* | southern pine |
| *Pinus strobus* | yellow pine |
| *Pinus sylvestris* | Scots pine |
| *Pinus taeda* *P. virginiana* | southern pine |
| *Podocarpus dacrydioides* | New Zealand white pine |
| *Podocarpus ensiculus* | podo |
| *Podocarpus ferrugineus* | miro |
| *Podocarpus gracilior* *P. milanjianus* | podo |
| *Podocarpus nubigenus* *P. salignus* | mañio |
| *Podocarpus spicatus* | New Zealand black pine |
| *Podocarpus totara* | totara |
| *Podocarpus usambarensis* | podo |
| *Pseudotsuga menziesii* | Douglas fir |
| *Sequoia sempervirens* | sequoia |
| *Taxodium distichum* | swamp cypress |
| *Taxus baccata* | yew |
| *Thuja plicata* | western red cedar |
| *Tsuga heterophylla* | western hemlock |

# Bibliography

The list below is not intended to be a complete bibliography but rather a selected list of books for further reading or reference.

The subject about which it is most difficult to suggest further reading is wood finishing. Probably the best book is *Wood Finishing* by John Collier, but this is out of print and only available from specialised libraries. *Staining and Polishing* by Charles Haywood concentrates mainly on the traditional methods and has relatively little to say about the more modern materials. The manufacturers are usually willing to give advice and information but their technical pamphlets tend to cater either for the completely amateur home decorator at the one extreme or the commercial user at the other

There are several references in the text of this book to the advisability of wearing a mask when working with some particular species. The toxic aspect of wood is dealt with very thoroughly in *Toxic Woods* by Woods and Calnan.

Bletchly, J. D., *Insect and Marine Borer Damage to Timber and Woodwork*, Forest Products Research Laboratory, HMSO, 1967.

British Standards Institution, *Glossary of Terms relating to Timber and Woodwork*, BS 565, 1972.

British Standards Institution, *Nomenclature of Commercial Timbers, including Sources of Supply*, BS 881 and 589, 1974.

Brown, W. H., *Timbers of the World*; Red booklets (9), TRADA, Hughender Valley, 1978–1979.

Cartwright, K. St. G., and Findlay, W. P. K., *Decay of Timber and its Prevention*, Forest Products Research Laboratory, HMSO, 1958.

Collier, John W., *Wood Finishing*, Pergamon Press, 1967.

Desch, H. E., *Timber – Its Structure and Properties*, Macmillan, Revised Edition, 1968.

Haywood, Charles H., *Staining and Polishing*, Evans, revised edition, 1960.

*Handbook of Hardwoods*, Building Research Establishment, HMSO, 1972.

*Handbook of Softwoods*, Building Research Establishment, HMSO, 1977.

*Identification of Hardwoods – A Lens Key*, Bulletin 25, Forest Products Research Laboratory, HMSO, 1960.

Johnston, David, *The Craft of Furniture Making*, B. T. Batsford, 1979.

Latham, B., *Timber – A Historical Survey*, George G. Harrap, 1957.

Miles, A., *Photomicrographs of World Woods*, Building Research Establishment, HMSO, 1978.

Rendle, B. J., *World Timbers*, E. Benn Ltd., 1969.

*Wood: decorative and practical*, Wood Information Section 2/3, Sheet 6, TRADA, Hughender Valley, revised 1981.

Woods, Brian and Calnan, C. D., *Toxic Woods*, British Journal of Dermatology, Volume 94, Supplement 13, 1976.

# Trade Associations and Suppliers

## UK

If any difficulty is experienced in obtaining a particular type of material the Branch Secretaries of the Timber Trades Federation will give advice. Their addresses are listed below:

Bristol Channel Timber Trades Association
27 Heol Hir, Llanishen, Cardiff, CF4 5AA.

East Anglian Timber Trades Association
7 Robin Hill, Lowestoft, Suffolk.

East Midlands Timber Trades Association
Nottinghamshire Chamber of Commerce & Industry
395 Mansfield Road, Nottingham, NG5 2DL.

Grimsby and Immingham Timber Importers Association
28 Dudley Street, Grimsby.

Hants and Dorset Timber Trade Association
'Hurstwood', 29 Melrose Road, Southampton.

Humber District Timber Trade Association
Samman House, Bowlalley Lane, Hull, HU1 1XT.

Irish Timber Importers Association
Crescent Trust Co., Gardner House, Ballsbridge, Dublin, 4.

London Area Timber Trade Association
Clareville House,
Whitcomb Street,
London, WC2H 7DL.

North East Coast Timber Trade Association
Pearl Assurance House, 7 New Bridge Street, Newcastle-on-Tyne, NE1 8BQ.

Northern Ireland Timber Importers Association
2 Greenwood Avenue, Belfast, 4.

North West Timber Trade Association
263a Monton Road, Monton, Eccles, Manchester, M2P 9LF.

Scottish Timber Trade Association
Thomson McLinlock & Co.,
24 Blytheswood Square, Glasgow, G2 4QS.

South East Timber Association
11 Riverhead house, Worships Hill, Riverhead, Sevenoaks, Kent, TN13 QAP.

Western Counties Timber Trade Association
Southernhay House, 38 Southernhay East, Exeter, EX1 1LF.

West Midlands Area Association
Heathfield, Breinton, Hereford, HR4 7PP.

British Wood Preserving Association (Affiliated Association)
150 Southampton Row, London, WC1B 5AL.

## USA

Southern Lumber Co.
1402 S. First St
San Jose 95110
California

Tech Plywood & Lumber Co.
110 Webb St
Hamden 06511
Connecticut

Paul Bunyan Hardwood Centre
12658 Paulina St
Calumet Park 60643
Illinois

Amherst Wood Working
Hubbard Ave
Northampton 01060
Massachusetts

Quality Woods
Box 205
Lake Hiawatha 07034
New Jersey

# Index

The species which are described in detail in chapters 8 and 9, in the alphabetical order of their common names, are not indexed unless they are mentioned in the earlier parts of these chapters. The numerous species discussed by their common and botanical names in the earlier parts of these chapters are indexed only by genera, unless a species of a different genus is included, colloquially, in a genus. For example, *Eucalyptus delegatensis* is indexed individually to oak because it is known as Tasmanian oak.